Healthy Slow Cooker Recipes Cookbook:

500 Easy Slow Cooker Recipes for Smart People on a Budget.

Helena Walker

Contents

INTRODUCTION

This book is written on an appliance that is often used in the kitchen and simmers food at a low temperature. It is the slow cooker which is also known as a crock-pot. A variety of dishes can be prepared using it, but it is a type of cooking that is different from baking, boiling or frying. People got the first sight of this appliance in 1950 when it came in an advertisement and was named Simmer Crock. This book tells us how Crock-pots are used to cook food, their design and operation. We will have a look at how they gives us benefits and what are the hazards related to this appliance.

WHY SLOW COOKER MEALS?

Crock-pot was given its name in 1971 and later modifications were made. A crock-pot is oval in shape, contains buttons for control and also has a digital timer. The cooking pot has a lid that is made up of glass. The Pot is made up of two materials. One is the glazed ceramic that is used to seal the inherent porosity of earthenware and on the outer surface is a metal surrounding container. The ceramic pot acts as a cooking container and heat reservoir at the same time. A crock-pot can hold 500 ml to 7 liters, depending on its capacity. It is possible that a crock-pot may not contain any heat setting or it may contain two heat settings. One is (low, medium, high) setting and the other is a keep warm setting.

The food to be cooked is placed within the pot with some liquid or sometimes we need to heat the liquid first. The temperature remains constant after the food is cooked. The recipe that is to be cooked in a slow cooker must be adjusted in quantities because there might be a little evaporation.

BENEFITS ATTAINED BY USING A ONE POT CROCK-POT:

A crock-pot is an appliance that works using electricity and replaces the use of extra utensils. All you need is some utensils to stir the food and you can cook your meal.

A crock-pot cooks food in a completely covered atmosphere so all the ingredients can fully blend. This blend enriches the flavors of ingredients and gives a delicious taste to the food.

It can give you ease of cooking by preventing any stress involved in standing near a stove while cooking. It relaxes you in a way that you could put your ingredients in the pot and then can come back to a delicious meal after a number of hours.

Keep food inside the crock-pot moist by adding sufficient liquid or sauces. This is good for cooking cheap cuts of meat like a beef chunk, pork shoulder, and brisket.

A crock-pot is able to cook some dishes that were the task of stoves and ovens. So, if we are planning a gathering of friends or family, this would be an intelligent approach because we could cook other dishes.

A crock-pot consists of a porcelain layer and a metal housing. It is beautifully designed to trap all heat inside. The heat stays within the pot and does not disturb or raise the temperature of your surroundings.

Because a crock-pot is able to hold all the ingredients placed in it tightly. It does not only heat, it also prevents the vapors of oil escaping from the pot. While cooking if oil escapes out of the pot, it causes the blackening of your surroundings. So, this entrapping design helps you ensure no extra work of cleaning.

Crock-pots work at a low temperature. They use a minimum amount of energy so they act as an energy saver. It is a way to avoid excessive energy consumption that occurs in an electric oven.

Food cooked in the pan may scorch but no such problem occurs if you are using crock-pot because of its low temperature.

A crock-pot helps you in easy cooking based on one or two steps. All you need to do is place ingredients within the pot, place the lid on, and press set.

BREAKFAST RECIPES

HUEVOS RANCHEROS

Servings: 2 | Prep Time: 3 hours 15 minutes

Ingredients:

- 1 tablespoon butter
- ½ cup black beans
- 2 tablespoons guacamole
- ¼ teaspoon cumin powder
- ¼ cup light cream

- ½ red onion, thinly sliced
- 2 eggs
- ½ oz. Mexican blend cheese, shredded
- 2 tablespoons red enchilada sauce

Directions: Put all the ingredients in a large bowl except guacamole and butter and mix thoroughly. Put butter in the crockpot and stir in the mixed ingredients. Cover and cook on LOW for about 3 hours. Dish out and top with guacamole to serve.

Nutrition Information: Calories: 264, Fat: 18g, Carbohydrates: 15g

TURKEY BREAKFAST CASSEROLE

Servings: 8 | Prep Time: 8 hours 30 minutes

Ingredients:

- 1-pound turkey sausages, cooked and drained
- 1 dozen eggs
- 1 (30 oz) package shredded hash browns, thawed
- 1 yellow onion, chopped

- 2 cups Colby Jack cheese, shredded
- 1 cup milk
- 1 teaspoon salt
- ½ teaspoon red pepper flakes, crushed
- 4 tablespoons flour
- ½ teaspoon black pepper

Directions: Grease a crockpot and layer with 1/3 of the hash browns, onions, sausages and cheese. Repeat these layers twice ending with the layer of cheese. Whisk together the rest of the ingredients in a large mixing bowl. Transfer this mixture into the crockpot and cover the lid. Cover and cook on LOW for about 8 hours. Dish out to serve the delicious breakfast.

Nutrition Information: Calories: 453, Fat: 25g, Carbohydrates: 26g

EGG CASSEROLE

Servings: 4 | Prep Time: 6 hours 30 minutes

Ingredients:

- ¾ cup milk

- ½ cup green bell pepper, chopped

- ½ teaspoon salt
- 8 large eggs
- ½ teaspoon dry mustard
- ¼ teaspoon black pepper
- 4 cups hash brown potatoes, partially thawed
- 4 green onions, chopped
- 12 ounces ham, diced
- ½ cup red bell pepper, chopped
- 1½ cups cheddar cheese, shredded

Directions: Whisk together eggs, dry mustard, milk, salt and black pepper in a large bowl. Grease the crockpot and put 1/3 of the hash brown potatoes, salt and black pepper. Layer with 1/3 of the diced ham, red bell peppers, green bell peppers, green onions and cheese. Repeat the layers twice, ending with the cheese and top with the egg mixture. Cover and cook on LOW for about 6 hours. Serve this delicious casserole for breakfast.

Nutrition Information: Calories: 453, Fat: 26g, Carbohydrates: 32.6g

CHEESY BREAKFAST POTATOES

Servings: 6 | Prep Time: 5 hours 20 minutes

Ingredients:

- 1 green bell pepper, diced
- 1½ cups cheddar cheese, shredded
- 1 can cream of mushroom soup
- 4 medium russet potatoes, peeled and diced
- 1 small yellow onion, diced
- 4 Andouille sausages, diced
- ¼ cup sour cream
- 1/3 cup water
- 1 teaspoon salt
- ¼ cup fresh parsley, chopped
- 1 teaspoon black pepper
- 1 teaspoon garlic powder

Directions: Mix together soup, sour cream, water, black pepper, season salt and garlic powder in a one pot crock pot until completely combined. Top with cheddar cheese and diced vegetables and stir well. Cover and cook on LOW for about 5 hours. Dish out and season with more salt and pepper if desired.

Nutrition Information: Calories: 479, Fat: 29.6g, Carbohydrates: 32g

APPLE OATMEAL

Servings: 3 | Prep Time: 7 hours 20 minutes

Ingredients:

- ¼ cup brown sugar
- ¼ teaspoon salt
- 2 cups milk
- 2 tablespoons honey
- 2 tablespoons butter, melted
- ½ teaspoon cinnamon
- 1 cup apple, peeled and chopped
- ½ cup walnuts, chopped
- 1 cup steel cut oats
- ½ cup dates, chopped

Directions: Grease a crock pot and add milk, honey, brown sugar, melted butter, cinnamon and salt. Mix well and stir in the oats, apples, walnuts and dates. Cover and cook on LOW for about 7 hours. Dish out and stir well before serving.

Nutrition Information: Calories: 593, Fat: 25.3g, Carbohydrates: 84.8g

BACON TATER

Servings: 4 | Prep Time: 8 hours 10 minutes

Ingredients:

- ½ pound Canadian bacon, diced
- ¼ cup Parmesan cheese, grated
- ½ cup whole milk
- Salt and black pepper, to taste
- 6 eggs
- 1 pound package frozen tater tot potatoes
- 2 onions, chopped
- 1½ cups Cheddar cheese, shredded
- 2 tablespoons flour

Directions: Grease a crockpot and layer 1/3 of the tater tots, bacon, onions, and cheeses. Repeat the layers twice, ending with cheeses. Mix together eggs, milk, flour, salt and black pepper in a medium mixing bowl. Drizzle this mixture over the layers in the crock pot and cover the lid. Cook on LOW about for 8 hours and dish out to serve.

Nutrition Information: Calories: 614, Fat: 36g, Carbohydrates: 36.6g

CARAMEL PECAN STICKY BUNS

Servings: 4 | Prep Time: 2 hours 40 minutes

Ingredients:

- ¾ cup packed brown sugar
- 15 ounces refrigerated biscuits
- 1 teaspoon ground cinnamon
- 6 tablespoons melted butter
- ¼ cup pecans, finely chopped

Directions: Mix together brown sugar, cinnamon and chopped nuts in a bowl. Dip refrigerator biscuits in melted butter to coat, then in the brown sugar mixture. Grease a crockpot and layer the biscuits in the crock pot. Top with the remaining brown sugar mixture and cover the lid. Cook on HIGH for about 2 hours and dish out to serve.

Nutrition Information: Calories: 583, Fat: 23.5g, Carbohydrates: 86.2g

FRIED APPLE SLICES

Servings: 6 | Prep Time: 6 hours 10 minutes

Ingredients:

- 1 teaspoon ground cinnamon
- 3 tablespoons cornstarch
- ¼ teaspoon nutmeg, freshly grated
- 1 cup sugar, granulated

- 3 pounds Granny Smith apples
- 2 tablespoons butter

Directions: Put the apple slices in the crock pot and stir in nutmeg, cinnamon, sugar and cornstarch. Top with butter and cover the lid. Cook on LOW for about 6 hours, stirring about halfway. Dish out to serve hot.

Nutrition Information: Calories: 234, Fat: 4.1g, Carbohydrates: 52.7g

CRANBERRY OATMEAL

Servings: 4 | Prep Time: 8 hours 15 minutes

Ingredients:

- 1 cup dried cranberries
- 1 cup steel cut oats
- 1 cup dates, chopped
- 4 cups water
- 2 tablespoons honey
- ½ cup half and half

Directions: Grease a crockpot and add all the ingredients except the half and half and honey. Cover and cook on LOW for about 8 hours. Stir in honey and half and half and dish out to serve.

Nutrition Information: Calories: 289, Fat: 5g, Carbohydrates: 59.7g

VEGETABLE OMELET

Servings: 4 | Prep Time: 2 hours 10 minutes

Ingredients:

- 6 eggs
- ½ cup milk
- ¼ teaspoon salt
- Black pepper, to taste
- 1/8 teaspoon garlic powder
- 1 cup broccoli florets
- 1 red bell pepper, thinly sliced
- 1 small yellow onion, finely chopped
- 1 garlic clove, minced
- 1/8 teaspoon chili powder

For Garnishing

- Chopped tomatoes
- Fresh parsley
- Shredded cheddar cheese
- Chopped onions

Directions: Mix together eggs, milk, garlic powder, chili powder, salt and black pepper in a large mixing bowl. Grease a crockpot and add garlic, onions, broccoli florets and sliced peppers. Stir in the egg mixture and cover the lid. Cook on HIGH for about 2 hours. Top with cheese and allow it to stand for about 3 minutes. Dish out the omelet into a serving plate and garnish with chopped onions, chopped tomatoes and fresh parsley.

Nutrition Information: Calories: 136, Fat: 7.4g, Carbohydrates: 7.8g

Quinoa Breakfast Casserole

Preparation Time: 4 Hours | Yield: 4 Servings

Ingredients:

- 1/2 cup quinoa rinsed well and uncooked
- 1 1/2 cups milk
- 6 large eggs
- 1/2 teaspoon salt
- 1/8 teaspoon pepper
- 1/2 cup frozen cut leaf spinach or use a handful of fresh!
- 3/4 cup grape tomatoes halved
- 1/4 cup shredded cheese colby, monterey jack, cheddar, etc.
- 1/4 cup shredded Parmesan cheese

Directions: In a mixing bowl whisk 6 eggs until beaten. Add quinoa, milk, salt and pepper and whisk until combined. Gently mix in spinach, tomatoes and 1/2 cup shredded cheese. Spray crock well with nonstick spray. Add egg and quinoa mixture to crock. Top with Parmesan cheese. Cover and cook on high for 2-4 hours until eggs are set and edges are lightly browned.

Nutritional Information: Calories: 270, Fat: 12g, Carbs: 20g

Cauliflower Hash Brown

Preparation Time: 5 Hours | Yield: 4 Servings

Ingredients:

- 12 eggs
- ½ cup milk
- ½ teaspoon dry mustard
- 1 teaspoon kosher salt
- ½ teaspoon pepper
- 1 head cauliflower shredded
- additional salt and pepper to season the layers
- up to one small onion diced (can omit or use less)
- two 5 oz packages pre-cooked breakfast sausages sliced (I used turkey sausage. Can also omit, or use about 1 lb bulk breakfast sausage cooked and crumbled, or bacon, vegetarian sausage crumbles, or chopped ham)
- 8 oz. or about 2 cups shredded cheddar cheese

Directions: Grease or coat a 6 quart slow cooker with cooking spray. Lightly beat together the eggs, milk, dry mustard, salt, and pepper. Place about a third of the shredded cauliflower in an even layer in the bottom of the slow cooker, and top with about a third of the onion. Season with salt and pepper, the top with about a third of the sausage and a third of the cheese. Repeat the layers two more times. Pour the egg mixture over the contents of the slow cooker. Cook on a low heat for 5-7 hours, or until eggs are set and the top is browned.

Nutritional Information: Calories: 131, Fat: 10g, Carbs: 6g

EASY BREAKFAST PIE

Preparation Time: 8 Hours | Yield: 4 Servings

Ingredients:

- 8 eggs, whisked
- 1 sweet potato or yam, shredded
- 1lb pork breakfast sausage, broken up
- 1 yellow onion, diced
- 1 tablespoon garlic powder
- 2 teaspoons dried basil
- salt and pepper, to taste
- any extra vegetables you want to put in there: peppers, squash, etc.

Directions: Grease your crockpot with a bit of oil to make sure none of the egg stuck to it. Shred your sweet potato, use the shredding attachment on my food processor to make it super quick, but you could use a grater as well. Add all ingredients to your crockpot and use a spoon to mix well. Set it and forget it!! Place on low for 6-8 hours. I cooked it for more than 7 to make sure the pork sausage was completely cooked through. Slice it like a pie.

Nutritional Information: Calories: 171, Fat: 6g, Carbs: 22g

TATER TOT EGG BAKE

Preparation Time: 8 Hours | Yield: 4 Servings

Ingredients:

- 30 oz pkg Tater Tots
- 6 oz diced Canadian bacon
- 2 onions chopped
- 2 c. shredded cheddar cheese
- 1/4 c. grated Parmesan cheese
- 12 eggs
- 1 c. milk
- 4 Tbsp all-purpose flour
- 1 tsp salt
- 1/2 tsp pepper

Directions: In a greased 5-quart or larger slow cooker, layer 1/3 of the Tots, Canadian Bacon, Onions and cheeses. Repeat these layers twice ending with the layer of cheeses. In a large mixing bowl whisk together the remaining ingredients and pour over the ingredients in the slow cooker. Cover and cook on low for 6-8 hours.

Nutritional Information: Calories: 618, Fat: 38g, Carbs: 33g

CARAMELIZED APPLE SLOW COOKER OATMEAL

Preparation Time: 9 Hours | Yield: 4 Servings

Ingredients:

- 2 pounds sweet or tart apples
- 3/4 cup brown sugar, more or less to taste
- juice from half a lemon (1-2 tablespoons)
- 2 cups rolled oats (gluten-free if necessary)

- pinch of sea salt
- 1 tablespoon cinnamon
- 1/2 teaspoon freshly-ground nutmeg
- 2 cups whole milk
- 2 eggs (optional)
- 1 1/2 cups water

Directions: Generously grease the bowl of a slow cooker (a deep 3-quart one works well). Toss the apples, brown sugar, salt, cinnamon, nutmeg, and lemon juice in a large bowl, then add the oats and stir again. Pour into the greased slow cooker insert. Either in the same bowl or a new one, whisk the eggs into the milk until the mixture is very smooth. Add the water and whisk again. Pour over the apple-oat mixture. Cook on low for 6-9 hours or on high for 4-5 hours. Cook time will vary considerably according to brand and size of slow cooker, so if you don't like crispy edges on your oatmeal, make this recipe for the first time during the day when you can gauge the progress of the oatmeal.

Nutritional Information: Calories: 167, Fat: 3g, Carbs: 30g

CHEESE SLOW COOKER SHRIMP AND GRITS

Preparation Time: 1 Hour | Yield: 4 Servings

Ingredients:

- 6 Cups Chicken Broth or Stock
- 1 1/2 Cups Quick Cooking Grits
- 1 Tablespoon Garlic Powder
- 1 Tablespoon Onion Powder
- 1 Teaspoon Dried Thyme or 2 Teaspoons Fresh Chopped Thyme
- Salt and Pepper to Taste
- 1 Cup Light Sharp Cheddar Cheese
- 4 Ounces Light Cream Cheese
- 1/2 Cup Grated Parmesan, Romano or Asiago Cheese. (Reserve a bit for garnish)
- 1/2 Teaspoon Hot Sauce (optional)
- 2 Pounds Raw Shrimp
- Scallions or Chives and Extra Cheese for garnish

Directions: Combine chicken broth and grits in slow cooker. Add all other ingredients except shrimp and green onions. Cook on low for 3 hours. Add shrimp and 1/2 cup cream or fat free half and half if desired. (If grits have absorbed all the liquid, add some more broth or some milk. It will depend on your slow cooker). Cook for 30 minutes to one hour, or until shrimp are done. Garnish with extra cheese. Garnish with green onions or chives and cheese.

Nutritional Information: Calories: 609, Fat: 33g, Carbs: 25g

APPLE GRANOLA CRUMBLE

Preparation Time: 4 Hours | Yield: 3 Servings

Ingredients:

- 2 Granny Smith apples
- 1 cup granola plus your favorite cereal, I mixed 1/2 cup granola and 1/2 cup bran flakes
- 2 tablespoons dairy free butter
- 1 teaspoon ground cinnamon
- 1/2 teaspoon ground nutmeg

- 1/8 cup maple syrup
- 1/4 cup apple juice

Directions: Peel, core and cut the apples into thick slices and then chunks. Cut the apple in half - then half again and then those halves in half. This gives you 8 thick slices. Cut those thick slices in chunks - like about 3 per slice. Add everything to the crock pot and stir well. Cover and cook on low for 4 hours.

Nutritional Information: Calories: 369, Fat: 15g, Carbs: 56g

OVERNIGHT QUINOA AND OATS

Preparation Time: 4 Hours | Yield: 6 Servings

Ingredients:

- 1 and 1/2 cups steel cut oats no substitutes
- 1/2 cup quinoa
- 4 and 1/2 cups water or almond milk
- 4 tablespoons brown sugar
- 2 tablespoons real maple syrup
- 1/4 teaspoon salt
- 1 and 1/2 teaspoons vanilla extract
- Optional: 1/4 teaspoon ground cinnamon, fresh berries, splash of milk, additional sugar for topping

Directions: Spray your slow cooker with non-stick spray. (Do not forget this step!) In a mesh strainer, rinse the quinoa really well. Combine the steel cut outs, rinsed quinoa, water or almond milk, brown sugar, maple syrup, salt, vanilla extract, and cinnamon (if desired) into the slow cooker. Stir really well and then set your slow cooker to low or, if you have a programmable slow cooker, set it to when you will wake up. This meal is ideal at 6-7 hours (best at 6 hours if you have a fast crockpot) and after that it becomes mushy and not so great. If you sleep 6-7 hours then turn it on low right before going to sleep or set the program to start preferably 6 hours before waking up. Once you wake up, immediately turn it off the heat and transfer to another dish or to breakfast bowls. Serve with a splash of milk, fresh berries, and additional brown sugar if desired.

Nutritional Information: Calories: 290, Fat: 6g, Carbs: 41g

PEACH AND BLUEBERRY OATMEAL

Preparation Time: 8 Hours | Yield: 6 Servings

Ingredients:

- 3 cups steel cut oats do not use regular oatmeal because it does not hold up well for slow cooking
- 8 cups water
- 1 pound frozen or fresh peaches unsweeetened
- 2 cups frozen blueberries
- 1 tablespoon real vanilla
- 1 1/2 - 2 teaspoons ground cinnamon
- 1 1/2 teaspoons sea salt

Directions: Spray slow cooker with cooking spray or use a crockpot liner. Combine all of the ingredients in the crockpot. The cinnamon and fruit will probably rise to the top, don't worry about it. They will cook up just fine. Cook overnight on low for 8 hours. Serve with sweetener of choice, butter or milk.

Nutritional Information: Calories: 172, Fat: 6g, Carbs: 30g

VEGETABLE OMELETTE

Preparation Time: 2 Hours │ Yield: 6 Servings

Ingredients:

- 6 eggs
- 1/2- cup milk
- 1/4 teaspoon salt
- fresh ground pepper, to taste
- 1/8 teaspoon garlic powder, or to taste

- 1 cup broccoli florets
- 1 red bell pepper, thinly sliced
- 1 small yellow onion, finely chopped
- 1 garlic clove, minced
- 1/8 teaspoon chili powder, or to taste

Garnish:

- shredded cheddar cheese
- chopped tomatoes

- chopped onions
- fresh parsley

Directions: Lightly grease the inside of the slow cooker/crock pot with cooking spray; set aside. In a large mixing bowl combine eggs, milk, salt, pepper, garlic powder and chili powder; using egg beaters or a whisk, beat the mixture until mixed and well combined. Add broccoli florets, sliced peppers, onions and garlic to the slow cooker; stir in the egg-mixture. Cover and cook on HIGH for 2 hours. Start checking at 1 hour 30 minutes. Omelette is done when eggs are set. Sprinkle with cheese and cover; let stand 2 to 3 minutes or until cheese is melted. Turn off the slow cooker. Cut the omelette into 8 wedges. Transfer to a serving plate. Garnish with chopped tomatoes, chopped onions and fresh parsley.

Nutritional Information: Calories: 144, Fat: 7g, Carbs: 8g

LUNCH RECIPES

LOW-CARB MEATBALLS

Servings: 4 | Prep Time: 4 hours 10 minutes

Ingredients:

- 1 pound pork, minced
- 1 pound beef, minced
- ½ large onion
- 2 eggs
- 2 tablespoons olive oil
- ½ cup Parmesan cheese, shredded
- 3 garlic cloves, minced

Directions: Put olive oil, onions and garlic in a pan and sauté for about 3 minutes. Transfer the onion mixture to a bowl and add the remaining ingredients. Make small-sized meatballs out of this mixture. Arrange these meatballs in a crockpot and cook, covered on LOW for about 4 hours. Dish out in a bowl and serve hot.

Nutrition Information: Calories: 521, Fat: 23.3g, Carbohydrates: 3.2g

MELT IN YOUR MOUTH MEATLOAF

Servings: 6 | Prep Time: 6 hours

Ingredients:

- 2 teaspoons onions, dried and minced
- 1 teaspoon salt
- ¾ cup milk
- 2 eggs
- 2/3 cup seasoned bread crumbs
- 1½ pounds ground beef
- ¼ cup ketchup
- ½ teaspoon rubbed sage
- ½ teaspoon Worcestershire sauce
- 1 teaspoon ground mustard
- ¼ teaspoon sugar

Directions: Combine together eggs, bread crumbs, milk, onions, sage and salt in a large bowl. Mix ground beef and shape into a round loaf. Transfer into a crock pot and cook, covered on LOW for about 5 hours 30 minutes. Whisk together Worcestershire sauce, ketchup, sugar and mustard in a bowl and spoon over the meat loaf. Cook for 15 more minutes and allow it to stand for about 10 minutes before cutting. Cut into slices and serve warm.

Nutrition Information: Calories: 272, Fat: 9.5g, Carbohydrates: 7.1g

SPICY SWISS STEAK

Servings: 4 | Prep Time: 8 hours 20 minutes

Ingredients:

- ¼ teaspoon kosher salt
- ½ tablespoon liquid smoke mesquite flavor
- ½ cup celery, sliced
- ¼ cup carrots, sliced
- 1 garlic clove, peeled and minced
- ½ teaspoon black pepper
- 1¼ pounds boneless round steak
- ½ (14½ oz.) can Rotel tomatoes (tomatoes with a hint of chili to give them some heat)
- ¾ cup beef broth
- ¼ cup onions, sliced
- ¼ cup red bell peppers

Directions: Put all the ingredients in a crock pot and mix well. Cover and cook on LOW for about 8 hours. Dish out and serve hot.

Nutrition Information: Calories: 332, Fat: 12.9g, Carbohydrates: 4.5g

BEEF BRISKET

Servings: 6 | Prep Time: 8 hours 15 minutes

Ingredients:

- ½ teaspoon vinegar
- 1/3 cup water
- ½ teaspoon salt
- ¼ teaspoon black pepper
- ¼ cup tomato sauce
- 2 pounds beef brisket, well-trimmed
- 2 bay leaves
- ¼ teaspoon thyme
- 2 cloves garlic

Directions: Put all the ingredients in a bowl and mix well. Arrange beef in the crock pot and pour the above mixture over beef. Cover and cook on LOW for about 8 hours. Dish out in a platter and serve hot.

Nutrition Information: Calories: 285, Fat: 9.5g, Carbohydrates: 1g

CROCK POT PIZZA

Servings: 8 | Prep Time: 5 hours 15 minutes

Ingredients:

- ¾ pound Italian sausage, cooked
- 3 cups mozzarella cheese, shredded
- 1 cup olives, sliced
- ¾ pound ground beef, cooked
- 1 (15 ounce) jar pizza sauce
- 3 cups fresh spinach
- 2 garlic cloves, minced
- 16 pepperoni slices
- 1 cup mushrooms, sliced
- ½ cup sweet onion, chopped
- ¼ cup sun-dried tomatoes, chopped
- ½ green pepper, chopped
- ¼ cup marinated artichoke hearts, chopped

Directions: Mix together sausage and ground beef with onions and sauce. Place half of the sauce mixture in the crock pot and layer with half of spinach. Arrange pepperoni on the spinach and top with half of the remaining ingredients ending with mozzarella cheese. Repeat the layering and cover the lid of the crock pot. Cook on LOW for about 5 hours and dish out.

Nutrition Information: Calories: 487, Fat: 37g, Carbohydrates: 7.6g

SAVORY CHOWDER

Servings: 6 | Prep Time: 6 hours 20 minutes

Ingredients:

- ¼ cup red onions, chopped
- 2 cups cauliflower, chopped
- ¼ teaspoon thyme
- 2 teaspoons parsley
- 1 can clams
- 1 cup organic chicken broth
- 1 pint half-and-half
- 2 slices bacon, cooked
- 1 teaspoon salt
- 1 garlic clove, minced
- 1/8 teaspoon pepper

Directions: Put all the ingredients in a crock pot and stir well. Cover and cook on LOW for about 6 hours. Ladle out in a bowl and serve hot.

Nutrition Information: Calories: 169, Fat: 12.2g, Carbohydrates: 9.2g

CARNE ADOVADA

Servings: 6 | Prep Time: 6 hours 20 minutes

Ingredients:

- 12 hot New Mexico red chili pods
- 1 teaspoon ground cumin
- 3 cups chicken broth
- 2 garlic cloves, minced
- ½ teaspoon salt
- 1/8 cup canola oil
- 2 pounds boneless pork shoulder, chunked
- 1 teaspoon Mexican oregano

Directions: Put canola oil and pork shoulder in a pan over medium heat and cook for about 2 minutes on each side. Transfer to a crock pot and stir in the remaining ingredients. Cover and cook on LOW for about 6 hours. Dish out and serve hot.

Nutrition Information: Calories: 280, Fat: 10.6g, Carbohydrates: 1.2g

TURKEY COLLARD GREENS

Servings: 4 | Prep Time: 5 hours 20 minutes

Ingredients:

- 1 bunch collard greens, woody stems removed and thinly sliced
- ½ teaspoon red pepper flakes
- 1 teaspoon kosher salt
- 2 tablespoons olive oil
- ½ teaspoon black pepper

- 2 teaspoons Frank's hot pepper sauce
- 1 pound smoked turkey wings, chopped in half
- ½ cup chicken broth
- 1 scoop stevia

Directions: Put the collard greens into the crockpot along with rest of the ingredients. Stir thoroughly and cover the lid. Cook on HIGH for about 5 hours and dish out into a serving bowl to serve.

Nutrition Information: Calories: 115, Fat: 10.4g, Carbohydrates: 1.9g

BACON SWISS PORK CHOPS

Servings: 8 | Prep Time: 8 hours 10 minutes

Ingredients:

- 12 bacon strips, cut in half
- 8 pork chops, bone-in
- 2 tablespoons butter
- Salt and black pepper, to taste
- 1 cup Swiss cheese, shredded

Directions: Season the pork chops with salt and black pepper. Put the butter, seasoned pork chops and shredded Swiss cheese in the crock pot. Cover and cook on LOW for about 7 hours. Stir in the cheese mixture and cook on low for 1 more hour.

Nutrition Information: Calories: 483, Fat: 40g, Carbohydrates: 0.7g

BEEF STROGANOFF

Servings: 6 | Prep Time: 8 hours 25 minutes

Ingredients:

- 1/8 teaspoon black pepper
- 1 teaspoon salt
- ¼ teaspoon garlic salt
- 1½ cups beef bouillon
- 2 pounds round steak
- ½ pound fresh mushrooms
- 1 cup sour cream

Directions: Season steaks with salt and black pepper. Place the seasoned steaks, garlic salt and beef bouillon in the crockpot. Cover and cook on LOW for about 8 hours. Add fresh mushrooms and sour cream. Cover and cook on HIGH for about 15 minutes. Dish out and serve hot.

Nutrition Information: Calories: 422, Fat: 22.9g, Carbohydrates: 3.5g

BAKED CHICKEN WITH SUMMER VEGETABLES

Preparation Time: 5 Hours | Yield: 6 Servings

Ingredients:

- about 3 pounds of chicken, cut up
- a bit of olive oil
- 4 large cloves garlic minced
- red bell pepper sliced

- 2 Tbs. dijon mustard
- salt and pepper
- 1 tsp. thyme
- 1 onion cut in thick wedges
- green bell pepper sliced
- 1 can diced tomatoes drained (or use fresh, chopped tomatoes)
- 1/2 cup white wine

Directions: Rub the inside of the crockpot with olive oil. Rinse and pat the chicken pieces dry with a paper towel.Rub the undersides of the chicken with dijon mustard and sprinkle with salt, pepper and thyme. Place them in the bottom of the crockpot, skin side down. Put the veggies and wine on top of the chicken. Cover and bake on high for 5 hours or so. Or bake on low 7-8 hours. Serve with angel hair pasta or baked potatoes.

Nutritional Information: Calories: 144, Fat: 3g, Carbs: 17g

BEEF SHWARMA

Preparation Time: 7 Hours | Yield: 6 Servings

Ingredients:

- 6 Tbs. lemon juice
- 6 Tbs. olive oil
- 1 tsp. salt
- 2 tsps. curry powder
- 2 dashes ground red pepper
- 2.5 - 3 lbs. thin cut boneless beef steak
- 8 oz plain or Greek yogurt
- 1 small cucumber chopped
- pita bread
- 3 garlic cloves crushed

Directions: Stir lemon juice, olive oil, salt, curry, cayenne pepper and garlic together in a small bowl. Place meat in slow cooker. Pour mixture over the top and stir to combine with meat. Cook on high 5-6 hours or low 7-8 hours. Combine yogurt and   cucumber. Serve cooked meat in pita bread with cucumber-yogurt sauce.

Nutritional Information: Calories: 505, Fat: 16g, Carbs: 38g

EASY CHICKEN CURRY

Preparation Time: 7 Hours | Yield: 6 Servings

Ingredients:

- 3 lbs. boneless chicken
- 1 onion chopped
- 1 cup salsa
- 3 Tbs. curry powder
- 1 can coconut milk
- 2 cups rice cooked

Directions: Place chicken, onion, salsa and curry powder in slow cooker. Cook on high 5-6 hours or low 7-8 hours. Remove the chicken from slow cooker. Add coconut milk to slow cooker. Stir into sauce. Return chicken to pot. Serve over cooked rice.

Nutritional Information: Calories: 505, Fat: 16g, Carbs: 38g

BEEF AND BEAN TOPPED BAKED POTATOES

Preparation Time: 7 Hours | Yield: 6 Servings

Ingredients:

- 1 lb. ground beef cooked
- 1/2 cup onion and bacon cooked
- 1 garlic clove pressed or minced
- 1 can kidney beans rinsed and drained
- 1 can chili ready diced tomatoes
- baking potatoes
- shredded cheddar cheese

Directions: Place all the ingredients, except the potatoes and cheese in the slow cooker or heat them together on the stove. Top baked potatoes and sprinkle with shredded cheese, if desired.

Nutritional Information: Calories: 398, Fat: 10g, Carbs: 60g

CHICKEN PHILLY SANDWICHES

Preparation Time: 8 Hours | Yield: 5 Servings

Ingredients:

- 2 lbs. boneless skinless chicken breasts
- 1 cup chicken broth
- ¼ tsp. salt
- ¼ tsp. pepper
- ¼ tsp. garlic powder
- ¼ tsp. paprika
- 1 large (or 2 small) bell peppers, sliced
- 1 medium onion, sliced
- 2 cups sliced mushrooms
- salt and pepper to season the bell peppers, onions, and mushrooms
- French bread or hoagie rolls for servings
- Swiss cheese for serving (use reduced-fat)

Directions: Place the chicken breasts into a 4-quart or larger slow cooker, and pour over the chicken broth. Season the chicken with the salt, pepper, garlic powder, and paprika (DON'T ADD THE VEGETABLES YET). Cover and cook on Low for 6.5 hours. After the chicken has cooked, add the sliced vegetables on top of the cooked chicken. Cover and cook on HIGH for 1.5 hours more. With 2 forks shred the chicken. Using tongs place the meat onto hoagies (tap as much liquid of the meat before placing on the bread), and top with cheese. Place the sandwiches open-faced under the broiler in the oven to toast the buns and melt the cheese. ENJOY!

Nutritional Information: Calories: 472, Fat: 16g, Carbs: 45g

CANTONESE SWEET AND SOUR CHICKEN

Preparation Time: 7 Hours | Yield: 6 Servings

Ingredients:

- 2 lbs. of chicken
- small onion sliced
- red pepper sliced
- 1/4 tsp. ground ginger
- 2 Tbs. cornstarch
- 1/4 cup cider vinegar

- green pepper sliced
- 20 oz can pineapple
- 1/4 cup brown sugar
- 1 clove garlic crushed
- 1/4 cup water
- 1 Tbs. soy sauce
- 1/2 tsp. salt

Directions: Put the chicken, onion and peppers in the crockpot. Drain the can of pineapple. Set the pineapple chunks aside for later. Mix the juice with the rest of the ingredients and pour over the chicken. Cook on low for 7-9 hours or high for about 4-5 hours. A bit before serving add the pineapple chunks. Serve over rice.

Nutritional Information: Calories: 250, Fat: 13g, Carbs: 24g

HONEY MUSTARD CHICKEN

Preparation Time: 7 Hours | Yield: 6 Servings

Ingredients:

- whole chicken cut up (or the equivalent in chicken pieces)
- 1/2 cup honey
- 1/4 cup dijon mustard
- salt and pepper to taste

Directions: Mix the honey, mustard, salt and pepper together in a small bowl. Put the chicken in the crockpot and pour the mixture over the top. Cook on high for 6-8 hours.

Nutritional Information: Calories: 293, Fat: 4g, Carbs: 30g

GARLIC ROSEMARY CHICKEN AND POTATOES

Preparation Time: 7 Hours | Yield: 6 Servings

Ingredients:

- Chicken, with or without bones 2-3 pounds
- About 10 garlic cloves, peeled but left whole
- 1 onion, sliced
- 6-7 medium potatoes, chopped
- 2 sprigs rosemary
- kosher salt and black pepper
- 1/2 cup white wine

Directions: Toss all the ingredients int to the slow cooker. Pour the wine over the top of everything. Cook 7-8 hours on low or 5-6 hours on high.

Nutritional Information: Calories: 540, Fat: 20g, Carbs: 30g

HONEY DIJON PORK CHOPS AND APPLES

Preparation Time: 7 Hours | Yield: 4 Servings

Ingredients:

- 1 1/2 lbs. pork chops boneless or bone-in
- 1 tsp. Dijon mustard

34

- 5 small apples peeled and sliced
- 1 onion sliced
- 3 Tbs. honey
- 1/2 tsp. Kosher salt
- generous grind black pepper

Directions: Place pork chops on bottom of crock. Stir honey, Dijon, salt and pepper together. Pour over apples and onions and toss to coat. Place apples and onions on top of pork chops in slow cooker. Cook 5-6 hours on high or 7-8 hours on low.

Nutritional Information: Calories: 293, Fat: 8g, Carbs: 17g

ITALIAN CHICKEN WITH TOMATOES

Preparation Time: 7 Hours | Yield: 6 Servings

Ingredients:

- 3-4 lbs. boneless chicken breast
- 1/3 cup olive oil
- 4 Tbs. red wine vinegar
- 1 tsp. oregano
- 1 tsp. basil
- 2 garlic cloves crushed
- salt and pepper to taste
- 15 oz can petite diced tomatoes
- 1/2 cup Italian blend shredded cheese

Directions: Place chicken in shallow dish. Whisk together all ingredients except tomatoes and cheese. Pour marinade over chicken. Refrigerate for 20-30 minutes or up to overnight. Brown chicken in olive oil in a skillet over medium heat. Place chicken in Crock-Pot. Add tomatoes to skillet, stirring to scrape up browned bits. Pour over chicken in Crock-Pot. Cook on low for 7-8 hours or high for 5-6 hours. Top with shredded cheese.

Nutritional Information: Calories: 225, Fat: 17g, Carbs: 10g

CHICKEN FAJITA CHILI

Preparation Time: 4 Hours | Yield: 6 Servings

Ingredients:

- 2 pounds skinless, boneless chicken breast halves, cut into 1-inch pieces
- 1 teaspoon fajita seasoning
- 2 cloves garlic, minced
- 1/2 teaspoon ground cumin
- 2 14 1/2 ounce can no-salt-added diced tomatoes, undrained
- 1 16 ounce package frozen yellow, green, and red peppers and onions
- 1 19 ounce can cannellini beans (white kidney beans), rinsed and drained
- 3 tablespoons shredded reduced-fat cheddar cheese (optional)
- 3 tablespoons light sour cream (optional)
- 3 tablespoons purchased guacamole (optional)
- 1 tablespoon chili powder

Directions: In a medium bowl combine chicken, chili powder, fajita seasoning, garlic, and cumin; toss gently to coat. Set aside. Coat a large skillet with cooking spray; heat skillet over medium-high heat. Cook half of the chicken mixture in hot skillet until brown, stirring occasionally. Transfer chicken mixture to a 3-1/2- or 4-quart slow cooker. Repeat with remaining chicken mixture. Stir tomatoes, frozen vegetables, and beans into chicken mixture in slow cooker. Cover and cook on low-heat setting for 4 to 5 hours or on high-heat setting for 2 to 2-1/2 hours. If desired, top each serving with cheese, sour cream, and guacamole.

Nutritional Information: Calories: 261, Fat: 2g, Carbs: 22g

CHICKEN TORTILLA SOUP

Preparation Time: 6 Hours | Yield: 4 Servings

Ingredients:

- 2 14 ounce can chicken broth with roasted garlic
- 1 14 1/2 ounce can Mexican-style stewed tomatoes, undrained
- 2 cups shredded cooked chicken (about 10 ounces)
- 2 cups frozen (yellow, green, and red) peppers and onion stir-fry vegetables
- 1 cup tortilla chips
- Sliced fresh jalapeno chile peppers (optional)

Directions: In a 3-1/2- or 4-quart slow cooker, combine broth, undrained tomatoes, chicken, and frozen vegetables. Cover and cook on low-heat setting for 6 to 7 hours or on high-heat setting for 3 to 3-1/2 hours. To serve, ladle soup into warm soup bowls and top with tortilla chips. If desired, top with chile peppers. Makes 4 servings.

Nutritional Information: Calories: 181, Fat: 4g, Carbs: 19g

WHITE QUESO DIP

Preparation Time: 2 Hours | Yield: 12 Servings

Ingredients:

- 16 oz white American cheese, cut into 1/2 inch cubes
- 8 oz cream cheese, cut into 1/2 inch cubes
- 2 Tablespoon salted butter
- 1 4oz can diced green chiles
- 1 4oz jar of pimentos, drained and diced
- 1 teaspoon of cumin
- 1/2 teaspoon of oregano
- 1/4 teaspoon of garlic powder
- 1/2 Tablespoon jalepenos, minced (plus extra for topping)
- 2 Tablespoons milk
- juice of 1/2 lime
- 2 Tablespoons cilantro, chopped fine

Directions: Combine the American cheese, cream cheese, butter, green chiles, pimentos, cumin, oregano, garlic powder and jalepenos in your crockpot. Cover and cook on low heat for 1.5 hours. Stir the mixture until until well combined and then add milk and lime juice. Cook for another 20 minutes, or until the cheese is completely melted and smooth. Top with cilantro and extra jalapenos. And serve with your favorite tortilla chips.

Nutritional Information: Calories: 223, Fat: 20g, Carbs: 2g

HOMEMADE BLACK BEANS

Preparation Time: 6 Hours | Yield: 6 Servings

Ingredients:

- 16 oz. (1 lb) dried black beans
- 8 cups water – or chicken or vegetable broth
- 1 tbsp minced garlic
- 1 tbsp salt
- 1 tsp black pepper
- 1/4 tsp cayenne pepper
- 1 tbsp ground cumin
- 1 tbsp oregano
- 1 tbsp onion powder
- 1 tsp smoked paprika
- 1 or 2 limes
- 1 bunch fresh cilantro, chopped (optional)
- 2 tbsp chopped green onions (optional)

Directions: Pour the beans into a colander in the sink and rinse the beans in cold water. Add the beans to a heavy bottomed sauce pan, dutch oven, or slow cooker and cover with 8 cups of water or broth. Stir in the garlic and all the dried spices. Cover and bring to a boil, if cooking on the stove top. If cooking in a slow cooker, just put on the lid and set it to low or high heat, depending on how long you want them to cook. Allow the beans to cook, covered, at a gentle simmer on the stove top, stirring from time to time, until tender – about 2 hours. If using a slow cooker, cook on high for about 4 hours or on low for 6-8. You want the beans to be tender, but not completely falling apart. Once cooked, you can drain the beans and they are ready to use. Or, you can let them simmer uncovered, stirring frequently, over a medium heat on the stove top until the liquid becomes a thick sauce – about 25-35 minutes. Add a few squeezes of fresh lime juice to taste, and sprinkle with cilantro and green onions if desired.

Nutritional Information: Calories: 181, Fat: 4g, Carbs: 19g

COOL RANCH PULLED CHICKEN

Preparation Time: 6 Hours | Yield: 6 Servings

Ingredients:

- 4 chicken breasts (about 1½ lbs)
- 1 packet of taco seasoning
- 1 packet of ranch dressing
- 14 ounces of chicken broth

Directions: Put chicken breasts, taco & ranch mixes and chicken broth in crock pot. Set crock pot on low for 5 hours. After 5 hours, shred chicken with 2 forks. Replace lid and continue cooking on low for 30 more minutes. Serve shredded chicken on a tostadas, tacos burritos or salad, with your favorite toppings!

Nutritional Information: Calories: 178, Fat: 2g, Carbs: 9g

MEXICAN CASSEROLE

Preparation Time: 6 Hours | Yield: 8 Servings

Ingredients:

- 1 tablespoon extra-virgin olive oil
- 1 pound ground turkey — or chicken, I used 93% lean ground turkey
- 1 medium yellow onion — diced
- 1 cup uncooked quinoa
- 2 cans red enchilada sauce — (10 ounce cans) (mild or medium) or 2 1/2 cups homemade red enchilada sauce
- 1 can black beans — (15 ounces), drained and rinsed
- 1 can of fire-roasted diced tomatoes in their juice — (15 ounces)
- 1 cup corn kernels — fresh or frozen
- 1 green bell pepper — cored and diced
- 2 tablespoons chili powder
- 1 tablespoon ground cumin
- 1 teaspoon garlic powder
- 1/2 cup water
- 1 cup shredded Mexican blend cheese — divided
- For serving: chopped fresh cilantro — diced avocado, chopped green onion, sour cream or plain Greek yogurt
- 1 red bell pepper — cored and diced

Directions: Heat the olive oil in a large skillet or Dutch oven over medium high. Add the turkey and onion. Cook and stir, breaking up the turkey as you go, until the turkey is no longer pink, about 5 minutes. Transfer to the bottom of a large slow cooker. To the slow cooker, add the quinoa, enchilada sauce, black beans, tomatoes, corn, red bell pepper, green bell pepper, chili powder, cumin, garlic powder, and 1/2 cup water. Stir to combine, then cover and cook on high for 2 1/2 to 3 hours or low for 5 to 6 hours, until the liquid is absorbed and the quinoa is tender. Remove the lid and stir. Taste and adjust any seasonings as desired. Stir in 1/2 cup of the shredded cheese, then sprinkle the remaining cheese over the top. Cover and cook on high until the cheese melts, about 10 to 15 minutes. Serve hot with any desired toppings.

Nutritional Information: Calories: 318, Fat: 11g, Carbs: 32g

SALSA CHICKEN

Preparation Time: 6 Hours | Yield: 6 Servings

Ingredients:

- 1 kg (2 lb.) chicken breasts, large cubes
- 2 cups salsa
- 2 Tbsp. taco seasoning
- 2 cups cheddar cheese, shredded

Directions: In a slow cooker, add the cubed chicken breasts and the taco seasoning. Mix together, so the chicken is coated with the seasoning. Pour the salsa over the chicken. Cook on low for 6-8 hours. Add the cheese on top of the chicken, cook for a further 30 minutes or until the cheese has melted. Serve & Enjoy

Nutritional Information: Calories: 385, Fat: 18g, Carbs: 10g

CROCKPOT MEXICAN CHICKEN

Preparation Time: 4 Hours | Yield: 16 Servings

Ingredients:

- 1 jar (16 oz.) of your favorite salsa
- 3 1/2 cups water
- 1 lb. chicken breasts
- 1 lb. dry pinto beans, rinsed
- 2-3 tablespoons taco seasoning
- 2 ounces or more light cream cheese (totally optional – just adds creaminess)
- salt to taste

Directions: Place the pinto beans, salsa, and water in a slow cooker or Crockpot. Stir to get the liquid in and around the beans. Place the chicken breasts on top. Cover and cook on high for 4-5 hours or low for 7-8 hours. After about 3 hours, remove the lid and check on the mixture. Stir to keep the beans from sticking to the bottom and add a little more water if necessary. Don't open the lid more than once or twice – it adds to the cooking time. When the beans and chicken are cooked, gently shred the chicken with two forks. It should shred very easily. Add the taco seasoning and cream cheese and let the mixture sit for another 15-30 minutes. Serve with rice, tortillas, or chips. Top with avocado, cheese, and cilantro. Serve & Enjoy

Nutritional Information: Calories: 120, Fat: 2g, Carbs: 14g

SLOW COOKER MEXICAN QUINOA CASSEROLE

Preparation Time: 3 Hours | Yield: 4 Servings

Ingredients:

- 1 cup Quinoa, uncooked
- 1 cup Frozen Corn
- 2/3 cup Reduced Sodium Chickpeas, drained and rinsed
- 1/2 cup Black Beans, drained and rinsed
- 1 cup Red Pepper, chopped, about 1 large pepper
- 1 cup Roma Tomato, chopped, about 2 tomatoes
- 1/2 cup Onion, roughly chopped, about 1/2 large onion
- 1 tablespoon Garlic, Minced
- 1/4 teaspoon Salt
- pinch of Black Pepper
- 1/2 tablespoons sauce from a can of chipotle peppers in adobo sauce
- cups Reduced Sodium Vegetable Broth
- Shredded Cheddar Cheese, for garnish
- Fresh Cilantro, for garnish
- 1/2 tablespoon Cumin

Directions: Spray your slow cooker with cooking spray and place the uncooked quinoa, corn, chickpeas, black beans, red pepper, tomato, onion cumin powder, garlic, salt, pepper and adobe sauce inside, stirring until well combined. Pour in in the vegetable broth, stir well, and cover the pot. Cook on high for 3-4 hours. Mine was perfect at 3 hours, so check it and make sure the quinoa isn't burning. Once cooked, season to taste with additional salt and pepper and garnish with cheese and cilantro.

Nutritional Information: Calories: 346, Fat: 6g, Carbs: 27g

SIMPLE WHOLE MEXICAN CROCKPOT CHICKEN

Preparation Time: 6 Hours | Yield: 6 Servings

Ingredients:

- 2 teaspoons paprika
- 1 tablespoon chili powder
- 1 teaspoon ground cumin
- teaspoons unrefined salt
- 1 whole chicken (3.5-4.5 lbs.), rinsed inside & out and patted dry
- 1 lime, quartered
- 2 garlic cloves, peeled and smashed
- 2 onions, halved and sliced
- 1 red bell pepper, sliced
- 1 green bell pepper, sliced
- 1/2 tsp black pepper

Directions: In a small bowl, combine the dry spices (paprika, chili powder, cumin, salt and pepper). Set aside. Rub the smashed garlic all over the chicken. Place the garlic and lime in the cavity. Rub the dry spices all over the chicken. Place the onions and peppers into the slow cooker. Place chicken on top of the vegetables. Cook on low for 4-6 hours – until the internal temperature of the leg is at 160 degrees F. Before serving, put the chicken in a roasting pan. Place it on the center oven rack and broil for about 3-4 minutes, until the skin is crispy and browned. (Watch it closely so it doesn't burn.) Allow the chicken to rest 5 minutes then serve.

Nutritional Information: Calories: 220, Fat: 6g, Carbs: 11g

SOUP, STEW AND CHILI RECIPES

BEEF BARLEY SOUP

Servings: 8 | Prep Time: 14 hours 20 minutes

Ingredients:

- 2 tablespoons butter
- ¼ cup onions
- 3 cups water
- 16 oz round beef steak
- ½ cup barley
- ½ teaspoon black pepper
- 1 cup celery, diced
- ¼ tablespoon dried basil
- ¼ teaspoon savory, ground
- 1 cup carrots, chopped
- ¾ fl oz red wine
- 2 cups beef broth

Directions: Put water, beef steaks, barley and beef broth in the one pot crock pot and cover the lid. Cook on LOW for about 13 hours and add the remaining ingredients. Cover and cook on LOW for 1 more hour. Dish out to serve hot.

Nutrition Information: Calories: 210, Fat: 9g, Carbohydrates: 10.9g

CHICKEN, CORN AND BEAN STEW

Servings: 10 | Prep Time: 5 hours 15 minutes

Ingredients:

- 3 pounds chicken tenders
- 1 cup Parmesan cheese, shredded
- 1 can seasoned diced tomatoes
- 1 can chili beans
- 1 can corn, drained

Directions: Arrange chicken at the bottom of a crockpot and stir in the remaining ingredients. Cover and cook on HIGH for about 5 hours. Sprinkle with Parmesan cheese and dish out to serve.

Nutrition Information: Calories: 338, Fat: 14g, Carbohydrates: 5.9g

HEARTY TURKEY CHILI

Servings: 5 | Prep Time: 8 hours 15 minutes

Ingredients:

- ¼ cup olive oil
- 1 pound ground turkey breast
- ½ teaspoon salt
- 1 can white beans, drained and rinsed
- 2 teaspoons dried marjoram
- 1 green pepper, chopped
- 1 can diced tomatoes
- 2 tablespoons chili powder
- 4 garlic cloves, minced

- 1 large onion, chopped
- 1 can no-salt-added tomatoes

Directions: Put olive oil, green peppers, onions and garlic in the crock pot and sauté for about 3 minutes. Add rest of the ingredients and cover the lid. Cook on LOW for about 8 hours and dish out in a bowl to serve hot.

Nutrition Information: Calories: 350, Fat: 17.6g, Carbohydrates: 18.1g

HAMBURGER SOUP

Servings: 8 | Prep Time: 7 hours 15 minutes

Ingredients:

- 1 pound ground meat, cooked
- 1 can diced tomatoes
- 1 can lima beans
- Salt, to taste
- 2 tablespoons olive oil
- 1 can kidney beans
- 1 can mixed vegetables
- 1½ teaspoons red chili powder
- 1 can beef broth

Directions: Put olive oil and ground meat in a crock pot and cook for about 5 minutes. Transfer the remaining ingredients into the crock pot and cover the lid. Cook on LOW for about 7 hours and ladle out into serving bowl to serve hot.

Nutrition Information: Calories: 262, Fat: 14.4g, Carbohydrates: 12.2g

SOUTHWESTERN TURKEY STEW

Servings: 6 | Prep Time: 7 hours 15 minutes

Ingredients:

- ½ cup red kidney beans
- ½ cup corn
- 2 cups diced canned tomatoes
- 15 oz ground turkey
- 1 cup red bell peppers, sliced
- ½ cup sour cream
- ½ cup cheddar cheese, shredded
- 1 garlic clove, minced
- 1½ medium red potatoes, cubed
- ½ medium onion, diced

Directions: Put all the ingredients in a bowl except sour cream and cheddar cheese. Transfer into the crock pot and cook on LOW for about 7 hours. Stir in the sour cream and cheddar cheese. Dish out in a bowl and serve hot.

Nutrition Information: Calories: 332, Fat: 15.5g, Carbohydrates: 17.1g

RABBIT STEW

Servings: 5 | Prep Time: 8 hours 15 minutes

Ingredients:

- ½ cup celery, diced
- 1 sausage, cubed
- 1 bay leaf
- 1 garlic clove, diced
- 1 cup Swiss chards, stalks
- ½ can water chestnuts, diced
- ½ cup apple cider vinegar
- 3 cups chicken broth
- ½ cup olive oil
- 1 pound rabbit, cubed
- Salt and black pepper, to taste
- 1 piece of bacon

Directions: Marinate rabbit in olive oil and apple cider vinegar and keep aside overnight. Put chicken broth in the crock pot and warm it up. Meanwhile, sear bacon and sausage in a pan and transfer it to the crock pot. Stir in rest of the ingredients and cover the lid. Cook on LOW for about 8 hours and dish out to serve hot.

Nutrition Information: Calories: 418, Fat: 30.7g, Carbohydrates: 2.7g

CHEESY MEATBALL SOUP

Servings: 6 | Prep Time: 8 hours 20 minutes

Ingredients:

For stock

- ½ green bell pepper, finely chopped
- ½ cup purple onion, chopped
- 2 cups organic beef broth
- ½ red bell pepper, finely chopped
- 1 celery stalk, chopped
- 5 large mushrooms, chopped
- 5 strips bacon

For meatballs

- 1 egg
- 1 pound ground beef
- ¼ cup ground flax seed meal
- 1 teaspoon oregano
- 1 tablespoons parsley
- ½ teaspoon pepper
- 1 teaspoon salt
- ½ teaspoon garlic powder

For cheese sauce

- 4 tablespoons heavy white cream
- 8 slices American cheese
- 4 tablespoons water
- 4 tablespoons butter

Directions:

For meatballs: Mix together the ingredients and roll into medium sized meatballs. Put this mixture in the crock pot along with the ingredients for stock and thoroughly stir. Cover and cook on LOW for about 8 hours.

For cheese sauce: Put all the ingredients in a microwave safe dish and microwave for about 3 minutes. Add this cheese sauce to the soup, gently stirring. Dish out and serve hot.

Nutrition Information: Calories: 419, Fat: 32g, Carbohydrates: 3.7g

MEXICAN CHICKEN STEW

Servings: 6 | Prep Time: 9 hours 20 minutes

Ingredients:

- 3 chicken breasts, boneless and skinless
- 1 can black beans, not drained
- 1 can corn
- 2 cans diced tomatoes and chilies
- ½ cup sour cream
- 1 cup onions, optional
- ½ cup Mexican cheese, shredded

Directions: Place chicken breasts at the bottom of the crock pot and top with tomatoes, beans and corns. Cover and cook on LOW for about 9 hours. Dish out and serve hot.

Nutrition Information: Calories: 286, Fat: 12.7g, Carbohydrates: 16.8g

BEEF CHILI

Servings: 8 | Prep Time: 3 hours 15 minutes

Ingredients:

- 29 ounces canned diced tomatoes, not drained
- 3 tablespoons chili powder
- 1 yellow onion, chopped
- 2 pounds lean ground beef
- ¼ cup tomato paste
- ½ cup saltine cracker crumbs, finely ground
- 1 jalapeno, minced
- 3 garlic cloves, minced
- 2 (16-ounce) cans red kidney beans, rinsed and drained
- 1 teaspoon Kosher salt
- 1 teaspoon ground cumin
- 1 teaspoon black pepper

Directions: Cook onions and beef over medium high heat in a pot until brown. Transfer to the crock pot along with the rest of the ingredients. Cover and cook on HIGH for about 3 hours and dish out to serve.

Nutrition Information: Calories: 638, Fat: 9.1g, Carbohydrates: 78.9g

BROCCOLI CHEESE SOUP

Servings: 6 | Prep Time: 6 hours 20 minutes

Ingredients:

- 1½ cups heavy cream
- 2½ cups water, ¾ teaspoon salt
- ½ cup red bell pepper, chopped
- 2 cups broccoli, chopped, thawed and drained
- 2 tablespoons chives, chopped
- 2 tablespoons butter
- ½ teaspoon dry mustard
- 8 ounces cheddar cheese, shredded
- 4 cups chicken broth
- ¼ teaspoon cayenne pepper

Directions: Put all the ingredients in a crockpot except chives and cheese and mix well. Cover and cook on LOW for about 6 hours. Sprinkle with cheese and cook on LOW for about 30 minutes. Garnish with chives and serve hot.

Nutrition Information: Calories: 353, Fat: 10g, Carbohydrates: 4g

CHICKEN POSOLE STEW

Preparation Time: 7 Hours | Yield: 6 Servings

Ingredients:

- 4 boneless chicken breasts or the equivalent in tenders
- 2 cans hominy, rinsed and drained
- 3 cups chicken broth
- 2 cans diced tomatoes, undrained
- 3 carrots, sliced thin
- 3 green onions, sliced
- 1 Tbs. cumin
- 2 tsps. chili powder
- 1 tsp. oregano
- 1/4 tsp. cayenne pepper, or to taste
- 1 tsp. salt, or to taste
- pepper to taste
- 3 cloves garlic, minced

Directions: Put the chicken in the bottom of the crockpot. Add the other ingredients on top, stirring to combine. Cook on high 5-6 hours or low 7-8 hours. Remove the chicken and shred with a fork. Return to the pot. Serve with tortilla chips and cheddar cheese, if desired.

Nutritional Information: Calories: 361, Fat: 15g, Carbs: 30g

THAI CHICKEN CURRY SOUP

Preparation Time: 7 Hours | Yield: 6 Servings

Ingredients:

- 2 lbs. bone-in chicken (I used 2 large chicken breasts)
- 1 onion diced
- 3 carrots diced
- 3 celery stalks diced
- 2 Tbs. curry powder
- 1/2 cup long-grain white rice
- 1 can coconut milk
- cilantro chopped, optional for topping
- Sriracha sauce optional for topping
- 2 - 32 oz boxes chicken broth

Directions: Place chicken on bottom of the slow cooker. Add onion, carrots, celery, curry powder and broth. Cook on high 5-6 hours or low 7-8 hours. Remove chicken from crock and pull meat from bones. Stir rice, coconut milk and chicken meat back into the soup. Cook for 20-30 more minutes or until rice is cooked. Serve with chopped cilantro and Sriracha sauce.

Nutritional Information: Calories: 190, Fat: 15g, Carbs: 10g

PUMPKIN BLACK BEAN CHICKEN CHILI

Preparation Time: 5 Hours | Yield: 6 Servings

Ingredients:

- 1 onion chopped
- 1 red or yellow bell pepper chopped
- 3-4 cloves garlic
- 4 cups chicken broth
- 1 can of pumpkin
- 2 cans black beans rinsed and drained
- 1 can diced tomatoes with juice
- 2 tsps. parsley flakes
- 2 tsps. chili powder
- 1 1/2 tsps. oregano
- 1 1/2 tsps. cumin
- 2-3 cups cooked chopped chicken

Directions: Put all ingredients in slow cooker. Cook on low 5 hours. Serve!

Nutritional Information: Calories: 190, Fat: 15g, Carbs: 10g

BLACK BEAN BUTTERNUT SQUASH CHILI

Preparation Time: 3 Hours | Yield: 6 Servings

Ingredients:

- 1 medium red onion chopped
- 4 garlic cloves chopped
- 1 tablespoon chili powder
- 1 tablespoon ground cumin
- 2 teaspoons unsweetened cocoa powder
- 1/4 teaspoon cinnamon
- 2 14 oz cans diced tomatoes
- 2 15.5 oz cans black beans
- 1 10 oz package of frozen butternut squash
- 1 cup water

Directions: Combine all ingredients in a slow cooker. (There is no need to thaw the frozen butternut squash beforehand.) Turn the slow cooker to high heat and allow to cook for 3 to 4 hours. Serve. Optional toppings: crushed tortilla chips, shredded cheddar, sour cream, chopped cilantro.

Nutritional Information: Calories: 218, Fat: 1g, Carbs: 56g

CHICKEN PARMESAN SOUP

Preparation Time: 7 Hours | Yield: 6 Servings

Ingredients:

- 1 1/2 - 2 lbs. frozen chicken tenders
- 46 oz tomato juice
- 32 oz chicken broth
- 4 garlic cloves crushed
- 1 cup shredded Parmesan cheese
- 1 tsp. basil
- 1 tsp. oregano
- salt and pepper to taste
- 6 - 8 oz small shaped pasta

Directions: Place all ingredients, except pasta in the slow cooker. Cook on high for 5-6 hours or low 7-8 hours. Remove the chicken and shred. Return chicken to the slow cooker. Add pasta and cook 30 minutes longer.

Nutritional Information: Calories: 287, Fat: 9g, Carbs: 33g

Chicken Vegetable Soup

Preparation Time: 5 Hours | Yield: 6 Servings

Ingredients:

- 2-3 lbs. bone in chicken thighs skin removed
- 1 onion chopped
- 3 cloves garlic crushed
- 4-6 parsnips chopped
- 3-4 carrots chopped
- 1/2 green pepper chopped
- 2 celery stalks chopped
- 46 oz tomato juice
- 4 cups water
- salt and pepper to taste

Directions: Place all ingredients in the slow cooker. Cook on high 5-6 hours or low 7-8 hours. Remove chicken and shred the meat. Place meat back in crock and season the soup.

Nutritional Information: Calories: 100, Fat: 3g, Carbs: 11g

Ham and Bean Soup

Preparation Time: 5 Hours | Yield: 6 Servings

Ingredients:

- 1 lb. Northern beans
- 1.5 lbs Ham steak with bone
- 6-7 cups of water
- salt to taste

Directions: Soak beans overnight or do a quick soak in the morning (cover with water, bring to boil and soak for 1 hour). Dice ham. Place beans, ham and the ham bone in slow cooker. Cover with 6-7 cups of water. Cook on high 7-8 hours. Taste and season with salt. Serve with cornbread.

Nutritional Information: Calories: 253, Fat: 4g, Carbs: 36g

Smoked Sausage and Sauerkraut Soup

Preparation Time: 5 Hours | Yield: 6 Servings

Ingredients:

- 1 lb. smoked sausage sliced
- 3 - 4 large potatoes or 6 - 8 small potatoes, chopped
- 2 15 oz cans sauerkraut drained and rinsed
- 1 can diced tomatoes
- 8 oz tomato sauce
- 2 32 oz chicken broth
- 1 onion chopped

Directions: Place all ingredients in slow cooker and stir. Cook on high 5-6 hours or low 7-8 hours.

Nutritional Information: Calories: 197, Fat: 12g, Carbs: 12g

WHITE CHICKEN CHILI

Preparation Time: 8 Hours | Yield: 6 Servings

Ingredients:

- 2 - 2 1/2 lbs. bone-in chicken pieces I used 2 very large chicken breasts
- 1 onion chopped
- 3 garlic cloves crushed
- 1 can chopped green chilies
- 1 lb. great northern beans soaked
- 2 tsp. cumin
- 1 tsp. oregano
- 1/2 - 1 tsp. chili powder
- 1 32oz box chicken broth
- 2 cups water
- salt to taste
- 2 Tbs. cornmeal
- 1 cup milk
- 1/8 tsp. cayenne pepper

Directions: Place all ingredients in the slow cooker, except the cornmeal and milk. Cook on high 6-7 hours or low 8-9 hours. Remove chicken from soup and shred. Return chicken to soup. Stir cornmeal and milk together and add to the soup to thicken. Adjust seasonings and serve.

Nutritional Information: Calories: 176, Fat: 5g, Carbs: 20g

CHICKEN COCK-A-LEEKIE SOUP

Preparation Time: 5 Hours | Yield: 6 Servings

Ingredients:

- 2 bone-in chicken breasts
- 3 leeks sliced and cleaned
- 3-5 carrots chopped
- 1/3 cup barley
- 1 onion chopped
- 1 bay leaf
- 1 tsp. thyme
- 2 32 oz boxes chicken broth
- salt and pepper to taste
- dried prunes diced for topping, optional

Directions: Place chicken breasts in slow cooker. Add leeks, carrots, barley, onion, bay leaf and thyme to slow cooker. Pour chicken broth over all ingredients. Cook on high 5-6 hours or low 7-8 hours. Remove chicken breasts and take meat off of bones. Return meat to the soup. Serve with diced prunes.

Nutritional Information: Calories: 220, Fat: 3g, Carbs: 36g

RICE RECIPES

SLOW COOKER BEEF BIRYANI

Servings: 6 | Prep Time: 4 hours 15 mins

Ingredients:

- 1 teaspoon garam masala
- 2 pounds stewing beef
- 1 teaspoon ground coriander
- ½ cup natural yogurt
- 1 knob ginger, grated
- 1 bunch coriander
- 1 teaspoon ground turmeric

- 1 tablespoon olive oil
- 2 cinnamon quills
- 2 cups basmati rice
- 4 garlic cloves, grated
- 4 onions, sliced
- 3 cups beef stock
- 1 teaspoon chili powder

Directions: Mix together yogurt, coriander, ginger, garlic and spices in a bowl. Stir in the beef to mix well and transfer into the crock pot and top with rice. Sauté onions in oil for about 3 minutes and layer over the rice. Pour in stock and cinnamon quills and cover the lid. Cook on HIGH for about 4 hours. Top with additional coriander leaves and serve hot.

Nutrition Information: Calories: 307, Fat: 10g, Carbohydrates: 32g

VEGETABLE RICE

Servings: 3 | Prep Time: 4 hours 45 minutes

Ingredients:

- ¼ cup sun-dried tomato, finely chopped
- 1 tablespoon lemon juice
- 1 cup rice
- ½ large onion, sliced
- 1 pinch ground turmeric
- ½ cup roasted red pepper, chopped
- 2 garlic cloves, minced
- ¼ cup green pepper, finely diced

- 1 stalk celery, sliced
- 1 carrot, sliced
- ¼ teaspoon black pepper
- 1 tablespoon fresh parsley, minced
- 2 cups vegetable stock
- ½ tablespoon extra-virgin olive oil
- ¾ cup frozen peas
- ¼ teaspoon salt

Directions: Heat oil in a large skillet and add carrots, onions, garlic and celery. Sauté for about 4 minutes and transfer into the crock pot. Add rice, sun-dried tomatoes, saffron, vegetable stock, salt and black pepper. Cover and cook for about 4 hours on LOW. Stir in the green pepper, peas, lemon juice and red pepper. Cover and cook for about 20 minutes on HIGH. Garnish with parsley to serve hot.

Nutrition Information: Calories: 333, Fat: 4.4g, Carbohydrates: 65.2g

VEGETARIAN SPANISH RICE

Servings: 3 | Prep Time: 6 hours 10 mins

Ingredients:

- 1 cup rice
- 1 cup vegetable broth
- ½ (15 ounce) can diced tomatoes
- ½ onion, diced
- ½ green bell pepper, diced
- 1 teaspoon chili powder
- 1/8 cup salsa
- ¾ teaspoons garlic powder
- ½ teaspoon onion powder

Directions: Place the rice in the crockpot and top with the remaining ingredients. Cover the lid and cook for about 6 hours on LOW. Dish out and serve hot.

Nutrition Information: Calories: 272, Fat: 1.2g, Carbohydrates: 57.5g

MOROCCAN BEEF RICE

Servings: 4 | Prep Time: 9 hours 20 minutes

Ingredients:

- 1 pound boneless beef, cut into 1-inch pieces
- 1 small apple, shredded
- 1 (6.9-oz.) package rice and vermicelli mix with chicken seasonings
- ¼ cup almonds, slivered
- ¼ cup raisins
- 1 teaspoon curry powder
- 1½ cups chicken broth

Directions: Mix together beef, curry powder, apple, broth and seasoning packet from rice mix in a crock pot. Cover the lid and cook for about 8 hours 30 minutes on LOW. Uncover and add rice, raisins and almonds. Cover the lid and cook for about 30 minutes on HIGH. Dish out to serve hot.

Nutrition Information: Calories: 475, Fat: 12.8g, Carbohydrates: 49.9g

COCONUT RICE

Servings: 6 | Prep Time: 3 hours 45 minutes

Ingredients:

- 4½ cups water
- 2 cups lengthy grain white rice
- 4 tablespoons butter
- 1 cup unsweetened coconut, grated
- 1 teaspoon salt
- 1 cup fresh parsley
- 1 teaspoon cinnamon powder

Directions: Put butter and rice in the crock pot and cook on HIGH for about 15 minutes. Add the remaining ingredients and cover the lid. Cook for about 3 hours 30 minutes on LOW and dish out to serve.

Nutrition Information: Calories: 181, Fat: 12.3g, Carbohydrates: 16.5g

CHICKEN AND OLIVE RICE

Servings: 6 | Prep Time: 6 hours 40 minutes

Ingredients:

- 2 stalks celery, sliced
- 1/8 teaspoon ground turmeric
- 1 tablespoon extra-virgin olive oil
- 2 small onions, sliced
- 4 cups vegetable stock
- ½ cup sun-dried tomato, finely chopped
- 2 tablespoons lemon juice
- 4 garlic cloves, minced
- 2 cups rice
- ½ teaspoon black pepper
- ½ cup green olives
- ½ teaspoon salt
- 1½ cups frozen peas
- 4 tablespoons coriander leaves, minced
- 1 pound chicken

Directions: Put oil in a large skillet over medium heat and add onions, celery and garlic. Sauté for about 5 minutes and transfer into the crockpot. Add chicken and sauté for about 10 minutes. Add rice, saffron, sun-dried tomatoes, vegetable stock, salt and black pepper. Secure the lid and cook for about 5 hours on LOW. Stir in the peas, green olives and lemon juice. Cover and cook for about 15 minutes on HIGH. Sprinkle with coriander leaves and serve.

Nutrition Information: Calories: 430, Fat: 6.6g, Carbohydrates: 61.1g

BEAN RECIPES

MEXICAN BEAN STEW

Servings: 5 | Prep Time: 4 hours 10 minutes

Ingredients:

- 1 (7.5 oz) can chopped tomatoes with green chilies
- ½ cup brown rice
- 1 cup water
- 1 (7.5 oz) can sweet corn
- 1 (7.5 oz) can butter beans
- ½ packet taco meat seasoning
- 1 (7.5 oz) can chili beans

Directions: Put all the ingredients in the crock pot and mix well. Cover and cook on LOW for about 4 hours. Dish out in a bowl and serve hot.

Nutrition Information: Calories: 169, Fat: 1.4g, Carbohydrates: 37.5g

BEAN AND CARROT STEW

Servings: 6 | Prep Time: 5 hours 20 minutes

Ingredients:

- 1 cup dried adzuki beans, soaked overnight and drained
- 1 tablespoon fresh ginger, chopped
- 1 large yellow onion, chopped
- 2 tablespoons rice vinegar
- 2 tablespoons olive oil
- 3 tablespoons tamari
- Salt, to taste
- 4 large carrots, peeled and sliced
- ½ cup fresh parsley, minced
- Freshly ground black pepper, to taste
- 4 cups water

Direction: Put all the ingredients in the one pot crock pot except vinegar, tamari and black pepper. Cover and cook on LOW for about 5 hours. Stir in vinegar, tamari and black pepper and remove from heat. Garnish with parsley and serve hot.

Nutrition Information: Calories: 191, Fat: 5g, Carbohydrates: 29.2g

BEANS WITH BACON

Servings: 6 | Prep Time: 2 hours 15 minutes

Ingredients:

- 3 (16-ounce) cans baked beans
- 6 strips bacon, cut in 1-inch pieces
- ¼ cup brown sugar, packed
- ½ cup ketchup
- ½ teaspoon mustard powder

Directions: Fry the bacon until it is brown and crispy. Pour the beans into the crock pot and add the bacon. Mix together brown sugar, mustard powder and ketchup in a bowl. Pour this mixture into the crock pot and cover the lid. Cook on HIGH for about 2 hours and dish out to serve hot.

Nutrition Information: Calories: 489, Fat: 19.8g, Carbohydrates: 59.8g

CROCK POT PINTO BEANS

Servings: 6 | Prep Time: 8 hours 20 minutes

Ingredients:

- 2 teaspoons extra-virgin olive oil
- 1½ teaspoons kosher salt, divided
- 2 cups pinto beans, rinsed
- 1 small yellow onion, diced
- 1 jalapeno, cored, seeded and finely chopped
- 3 garlic cloves, minced
- 1 teaspoon ground cumin
- ¼ teaspoon cayenne pepper
- 4 cups low-sodium chicken broth
- 2 bay leaves
- 1 teaspoon dried oregano
- 3 cups water

Directions: Place the pinto beans in the crock pot and keep aside. Heat the oil in a skillet over a medium-high heat and add onions, garlic and jalapeno. Sauté for about 3 minutes and transfer to the crock pot along with the bay leaves, oregano, cumin, cayenne and salt. Top with broth and water and cover the lid. Cook on HIGH for about 8 hours and dish out to serve hot.

Nutrition Information: Calories: 73, Fat: 3.7g, Carbohydrates: 8g

BABY LIMA BEANS WITH HAM

Servings: 4 | Prep Time: 7 hours 20 minutes

Ingredients:

- 1 quart water, for soaking
- 4 cups water, to cover
- ½ pound baby lima beans, soaked overnight
- 1 medium onion, coarsely chopped
- 1 teaspoon Creole seasoning blend
- 1 pound ham, diced
- Dash cayenne pepper
- ¼ teaspoon freshly ground black pepper
- Salt, to taste

Directions: Place the lima beans in crock pot and stir in the chopped onions, ham and water. Cover and cook the beans on HIGH for about 3 hours. Add Creole seasoning, salt, black and cayenne peppers and cover the lid. Cook on LOW for about 4 hours and dish out to serve hot.

Nutrition Information: Calories: 120, Fat: 2.6g, Carbohydrates: 4.7g

BAKED BEANS WITH SALT PORK

Servings: 8 | Prep Time: 12 hours 15 minutes

Ingredients:

- 6 cups water, to cover
- 1 pound white beans, rinsed and soaked overnight
- 1/3 cup molasses
- 1 tablespoon Dijon mustard
- 1 cup onion, chopped
- ¼ cup brown sugar, packed
- ¼ pound salt pork, rinsed and diced

Directions: Put all the ingredients in the crock pot except Dijon mustard. Cover and cook on LOW for about 8 hours, stirring occasionally. Add Dijon mustard and cook for about 30 minutes on LOW. Dish out and serve hot.

Nutrition Information: Calories: 343, Fat: 10g, Carbohydrates: 50.3g

FISH AND SEAFOOD RECIPES

SALMON STEW

Servings: 6

Prep Time: 5 hours 15 minutes

Ingredients:

- 2 tablespoons butter
- 2 pounds salmon fillet, cubed
- 2 medium onions, chopped
- Salt and black pepper, to taste
- 2 cups homemade fish broth

Directions: Put all the ingredients in the one pot crock pot and thoroughly mix. Cover and cook on LOW for about 5 hours. Dish out and serve hot.

Nutrition Information: Calories: 293, Fat: 8.7g, Carbohydrates: 16.3g

PAPRIKA SHRIMP

Servings: 3 | Prep Time: 4 hours 20 minutes

Ingredients:

- 1 pound tiger shrimp
- Salt, to taste
- ½ teaspoon smoked paprika
- 2 tablespoons tea seed oil

Directions: Mix together all the ingredients in a large bowl until well combined. Transfer the shrimp in the crock pot and cover the lid. Cook on LOW for about 4 hours and dish out to serve with roasted tomatoes and jalapenos.

Nutrition Information: Calories: 231, Fat: 10.4g, Carbohydrates: 0.2g

MOROCCAN FISH

Servings: 9 | Prep Time: 3 hours 20 minutes

Ingredients:

- 1 pound cherry tomatoes, crushed slightly
- 1 teaspoon tea seed oil
- 1 teaspoon red pepper flakes, crushed
- 3 pounds salmon fillets
- 2 garlic cloves, crushed
- Salt, to taste
- 1 tablespoon fresh basil leaves, torn
- 1 teaspoon dried oregano, crushed

Directions: Put the tea seed oil and salmon fillets in the crock pot and cover the lid. Cook on LOW for about 2 hours and add cherry tomatoes, garlic, oregano, salt and red pepper flakes. Cook on HIGH for about 1 hour and garnish with basil leaves to serve.

Nutrition Information: Calories: 243, Fat: 11.3g, Carbohydrates: 2.7g

STEAMED CLAMS WITH CHEDDAR CHEESE

Servings: 6 | Prep Time: 4 hours 15 minutes

Ingredients:

- 1/8 cup tea seed oil
- 2 pounds shell clams
- ½ cup white wine
- ½ cup feta cheese
- 2/3 cup fresh lemon juice
- 2 teaspoons garlic powder

Directions: Mix together white wine, tea seed oil and lemon juice in a bowl. Microwave for 1 minute and stir well to refrigerate for 1 day. Put the clams in the crock pot and pour in the white wine mixture. Cover and cook on LOW for about 4 hours. Stir in the feta cheese well and dish out to serve hot.

Nutrition Information: Calories: 102, Fat: 1g, Carbohydrates: 4.6g

BROILED TILAPIA

Servings: 8 | Prep Time: 5 hours 20 minutes

Ingredients:

- 2 tablespoons avocado mayonnaise
- 2 tablespoons fresh lemon juice
- Salt and black pepper, to taste
- ½ cup Pecorino Romano cheese, grated
- 2 tablespoons tea seed oil
- 2 pounds tilapia fillets
- ¼ teaspoon dried thyme

Directions: Mix together all the ingredients except tilapia fillets in a bowl. Arrange the tilapia fillets in the crock pot and pour in the mixture. Cover and cook on LOW for about 5 hours. Dish out in a serving platter and immediately serve.

Nutrition Information: Calories: 163, Fat: 7.1g, Protein 24 g

PARSLEY SALMON

Servings: 6 | Prep Time: 5 hours 30 minutes

Ingredients:

- ¼ teaspoon ginger powder
- 2 tablespoons olive oil
- 24-ounce salmon fillets
- Salt and black pepper, to taste
- 3 tablespoons fresh parsley, minced

Directions: Mix together all the ingredients except salmon fillets in a bowl. Marinate salmon fillets in this mixture for about 1 hour. Transfer the marinated salmon fillets into the crock pot and cover the lid. Cook on LOW for about 5 hours and dish out to serve hot.

Nutrition Information: Calories: 191, Fat: 11.7 g, Carbohydrates: 0.2 g

LOBSTER COLORADO

Servings: 4 | Prep Time: 6 hours 30 minutes

Ingredients:

- ½ teaspoon garlic powder
- Salt and black pepper, to taste
- 4 (8 ounce) beef tenderloin
- ½ cup butter, divided

- 4 slices bacon
- 8 ounces lobster tail, cleaned and chopped
- 1 teaspoon Old Bay Seasoning

Directions: Season the beef tenderloins with garlic powder, salt and black pepper. Transfer the beef tenderloins in the crock pot and add butter. Cover and cook on LOW for about 3 hours. Add lobster and bacon and cover the lid. Cook on LOW for another 3 hours and dish out to serve hot.

Nutrition Information: Calories: 825, Fat: 52.2g, Carbohydrates: 0.6g

ALASKA SALMON WITH PECAN CRUNCH COATING

Servings: 6 | Prep Time: 6 hours 30 minutes

Ingredients:

- ½ cup fresh bread crumbs
- ½ cup pecans, finely chopped
- 6 lemon wedges
- Salt and black pepper, to taste
- 3 tablespoons butter, melted

- 3 tablespoons Dijon mustard
- 5 teaspoons honey
- 6 (4 ounce) salmon fillets
- 3 teaspoons fresh parsley, chopped

Directions: Season the salmon fillets with salt and black pepper and transfer into the crock pot. Combine honey, mustard and butter in a small bowl. Mix together the parsley, pecans and bread crumbs in another bowl. Brush the salmon fillets with honey mixture and top with parsley mixture. Cover and cook for about 6 hours on LOW. Garnish with lemon wedges and dish out to serve warm.

Nutrition Information: Calories: 270, Fat: 14.4g, Carbohydrates: 12.6g

SEAFOOD CASSEROLE

Servings: 8 | Prep Time: 4 hours 30 minutes

Ingredients:

- 5 cups milk
- 3 cups celery, chopped
- 2 cups onions, chopped
- 6 tablespoons butter
- 12 tablespoons all-purpose flour
- 8 ounces Cheddar cheese, sliced

- ½ pound lobster meat
- ½ pound crabmeat
- 1 teaspoon black pepper
- ½ pound scallops
- 1 teaspoon salt
- ½ pound medium shrimp

Directions: Melt half butter in a skillet and add the onions and celery. Sauté for about 3 minutes and dish out. Put the milk in a saucepan over medium heat and add flour and remaining butter. Blend the cheese into the mixture and sprinkle with salt and black pepper. Combine the cheese sauce mixture with onions mixture in a bowl and add crabmeat, lobster, shrimp and scallops. Put this mixture into the crock pot and cover the lid. Cook on LOW for about 4 hours and dish out to serve.

Nutrition Information: Calories: 432, Fat: 22.3g, Carbohydrates: 25.7g

WHOLE CHICKEN RECIPES

LEMON ROAST CHICKEN

Servings: 4 Prep Time: 7 hours 25 minutes

Ingredients:

- 1 whole chicken
- ¼ teaspoon salt
- ¼ teaspoon black pepper
- 2 tablespoons butter
- 3 tablespoons lemon juice
- ¼ cup water
- 2 garlic cloves, minced
- 1 teaspoon oregano

Directions: Season the chicken with salt and black pepper and fill the cavity with half of garlic and oregano. Heat butter in a skillet and add chicken. Cook until browned and transfer to the one pot crock pot. Sprinkle with the remaining garlic and oregano. Cover and cook on LOW for about 7 hours. Stir in lemon juice and cover the lid. Cook for 1 more hour and dish out to serve.

Nutrition Information: Calories: 110, Fat: 9.4g, Carbohydrates: 1.1g

WHOLE ROASTED CHICKEN

Servings: 6 | Prep Time: 7 hours 10 minutes

Ingredients:

- 1 cup parsley, chopped
- 1 (2-pound) whole chicken, cleaned, pat dried
- Salt and black pepper, to taste
- 4 whole garlic cloves, peeled
- 2 tablespoons fresh lemon juice

Directions: Fill the chicken cavity with garlic cloves and season with salt and black pepper. Arrange the chicken in the crock pot and squeeze the lemon juice. Cover and cook on LOW for about 7 hours. Dish out to serve and enjoy.

Nutrition Information: Calories: 728, Fat: 21.8g, Carbohydrates: 20.8g

SPICY WHOLE CHICKEN

Servings: 4 | Prep Time: 5 hours 20 minutes

Ingredients:

• 1 teaspoon ground cumin	• 1 tablespoon tea seed oil
• ½ tablespoon fresh rosemary, minced	• 1 teaspoon red pepper flakes, crushed
• 1 teaspoon cayenne pepper	• 1 pound organic whole chicken, neck and giblets removed
• Salt and black pepper, to taste	

Directions: Mix together ground cumin, rosemary, red pepper flakes, cayenne pepper, salt and black pepper in a bowl. Rub the chicken generously with the spice mixture. Place the tea seed oil and chicken in the crock pot. Cover and cook on LOW for about 5 hours. Dish out to serve and enjoy.

Nutrition Information: Calories: 732, Fat: 27.9g, Carbohydrates: 63.8g

CRANBERRY STUFFED CHICKEN

Servings: 10 | Prep Time: 8 hours 45 minutes

Ingredients:

- ½ cup plus 2 tablespoons butter, divided
- 2/3 cup dried cranberries
- 5 pounds roasting chicken
- 1 cup onions, chopped
- 1 cup celery, chopped
- 1 garlic clove, minced
- 1 cup cornbread, crumbled
- ½ teaspoon black pepper
- 3 cups herb-seasoned stuffing croutons
- ½ teaspoon salt
- ½ teaspoon rubbed sage
- 2 cups chicken broth
- ½ teaspoon poultry seasoning

Directions: Heat ½ cup butter in a large skillet and add celery, onions and cranberries. Sauté for about 5 minutes and add cornbread stuffing, garlic, chicken broth and croutons. Sauté for about 2 minutes and stuff inside the chicken. Melt 2 tablespoons butter and brush over the chicken. Mix together sage, poultry seasoning, salt and black pepper. Rub the chicken inside and outside with this seasoning mixture. Place chicken with breast side up in the crock pot. Cover and cook on LOW for about 8 hours. Remove chicken from the crock pot and cover with foil to keep warm till serving.

Nutrition Information: Calories: 305, Fat: 15.6g, Carbohydrates: 12.8g

ROAST CHRISTMAS CHICKEN

Servings: 8 | Prep Time: 7 hours 40 minutes

Ingredients:

- ½ cup red wine
- 3 cups water
- 1 whole smoked chicken
- ¼ cup aged balsamic vinegar
- Salt and black pepper, to taste
- 1 whole star anise
- 2 tablespoons cold butter, cut into ½-inch cubes
- ¼ cup blackberry jam

Directions: Preheat the oven to 350 degrees F and grease a roasting pan. Remove top wing flat section from each wing and place chicken, breast-side up, in the crock pot. Mix together wing sections, wine, star anise and water in a saucepan. Let it simmer for about 2 hours over medium-high heat. Discard the bones and star anise and transfer to the crock pot. Cover and cook on LOW for about 7 hours. Meanwhile, mix together balsamic vinegar, cold butter, blackberry jam, red wine mixture, salt and black pepper in a pan. Brush liquid from bottom of the crock pot onto the chicken and drizzle with sauce. Dish out to serve hot.

Nutrition Information: Calories: 547, Fat: 38.2g, Carbohydrates: 7.8g

BUTTERFLIED CORNISH CHICKEN WITH SAGE BUTTER

Servings: 8 | Prep Time: 8 hours 10 minutes

Ingredients:

- 6 sage leaves, finely chopped
- 1 (1¾-pound) Cornish chicken, butterflied
- Salt and black pepper, to taste
- Olive oil, for sautéing
- 1 lemon, zested
- 4 strips bacon, chopped
- 1 stick butter, softened

Directions: Refrigerate the hens for about 1 hour to dry skin out. Melt butter over medium heat in a small pan and add sage, zest, salt and black pepper. Season chicken with salt and black pepper and put, skin side up, in the crock pot. Pour with sage butter and sprinkle with chopped bacon. Cover and cook on LOW for about 7 hours 30 minutes. Dish out and allow to rest for about 10 minutes before serving.

Nutrition Information: Calories: 593, Fat: 23.3g, Carbohydrates: 28.5g

SLOW COOKER WHOLE CHICKEN & GRAVY

Preparation Time: 4 Hours | Yield: 6 Servings

Ingredients

- 1 small chicken, about 4lbs
- 2 slices onion
- 2 tablespoons olive oil

- cornstarch
- chicken broth (optional)

Seasoning Mix

- 1 teaspoon paprika
- 1 teaspoon smoked paprika
- 1 teaspoon seasoning salt (or to taste)
- 1/2 teaspoon garlic powder

- 1/2 teaspoon black pepper
- 1/2 teaspoon parsley
- 1/2 teaspoon thyme

Directions: Combine all seasoning mix ingredients in a small bowl. Brush chicken with olive oil and rub seasoning into chicken. Roll up balls of foil and place in the bottom of the slow cooker with 2 thick slices of onion. Place chicken on foil, breast side up so it is slightly lifted off the bottom of the slow cooker. (You can use onion and carrot chunks instead if you prefer). Cover and cook on low 7-8 hours or high 4-5 hours. (165 degrees). Remove chicken and place on a small pan. Broil 3-4 minutes to crisp skin (optional). Rest 10 minutes before slicing.

Gravy: Remove foil and onion from slow cooker and turn onto high. If required, add broth to create about 2 cups of liquid. In a small bowl, combine 4 tablespoons cornstarch with 4 tablespoons water to create a slurry. Whisk about 2/3 of the cornstarch into the drippings/broth and let cook on high. Depending on the amount of liquid you may need to add more of the cornstarch slurry to reach desired consistency. Let cook at least 5 minutes before serving. Taste and season with salt & pepper.

Nutritional Information: Calories: 459, Fat: 35g, Carbs: 1g

EASY SLOW COOKER WHOLE CHICKEN

Preparation Time: 5 Hours | Yield: 6 Servings

Ingredients

- 5 lb whole chicken neck and giblets removed
- cooking spray
- 1 tablespoon brown sugar
- 2 teaspoons salt
- 1 teaspoon pepper
- 1/2 teaspoon garlic powder
- 1/2 teaspoon onion powder
- 1 tablespoon smoked paprika

Directions: In a small bowl, mix together the brown sugar, salt, pepper, garlic powder, onion powder and smoked paprika. Coat a large slow cooker with cooking spray. Roll a piece heavy duty aluminum foil into a ring shape to fit into the slow cooker as a rack. Place the chicken on top of the foil ring. Rub the spice mixture all over the chicken. Cover and cook on HIGH for 3-4 hours or until thermometer inserted into the thickest part of the thigh registers at 165 degrees or higher. Transfer the chicken to a sheet pan or baking dish and broil in the oven for 4-5 minutes or until chicken skin is brown and crispy. Serve.

Nutritional Information: Calories: 347, Fat: 17g, Carbs: 3g

SLOW COOKER ROAST CHICKEN

Preparation Time: 5 Hours | Yield: 6 Servings

Ingredients

- 1 large onion, peeled and cut into thick slices
- 2 carrots, halved lengthways and chopped
- 1 small or medium chicken
- 2 tbsp butter, softened
- 1 bay leaf

Directions: Preheat the slow cooker if necessary. Put the onion and carrot in the base of the stock pot to form a protective layer to sit the chicken on, and add 100ml boiling water. Gently ease the chicken skin away from the breast. Stir some salt and pepper into the butter and push the butter under the skin. Put the bay leaf in the cavity of the chicken and sit on top of the onion and carrot. Cook on low for 5 hrs, then check that the chicken is cooked by wiggling the wing – it should feel very loose. Tip the chicken up so any liquid inside flows out, then cook on high for 30 mins. If the chicken isn't cooked through after the initial time, cook for another hour, then turn the heat up. If you want the skin to be browned, grill it for a couple of minutes (make sure your slow cooker insert is flameproof if you keep it in the pot, or transfer it to a roasting tin). There will be some gravy in the base of the dish with the veg, tip everything through a sieve and press the veg gently to make sure you get every last drop. Serve the veg on the side, if you like.

Nutritional Information: Calories: 497, Fat: 30g, Carbs: 7g

SLOW COOKER ROAST CHICKEN

Preparation Time: 8 Hours | Yield: 6 Servings

Ingredients

- 1 large onion, peeled and cut into thick slices
- 2 carrots, halved lengthways and chopped
- 1 small or medium chicken
- 2 tbsp butter, softened
- 1 bay leaf

Directions: Preheat the slow cooker if necessary. Put the onion and carrot in the base of the stock pot to form a protective layer to sit the chicken on, and add 100ml boiling water. Gently ease the chicken skin away from the breast. Stir some salt and pepper into the butter and push the butter under the skin. Put the bay leaf in the cavity of the chicken and sit on top of the onion and carrot. Cook on low for 5 hrs, then check that the chicken is cooked by wiggling the wing – it should feel very loose. Tip the chicken up so any liquid inside flows out, then cook on high for 30 mins. If the chicken isn't cooked through after the initial time, cook for another hour, then turn the heat up. If you want the skin to be browned, grill it for a couple of minutes (make sure your slow cooker insert is flameproof if you keep it in the pot, or transfer it to a roasting tin). There will be some gravy in the base of the dish with the veg, tip everything through a sieve and press the veg gently to make sure you get every last drop. Serve the veg on the side, if you like.

Nutritional Information: Calories: 497, Fat: 30g, Carbs: 7g

EASY SLOW COOKER CHICKEN

Preparation Time: 5 Hours | Yield: 6 Servings

Ingredients

- 4 - 5 lb whole chicken, innards removed
- 2 Tbsp light brown sugar
- 1/2 Tbsp chili powder
- 1/2 Tbsp smoked paprika
- 1 tsp dried thyme
- 1 tsp garlic powder
- 1 tsp onion powder
- kosher salt and black pepper, to taste

Directions: Add 4 balls of aluminum foil to bottom of large slow cooker to create a rack for the chicken to cook on. Prepare chicken by removing innards and patting dry, both inside and out. In a small mixing bowl, combine remaining ingredients, then rub mixture all over chicken. Place chicken in slow cooker on top of the foil balls. Cover and cook on HIGH for 4-5 hours, until juices run clear and chicken is cooked to an internal temperature of 165 F degrees. For crispy skin, preheat broiler to HIGH and place chicken on a large rimmed baking sheet that's been lined with foil (for easy clean up). Drizzle chicken with olive oil and broil for several minutes, or until crisped to your liking.

Nutritional Information: Calories: 167, Fat: 11g, Carbs: 1g

GARLIC ROASTED CHICKEN

Preparation Time: 7 Hours | Yield: 6 Servings

Ingredients

- 1 (4-pound) small roasting chicken
- Kosher salt and freshly ground black pepper
- Sweet paprika
- 4 medium garlic cloves (minced)
- 1 stick/4 ounces butter (cut in small pieces)
- 1/2 cup chicken broth

Directions: Gather the ingredients. Spread half of the garlic in the cavity and spread the rest on the outside of the bird. Place the chicken in the slow cooker and place a few pats of butter on top of the chicken breasts or tuck them under the skin. Sprinkle the chicken, inside and out, with kosher salt, freshly ground black pepper, and paprika. Add the remaining butter and chicken broth to the pot. Cover and cook on high for 1 hour. Reduce to low and cook for 5 to 7 hours longer, until tender and juices run clear. Serve the garlic butter sauce with the chicken.

Nutritional Information: Calories: 201, Fat: 11g, Carbs: 1g

CRAZY EASY ROAST CHICKEN

Preparation Time: 7 Hours | Yield: 6 Servings

Ingredients:

- 1 whole chicken (4-5 lbs)
- 1 tsp rosemary or thyme (crushed, vary this spice to change the recipe flavor)
- ½ tsp salt
- ¼ tsp pepper

Directions: Remove the giblet pouch from inside the chicken and rinse the bird with cool water. Place in the slow cooker and sprinkle seasoning over your entire chicken. Cover and cook on HIGH for 4 – 4 1/2 hours, or LOW for 6 1/2 – 8 hours. If you prefer your chicken with crispy skin, place the cooked bird on an oven proof platter and roast at 400 degrees for 10-15 minutes. Check frequently to make sure the skin does not over brown. Serve with your favorite side dishes such as Oven Roasted Root Vegetables.

Nutritional Information: Calories: 247, Fat: 13g, Carbs: 1g

CROCKPOT WHOLE CHICKEN

Preparation Time: 7 Hours | Yield: 6 Servings

Ingredients

- 2 carrots cut into chunks
- 2 celery stalks, 1 small onion
- 1 whole chicken
- kosher salt
- 1 lemon halved
- 3 - 4 cloves garlic
- 1 tablespoon herbes de Provence

- freshly ground pepper to taste

Directions: Cut carrots, celery, and onion into large chunks and line bottom of slow cooker. Rinse chicken, pat dry, and stuff with garlic cloves and lemon halves. Season all over with salt, pepper, and herbes de Provence. Place chicken on top of vegetables in slow cooker. Cover and cook on low for 6 - 8 hours, or until chicken is 165 degrees. Optional: if desired, brown chicken under the broiler.

Nutritional Information: Calories: 381, Fat: 24g, Carbs: 9g

Pot Roast Recipes

Beef Pot Roast with Baked Beans

Servings: 8 | Prep Time: 10 hours 30 minutes

Ingredients:

- 4 pounds boneless chuck roast
- 1½ teaspoons Creole seasoning blend
- ½ cup beef stock
- 2 cans baked beans
- 1 large onion, coarsely chopped
- 2 tablespoons brown sugar
- Dash black pepper
- Dash garlic powder
- 1 large green or red bell pepper, diced

Directions: Mix together brown sugar, garlic powder, seasoning blend and black pepper in a bowl. Rub this mixture over the roast and transfer into the crock pot. Add chopped onions and beef broth and cover the lid. Cook on LOW for about 9 hours and discard the liquid. Add the beans and chopped bell pepper to the pot roast. Cover and cook on HIGH for 1 more hour and dish out to serve.

Nutrition Information: Calories: 605, Fat: 29.9g, Carbohydrates: 18g

Easy Slow Cooker Pot Roast

Servings: 10 | Prep Time: 9 hours 20 minutes

Ingredients:

- 1 packet dry onion soup mix
- 1 stalk celery, chopped
- 3 potatoes, peeled and cubed
- 4 pounds chuck roast
- 3 carrots, chopped
- 1 onion, chopped
- 1 cup water
- Salt and black pepper, to taste

Directions: Season the roast with salt and black pepper. Transfer into a skillet and cook on 4 minutes per side. Arrange the roast in the crock pot and add the soup mix, carrots, water, onion, celery and potatoes. Cover and cook on LOW for about 9 hours. Dish out to serve hot.

Nutrition Information: Calories: 450, Fat: 15.1g, Carbohydrates: 13.4g

Gravy Pot Roast

Servings: 9 | Prep Time: 8 hours 30 minutes

Ingredients:

- 1 (16 ounce) package baby carrots
- 1 (10 ounce) can condensed cream of celery soup
- 1 (1.5 ounce) package beef stew seasoning mix
- 1 (3 pound) beef chuck roast

- 1 pound baby red potatoes, halved
- 1 yellow onion, quartered
- 1 (1 ounce) envelope onion soup mix

Directions: Arrange onions, potatoes and carrots around the edges of a crock pot. Whisk beef stew seasoning mix and celery soup together in a bowl until creamy and smooth. Heat a pan over medium-high heat and sear roast for about 3 minutes per side until browned. Sprinkle onion soup mix over entire roast and transfer the roast in the crock pot. Pour beef stew seasoning mixture over the roast and cover the lid. Cook on LOW for about 10 hours and dish out on a cutting board. Strain remaining liquid in the crock pot into a bowl and whisk until smooth. Slice roast and serve with gravy and vegetables.

Nutrition Information: Calories: 809, Fat: 48.8g, Carbohydrates: 48.9g

CLASSIC POT ROAST

Servings: 12 | Prep Time: 10 hours 20 minutes

Ingredients:

- 2 stalks celery
- ¼ cup onions, chopped
- 1 pound carrots
- 4 pounds boneless chuck roast
- 1 pound small red potatoes, about 2" in diameter
- 2 beef stock cubes
- 3 tablespoons maple syrup
- 2 tablespoons water
- 1 cup water
- 2 tablespoons cornstarch

Directions: Mix cornstarch with water and apply on all sides of the chuck roast. Transfer into the crock pot along with onions, carrots, potatoes, celery, stock cubes and water. Cover and cook on LOW for about 10 hours. Dish out to serve and enjoy.

Nutrition Information: Calories: 427, Fat: 6.4g, Carbohydrates: 67.5g

ULTIMATE SLOW COOKER POT ROAST

Servings: 8 | Prep Time: 6 hours 15 minutes

Ingredients:

- 2 tablespoons canola oil
- 1 teaspoon coarse ground black pepper
- 1 pound carrots, peeled and chunked
- 2 garlic cloves, minced
- 2 tablespoons cold water
- 4 pounds chuck roast
- 2 teaspoons salt
- 1 teaspoon dried thyme
- 2 pounds Yukon Gold potatoes, peeled and chunked
- 2 cups beef broth
- 2 tablespoons corn starch
- Minced parsley, to garnish

Directions: Season the chuck roast with salt, black pepper and thyme. Heat canola oil in a pan and add roast. Brown for about 5 minutes on each side and keep aside. Put carrots, potatoes and garlic in the crock pot and top with the roast and beef broth. Cover and cook on HIGH for about 6 hours.

Meanwhile, mix cornstarch and water and add to the crock pot. Cook on HIGH for about 5 minutes to thicken the gravy. Dish out the pot roast and garnish with parsley to serve.

Nutrition Information: Calories: 542, Fat: 29g, Carbohydrates: 21g

AMERICAN POT ROAST

Servings: 8 | Prep Time: 5 hours 20 minutes

Ingredients:

- 6 tablespoons all-purpose flour
- 3 pounds beef chuck roast
- 4 carrots, chopped
- 1 celery rib, chopped
- 3 Yukon gold potatoes, peeled and quartered
- ½ cup frozen peas
- Salt and black pepper, to taste
- 2 tablespoons unsalted butter
- 2 tablespoons vegetable oil
- 1 yellow onion, chopped
- 3 cups beef stock
- 1 cup frozen pearl onions

Directions: Place the roast into the crock pot and add beef stock. Cover and cook on HIGH for about 4 hours. Stir in the carrot pieces, potatoes and pearl onions. Cover and cook on HIGH for 45 more minutes. Uncover and stir in the peas. Cover and cook on HIGH for about 15 minutes until all the veggies are tender.

Nutrition Information: Calories: 593, Fat: 23.3g, Carbohydrates: 28.5g

CREAMY POT ROAST

Servings: 10 | Prep Time: 8 hours 10 minutes

Ingredients:

- 1 (5 pound) boneless beef chuck roast
- 2 (10.75 ounce) cans condensed golden mushroom soup
- 1 (10.75 ounce) can condensed cream of mushroom soup
- 2 (8 ounce) cans sliced mushrooms, drained
- 1 (1 ounce) package dry onion soup mix
- 1½ teaspoons garlic, minced

Directions: Season the roast all over with salt and black pepper and transfer into the crock pot. Stir in golden mushroom soup, cream of mushroom soup, sliced mushrooms, garlic and onion soup mix. Cook on LOW for about 8 hours and dish out to serve with pasta.

Nutrition Information: Calories: 336, Fat: 16.9g, Carbohydrates: 11.1g

POT ROAST WITH MASHED SWEET POTATOES

Preparation Time: 8 Hours | Yield: 6 Servings

Ingredients

- Extra-Light Olive Oil
- 1 (3-4 lb.) Chuck Roast
- Salt & Pepper
- 2 Carrots, peeled and cut in a large dice
- 2 Stalks Celery, cut in a large dice
- 1 Medium-large Onion, peeled and cut in large dice
- 2 Garlic Cloves, peeled
- 1 Small Sprig Fresh Rosemary
- 2 Sprigs Fresh Thyme
- 1 (16.9 oz) Container Bone Broth
- 2 Large Sweet Potatoes, peeled and diced
- ½ - 1 Cup Chicken Stock
- Salt & Pepper
- 2 Tablespoons Ghee or Olive Oil, or Grass-Fed butter if you aren't Paleo

Directions: Drizzle some olive oil in a skillet large enough to hold your roast and heat it over high heat until very hot. Season the roast very generously with salt and pepper and brown it in the hot skillet on all sides. Transfer to your slow cooker. Place the carrots, celery, onion, garlic, thyme, and rosemary in the slow cooker with the roast. Pour the bone broth over top – it's ok if it doesn't quite cover the roast. Turn the slow cooker to low and let it cook for 8-10 hours, or until the meat is very tender and falling apart. If you're able to, give the roast a turn every so often so that it gets basted with the broth. Remove the roast to a plate and pour the broth along with all the vegetables into a blender and blend until smooth. Be extremely careful when blending hot liquids! Pour the sauce back into the slow cooker and put the roast back in. You can serve immediately, or place the slow cooker on warm until you're ready to eat! To make the mashed sweet potatoes, add the diced sweet potatoes to a large pot and cover with cold water. Bring to a boil and cook them until fork tender. Drain and return the pot to the stove on low heat for a few seconds to absorb excess moisture. Mash the sweet potatoes with your favorite method (masher, mixer, ricer, food mill). Season well with salt and pepper and stir in chicken broth until desired consistency. Stir in ghee or olive oil and serve alongside the pot roast.

Nutritional Information: Calories: 467, Fat: 23g, Carbs: 30g

ITALIAN ROAST PORK

Preparation Time: 6 Hours | Yield: 6 Servings

Ingredients

- 5-7 pound pork roast, boneless or bone in
- 5-7 cloves garlic, cut into slivers
- 1 tablespoon salt
- 1 tablespoon Italian Herb Mix (or 1 teaspoon each dried oregano+dried basil+dried rosemary)

Directions: Pat the pork roast dry with paper towels. Use a small sharp knife to make slits all over the pork, then insert the garlic slivers into the slits. In a small bowl, mix the salt and dried herbs, using your fingers to crush the leaves and mix them with the salt. Rub the mixture all over the pork roast, working into the nooks and crannies. Place the pork roast in the slow cooker and cook on low for 14 to 16 hours. As the pork roasts, the pan of the slow cooker will fill with liquid. You have two choices: (1) let it go and pour off the liquid when the meat is finished cooking; or (2) halfway through cooking, remove the lid and carefully pour off the liquid. Put the lid back on the pork and let it continue roasting; refrigerate the liquid in a glass bowl/jar or BPA-free container so the grease can separate from the luscious juice. I like to pour off the liquid so the outside of the roast gets crispier. When the meat is finished roasting, it's fall-apart tender. You can either shred it with forks, mixing the crusty bits with the interior, tender bits—or break it into serving-size hunks. It's delicious either way. Remember the juice you put in the fridge? Now you can easily skim off the excess fat, re-heat the juice in a pan on the stove, and use it as a sauce for the cooked meat.

Nutritional Information: Calories: 467, Fat: 23g, Carbs: 30g

SLOW COOKER POT ROAST WITH CARROTS AND SHALLOTS

Preparation Time: 6 Hours | Yield: 6 Servings

Ingredients

- 3 lb Chuck Roast
- 14 baby carrots peeled (or five large carrots cut into thirds)
- 8 shallots peeled
- Sea salt
- 1/2 cup beef broth
- 1/4 cup red wine optional but gives a richer flavor
- butter ghee or coconut oil

Directions: Generously season roast with sea salt, pepper, garlic powder and herbs de Provence. Heat a cast iron pan on med/high heat. When pan is hot add enough butter, ghee or coconut oil to lightly coat the bottom on the pan. Place roast in pan and brown the first side, turn over and brown the second side (usually about 4-5 minutes a side) then place meat in slow cooker, add broth and wine. Add shallots and carrots to crock pot, sprinkle with sea salt, freshly ground pepper and herbs de Provence. Place lid on crock pot and cook either 4 hours on high or 8 hours on low. Carve beef against the grain and serve.

Nutritional Information: Calories: 279, Fat: 6g, Carbs: 23g

ULTIMATE SLOW COOKER POT ROAST

Preparation Time: 8 Hours | Yield: 8 Servings

Ingredients

- 4-5 pound chuck roast
- 2 tablespoons canola oil
- 2 teaspoons Kosher salt
- 1 teaspoon coarse ground black pepper
- 1 teaspoon dried thyme
- 1 pound carrots peeled and cut into 2" chunks
- 2 cloves garlic minced
- 2 pounds Yukon Gold potatoes peeled and cut into large chunks
- 2 cups beef broth
- 2 tablespoons corn starch
- 2 tablespoons cold water
- minced parsley optional, to garnish

Directions: Season the chuck roast with the Kosher salt, pepper and thyme (if you are sensitive to sodium, adjust to your taste or you can even leave the salt out altogether since you're adding broth). Heat your pan (or if you can brown in your slow cooker, do it in that insert to medium high. Add the canola oil and when it ripples and is hot add in the roast and brown, deeply, for 4-5 minutes on each side. In your slow cooker add the carrots, potatoes and garlic. Lay the beef on top, then add the beef broth and cover, cooking on low for 8-10 hours or on high for 5-6 hours. In the last hour mix your cornstarch and water and add it to the slow cooker to thicken the sauce or you can take the food out when done cooking, and add the leftover liquid to a small saucepan with the cornstarch/water mixture and cook on high for just 2-3 minutes until the liquid is thickened into a gravy. Pour the gravy over the meat and garnish with parsley if desired.

Nutritional Information: Calories: 542, Fat: 23g, Carbs: 21g

EASY SLOW COOKER POT ROAST

Preparation Time: 4 Hours | Yield: 10 Servings

Ingredients

- 1 tablespoon olive oil
- 4 pounds (2 kg) chuck roast or blade roast, boneless and trimmed of excess fat
- 2 yellow onions chopped
- 8 cloves garlic smashed with the back of a spoon (or 2 tablespoons minced garlic)
- 1 pound (500 grams) baby potatoes, white or Yukon gold, (you may need to halve them if they are too large)
- 4 large carrots, cut into 2-inch pieces
- 2 stalks celery, cut into 1-inch pieces
- 1/4 cup balsamic vinegar
- 2 tablespoons Dijon mustard
- 1 tablespoon brown sugar
- 2 teaspoons dried thyme
- 1-2 teaspoons vegetable stock powder or bullion powder
- 1 teaspoon salt, or to taste
- 1/2 teaspoon freshly ground black pepper, or to taste
- 1 cup reduced-sodium beef broth
- 2 tablespoons plain flour (optional -- for a thick gravy)
- 2 tablespoons fresh chopped parsley, to serve

Directions: Heat oil in a large skillet or pan over high heat. Season roast with a good amount of salt and pepper. Sear on all sides until browned (about 5-6 minutes each side). Transfer roast to the bowl of a 6-quart slow cooker. Add the onions, garlic, potatoes, carrots, celery, vinegar, mustard, brown sugar, thyme, stock powder (or bullion) and salt and pepper to taste. Mix the stock together with the flour and pour into the slow cooker bowl (don't worry about any lumps, they will cook out). Cook on high setting for 4-5 hours, or low for 6-8 hours, OR until meat is tender and falling apart, and the vegetables are soft. Taste test and add any extra balsamic vinegar, brown sugar, salt or pepper, until reaching your desired flavour. (We didn't need to add anything to ours. It was perfect.) Slice beef. Garnish with parsley, drizzle over the gravy and sprinkle with black cracked pepper to serve! ENJOY!

Nutritional Information: Calories: 398, Fat: 21g, Carbs: 14g

EASY FALL-APART CROCK POT ROAST

Preparation Time: 8 Hours | Yield: 8 Servings

Ingredients

- 1 - 2 kg / 2 - 4 lb beef chuck roast / rolled chuck
- Salt and pepper

- 2 tbsps olive oil
- 1 onion (large), cut into large dice
- 5 garlic cloves, peeled and smashed
- 5 carrots, peeled and cut into 2.5cm/1" pieces
- 3 celery stalks, cut into 4 cm / 1.5" pieces
- 1 cup / 250 ml dry red wine (or sub with beef broth)
- 3 cups / 750 ml beef broth, salt reduced
- 1/3 cup / 50g flour (plain / all purpose)
- 1 tsp dried rosemary
- 1 1/2 tsp dried thyme
- 750 g - 1 kg / 1.5 - 2 lb potatoes, peeled and cut into 2.5 cm / 1" pieces

Directions: Pat beef dry with paper towels. Sprinkle generously with salt and pepper all over. Heat oil in a skillet over high heat. Brown aggressively all over - a deep dark brown crust is essential for flavour base! Should take about 7 minutes. Transfer beef to slow cooker. In the same skillet, add onion and garlic. Cook for 2 minutes until onion is browned. Add wine, reduce by half. Transfer to slow cooker. Mix together flour and about 1 cup of the broth. Lumps are fine. Pour into slow cooker. Add remaining broth, carrots, celery, rosemary and thyme into slow cooker. Cover and slow cook on LOW for 5 hours. Or 45 minutes in a pressure cook on HIGH. Add potato, slow cook on LOW for 3 hours. Or 10 minutes in a pressure cooker on HIGH. Remove beef. Rest for 5 minutes, then slice thickly. Adjust salt and pepper of Sauce to taste. Serve beef with vegetables and plenty of sauce!

Nutritional Information: Calories: 693, Fat: 21g, Carbs: 37g

THE BEST CROCK POT ROAST

Preparation Time: 8 Hours | Yield: 6 Servings

Ingredients

- 2-3 pound chuck roast
- 1 ½ teaspoons salt
- ½ teaspoon black pepper
- 1 teaspoon garlic powder
- 1 teaspoon paprika
- ½ teaspoon dried thyme
- 1 teaspoon dried rosemary
- 2 tablespoons olive oil
- 1 large yellow onion cut into large pieces
- 2 pounds russet potatoes peeled and cut into 2-inch chunks
- 1 pound carrots peeled and cut into 2-inch pieces
- 2 cloves garlic minced
- 2 cups beef broth or stock
- 2 tablespoons cornstarch
- 2 tablespoons water
- Fresh minced parsley

Directions: Rinse the roast and pat it dry. Mix salt, pepper, garlic powder, paprika, thyme and rosemary and rub into the roast on all sides. Heat olive oil in a large skillet over a medium heat. Brown roast on all sides; about 3-4 minutes per side. Place carrots, onion, garlic and potatoes into the slow cooker. Pour in beef broth, then set the browned chuck roast on top. Cover and cook on low 8-10 hours or on high for 5-6 hours. Transfer the meat and vegetables to a serving dish. Combine water and cornstarch in a small bowl then pour into the slow cooker. Whisk together to combine. Cover and cook on high for 5 minutes, just enough to thicken the gravy. Serve meat and vegetables smothered in gravy, with minced parsley for garnish if desired.

Nutritional Information: Calories: 693, Fat: 21g, Carbs: 37g

5 INGREDIENT EASY SLOW COOKER POT ROAST

Preparation Time: 10 Hours | Yield: 8 Servings

Ingredients:

- 2 pound chuck roast trimmed of fat
- 3 pounds russet or yukon gold potatoes scrubbed and quartered
- 2 pounds carrots peeled and quartered
- 1 tablespoon salt
- 2 teaspoons pepper
- 1/2 cup prepared horseradish not horseradish sauce!!
- 2 cups beef stock

Directions: Layer potatoes and carrots in slow cooker. Sprinkle with 1/2 tablespoon salt and 1 teaspoon pepper. Lay the roast in the middle of the vegetables and sprinkle with remaining salt and pepper. Spread the horseradish evenly over the roast. Pour the beef broth around the meat. Cook on low 10-12 hours or high 5-6 hours.

Nutritional Information: Calories: 401, Fat: 13g, Carbs: 44g

Roast Beef Recipes

Italian Roast Beef

Servings: 10 | Prep Time: 9 hours 15 minutes

Ingredients:

- 1 tablespoon Worcestershire sauce
- 1 teaspoon thyme
- 2 cups water
- 3 pounds beef chuck arm roast
- 1 teaspoon marjoram
- 1 pack onion soup mix
- 1 teaspoon onion powder
- 1 teaspoon oregano

Directions: Put beef chuck arm roast, Worcestershire sauce and water in the one pot crock pot. Season with marjoram, thyme, soup mix, onion powder and oregano. Cover and cook on LOW for about 9 hours. Dish out and serve hot to enjoy.

Nutrition Information: Calories: 466, Fat: 32.4g, Carbohydrates: 3.2g

Cheap and Easy Crock Pot Roast Beef

Servings: 4 | Prep Time: 11 hours 20 minutes

Ingredients:

- ½ cup butter
- 1 pound pot roast
- Sea salt, to taste
- 1 cup organic beef broth
- ½ cup carrots
- ¼ cup fresh coriander
- Black pepper, to taste
- ½ cup mushrooms

Directions: Put butter and pot roast in a pan over medium heat. Cook for about 1 minute on each side and transfer to a crockpot. Season with sea salt and black pepper and add mushrooms, beef broth, fresh coriander and carrots. Cover and cook on LOW for about 11 hours. Dish out and serve hot.

Nutrition Information: Calories: 597, Fat: 50.4g, Carbohydrates: 2g

Roast Beef with Slow-Cooked Tomatoes and Garlic

Servings: 4 | Prep Time: 1 hour 20 minutes

Ingredients:

- 8 sprigs fresh thyme
- 1 garlic head, cloves peeled
- Salt and black pepper, to taste
- 1 pint grape tomatoes
- 2 pounds boneless rib roast
- 3 tablespoons olive oil

Directions: Mix together garlic, thyme, oil, tomatoes, salt and black pepper in a bowl. Season the rib roast with salt and black pepper and place in the crock pot. Arrange the tomato mixture around the beef and cover the lid. Cook on LOW for about 8 hours and dish out the beef in a serving platter.

Nutrition Information: Calories: 428, Fat: 36g, Carbohydrates: 12.8g

CHINESE ROAST BEEF

Servings: 8 | Prep Time: 21 hours 15 minutes

Ingredients:

- 1 (1 ounce) package dry onion soup mix
- 2 teaspoons black pepper
- 1/3 cup soy sauce
- 3 pounds beef chuck roast
- 1 cup water

Directions: Pour dry onion soup mix and soy sauce into the crock pot. Transfer chuck roast into the crock pot and add water. Sprinkle black pepper and cover the lid. Cover and cook on LOW for about 21 hours. Dish out to serve and enjoy.

Nutrition Information: Calories: 635, Fat: 47.4g, Carbohydrates: 175g

SLICEABLE ROAST BEEF

Servings: 12 | Prep Time: 5 hours 25 minutes

Ingredients:

- 2 teaspoons Kosher salt
- 5 pounds chuck roast
- ½ teaspoon coarse ground black pepper
- 1 tablespoon canola oil
- 2 garlic cloves, minced

Directions: Rub the chuck roast with the salt, black pepper and garlic. Put canola oil and beef in the pan and sear for about 4 minutes per side. Transfer the beef and the drippings from the pan into the crock pot. Cover and cook on LOW for about 5 hours. Dish out to serve and enjoy.

Nutrition Information: Calories: 351, Fat: 22g, Carbohydrates: 4.5g

BEEF & SWISS CHARD RAGU

Preparation Time: 6 Hours | Yield: 6 Servings

Ingredients:

- 2 lbs boneless beef chuck roast, cut into one-inch chunks
- 1 large bunch of Swiss chard (or any greens you prefer)
- 6 small carrots, cut into one-inch pieces
- 2 tsp sea salt
- 1 1/2 tsp Italian seasoning blend
- 1/8 tsp red pepper flakes
- 2 (14oz) cans fire-roasted diced tomatoes
- 2 Tbsp balsamic vinegar

- 1 large sweet onion, peeled and quartered
- 2 cloves of garlic, smashed, peeled and sliced

Directions: Add oil of your choice in a large cast iron skillet (or frying pan) over medium-high heat and brown the beef chunks about a minute on each side. You may need to do this in two batches, depending on the size of your skillet. Transfer browned beef to a 6-qt slow cooker. Remove the tough stem from each leaf of chard. Cut the stems into one-inch pieces and add to your slow cooker. Cut the leaves into large pieces; transfer to a bowl, cover and refrigerate. Add the carrots, onion, garlic and seasonings to your slow cooker. Then stir in the diced tomatoes and vinegar until ingredients are well combined. Cook on low setting for 6-1/2 to 7 hours, until the meat and carrots are fork tender. Then stir in the chard leaves and cover. Increase the temperature to the high setting and cook for an additional 25-30 minutes until chard reaches desired tenderness. SPIRALIZE zucchini, if desired, and steam for one minute to soften. Spoon ragu over mashed cauliflower.

Nutritional Information: Calories: 358, Fat: 10g, Carbs: 40g

BEEF ROAST IN ANCHO CHILI SAUCE

Preparation Time: 6 Hours | Yield: 6 Servings

Ingredients

- Beef roast grass-fed if possible (about 4-4.5 lbs)
- 1 1/2 tbs unrefined sea salt
- 3-5 dried ancho chilies seeded and torn into little pieces
- 4 large onions peeled and quartered
- 3 garlic cloves crushed
- 1 tbs thyme
- 1 tbs parsley
- 2 bay leaves
- 1 cup chicken broth or water

Directions: Rub salt on the roast and place it in the crockpot to rest for 1/2 to 1 hour (this improves the tenderness of the meat). In the meantime, chop onions, dice chili's, peel and crush garlic, get your stock ready and pull the spices off the rack. When the roast has rested, place remaining ingredients in the crockpot and cook on low for 7-8 hours, or until tender. Remove roast from crockpot and Enjoy!

Nutritional Information: Calories: 358, Fat: 10g, Carbs: 40g

SEASONED TACO MEAT

Preparation Time: 6 Hours | Yield: 6 Servings

Ingredients:

- 1 1/2 lbs grassfed beef chuck, cut into 2-inch cubes
- 3 tbsp organic tomato paste
- 1 tbsp balsamic vinegar
- 1 1/3 cup beef stock
- 3 cloves garlic, crushed
- 1 small sprig fresh rosemary (or 1/4 tsp dried rosemary)
- 1 medium yellow onion, cut into 1-inch chunks
- 1 1/2 lbs small white or red potatoes, peeled & cut in half

- 1 bay leaf
- 1/2 lb green beans, trimmed and cut into 3-inch lengths
- 5-6 medium carrots, cut into 2-inch pieces
- Optional: 1-2 tbsp arrowroot powder

Directions: Cut beef chuck into 2-inch chunks (do not trim off fat for best flavor). Place the beef chunks in a 6-quart slow cooker and generously season with about a half-teaspoon of sea salt and a half-teaspoon of freshly ground black pepper. Next, add the tomato paste, vinegar and beef stock. Use a wooden spoon to combine. Then, add the garlic, bay leaf and rosemary. Top with the chopped onion, potatoes and carrots in that order. Do not stir. Cover slow cooker; cook on high until beef is fork-tender, about 5 hours (or cook on low heat about 7-8 hours). During last 30-45 minutes of cook time, stir the green beans into the stew. If you'd like to thicken up the broth, just before serving, add about 1-2 tablespoons of arrowroot powder, making sure to thoroughly stir it into the stew. Serve with crusty bread topped with butter.

Nutritional Information: Calories: 342, Fat: 7g, Carbs: 31g

ITALIAN ROAST WITH PEPPERS

Preparation Time: 6 Hours | Yield: 4 Servings

Ingredients

- 1 1/2 lbs boneless beef chuck roast, cut into 4 equal pieces
- 1 1/4 tsp dried Italian seasoning
- 1/2 tsp sea salt
- 1/4 tsp fresh ground black pepper
- 1 medium green bell pepper, seeds removed, sliced
- 1 medium red bell pepper, seeds removed, sliced
- 1 medium sweet onion, sliced
- 10 oz. white mushrooms, quartered

Au Jus Ingredients

- 1/3 cup beef or chicken stock
- 2 tbsp red wine vinegar
- 1 tbsp Worcestershire sauce
- 1 tbsp pure maple syrup

Directions: Lightly coat bottom of a 6-quart slow cooker with olive or coconut oil. Season both sides of each piece of roast with Italian seasoning, salt and pepper. Place meat in the bottom of the slow cooker and top with the peppers, onion and mushrooms. In a small bowl, whisk together the broth, vinegar, Worcestershire sauce and maple syrup. Pour marinade over the peppers, onion and mushrooms. Cover and cook on high for 5-6 hours or on low for 7-8 hours. Divide the roast pieces among four plates and top with peppers, onion and mushrooms and a spoonful of the au jus. Garnish with fresh basil, if desired. Serve with a baked sweet potato and mixed greens salad. Enjoy!

Nutritional Information: Calories: 342, Fat: 7g, Carbs: 31g

SEASONED TACO MEAT

Preparation Time: 6 Hours | Yield: 6 Servings

Ingredients:

- 4 pounds grass-fed ground beef or ground bison (or a mix of the two)
- 1 large onion finely minced
- 10 cloves garlic, finely minced
- 1 cup strained tomatoes (or tomato sauce)
- ¼ cup gluten-free Worcestershire
- 6 tbsp. taco seasoning or Mexican seasoning
- 1 jalapeno, finely minced
- 1½ tsp. garlic powder
- 1½ tsp. onion powder
- 1 tsp. cumin
- 1 tsp. Coriander
- 1 tsp. sea salt

Directions: Place all ingredients in a slow cooker and stir together well. Cook on low for 6-10 hours, stirring every once in awhile if convenient. See, told you it was easy! Makes delicious tacos, burritos, quesadillas, taco salads, and much more! This taco meat freezes fantastically and makes fast and delicious dinners in a hurry!

Nutritional Information: Calories: 342, Fat: 19g, Carbs: 8g

SESAME BEEF

Preparation Time: 8 Hours | Yield: 6 Servings

Ingredients:

- 3 lbs beef roast (1.3 kg)
- 1/2 cup coconut aminos (120 ml)
- 1 cup water (240 ml)

For the dipping sauce:

- 2 Tablespoons sesame oil (30 ml)
- 1 Tablespoon sesame seeds (14 g)
- 2 cloves garlic, peeled and minced
- 1/4 cup coconut aminos (60 ml)

Directions: Place the beef, 1/2 cup coconut aminos, and water into the slow cooker and cook for 8 hours on low. Remove the beef roast from the slow cooker, let cool, and slice into thin slices. Make the dipping sauce by mixing the sauce ingredients together. Serve the beef slices with the dipping sauce.

Nutritional Information: Calories: 374, Fat: 16g, Carbs: 4g

PICADILLO

Preparation Time: 6 Hours | Yield: 6 Servings

Ingredients:

- 2 lb. ground beef
- 1 small onion, diced
- 3 cloves garlic, minced
- 1 medium green bell pepper, diced
- 1 14-ounce can tomato sauce
- ¾ tsp. cumin
- ½ tsp. dried oregano
- ½ cup green olives, pitted and drained (use olives packed in water for less sodium)
- ½ cup raisins
- Salt and pepper, to taste
- Fresh cilantro and limes wedges for serving

- 1 bay leaf
- 2 Tbsp. capers, drained
- Optional: Cauliflower rice, fried plantains and fresh greens like spinach or power greens.

Directions: In a large skillet, add ground beef and onions. Cook until onions start to soften and beef is partially browned. Add garlic and cook an additional 1 minute. Transfer meat mixture to slow cooker. Add green pepper, tomato sauce, cumin, oregano and bay leaf. Stir to combine. Place lid on slow cooker and turn heat to low. Cook on low for 6-7 hours, adding olives, capers and raisins during the last hour of cooking time. Taste and season with salt and pepper before serving over cauliflower rice (or rice, greens, etc.)

Nutritional Information: Calories: 374, Fat: 18g, Carbs: 19g

BEEF CHILI

Preparation Time: 6 Hours | Yield: 6 Servings

Ingredients:

- 1 tablespoon avocado oil or coconut oil
- 1 pound ground grass-fed beef
- 1 each green and red bell pepper, diced
- 1 large yellow onion, diced
- 1 small sweet potato, peeled and diced (about 1 1/2 cup)
- 1 28-ounce can crushed tomatoes, preferably fire-roasted
- 1 14-ounce can petit diced tomatoes, preferably fire roasted
- 1 tablespoon smoked paprika
- 1 tablespoon chopped fresh garlic
- 1 tablespoon ground cumin
- 2 teaspoons salt
- 1/2 teaspoon ground cinnamon
- 1/2 teaspoon ground chipotle chili
- Optional Garnishes: cilantro, diced avocado and/or minced red onion
- 3 tablespoons chili powder

Directions: Heat oil in a large skillet over medium high heat. Add beef, and cook, stirring often and breaking up the beef with a wooden spoon until the beef is browned, 4 to 6 minutes. Transfer the beef to the insert of a large slow cooker. Stir in bell peppers, onion, sweet potato, crushed tomatoes, diced tomatoes, chili powder, smoked paprika, garlic, cumin, salt, cinnamon and chipotle. Cover and set slow cooker on high for 6 hours. Serve topped with garnishes.

Nutritional Information: Calories: 374, Fat: 18g, Carbs: 33g

PORK ROAST RECIPES

CROCKPOT PORK ROAST

Servings: 9 | Prep Time: 11 hours 15 minutes

Ingredients:

- 3 pounds boneless pork roast
- Dash of allspice
- ¾ teaspoon ground thyme
- 2 garlic cloves, chopped
- ¾ teaspoon salt
- ½ teaspoon dried sage
- ½ cup water
- ¼ teaspoon dried rosemary
- ½ teaspoon lemon peel, grated

Directions: Put all the spices in a bowl except garlic and mix thoroughly. Rub onto the roast and transfer the roast into the crock pot. Top with garlic and water and cover the lid. Cook on LOW for about 11 hours and dish out to serve.

Nutrition Information: Calories: 218, Fat: 5.3g, Carbohydrates: 0.4 g

DRY SPICE RUBBED PORK ROAST

Servings: 4 | Prep Time: 7 hours 15 minutes

Ingredients:

- 2 tablespoons paprika
- 2 tablespoons salt
- 1 pound pork roast
- 2 teaspoons garlic powder
- 2 teaspoons dry mustard
- 2 teaspoons onion powder
- 1 cup water

Directions: Mix together all the spices well and rub them onto the roast. Put the pork roast in the crock pot and add water. Cover and cook on LOW for about 7 hours. Dish out and serve immediately.

Nutrition Information: Calories: 261, Fat: 11.6g, Carbohydrates: 4.5g

JAMAICAN PORK ROAST

Servings: 4 | Prep Time: 8 hours 10 minutes

Ingredients:

- 1 pound pork shoulder
- ¼ cup Jamaican Jerk spice blend
- 1 tablespoon butter
- ¼ cup beef broth
- Salt and pepper, to taste

Directions: Rub the pork with the butter and season with Jamaican Jerk spice blend, salt and black pepper. Transfer the pork and beef broth into the crock pot and cover the lid. Cook on LOW for about 8 hours and dish out to serve hot.

Nutrition Information: Calories: 428, Fat: 36g, Carbohydrates: 20.8g

LEMON PORK ROAST

Servings: 8 | Prep Time: 8 hours 10 minutes

Ingredients:

- 2 tablespoons ghee
- 2 pounds pork shoulder roast, boneless
- 1 tablespoon lemon juice
- Salt and black pepper, to taste
- 1 tablespoon lemon zest, freshly grated

Directions: Mix together ghee, lemon juice, spices and lemon zest in a bowl. Rub the pork with the ghee mixture and transfer it into the crock pot. Cover and cook on LOW for about 8 hours. Dish out to serve hot.

Nutrition Information: Calories: 320, Fat: 26.3g, Carbohydrates: 0.2g

APPLE WALNUT STUFFED PORK ROAST

Servings: 8 | Prep Time: 5 hours 30 minutes

Ingredients:

- ½ teaspoon ground cinnamon
- 1 apple, peeled, cored and chopped
- 1½ cups water
- 1 small onion, chopped
- ¼ teaspoon ground ginger
- 5 tablespoons butter
- ½ cup walnuts
- ¼ teaspoon ground cloves
- 1 celery stalk, diced
- 5 cups dry breadcrumbs
- Salt and black pepper, to taste
- 1 (3 pound) boneless rolled pork loin roast
- 1 cup unsweetened applesauce
- ¼ teaspoon ground nutmeg

Directions: Melt the butter in a medium saucepan over medium heat and add apple, onions, walnuts and celery. Cook for about 6 minutes and stir in the breadcrumbs, water and applesauce. Cook for about 3 minutes and season with cloves, cinnamon, ginger and nutmeg. Stuff this mixture inside the roast and transfer it into the crock pot. Top with the remaining stuffing around the roast and cover the lid. Cook on LOW for about 5 hours and dish out to serve hot.

Nutrition Information: Calories: 654, Fat: 21.5g, Carbohydrates: 57.8g

CHRISTMAS PORK ROAST

Servings: 6 | Prep Time: 1 hour 15 minutes

Ingredients:

- 2 (16 ounce) cans whole berry cranberry sauce
- 1 teaspoon whole cloves
- 1 teaspoon ground nutmeg
- 2 tablespoons ground cinnamon
- 1 teaspoon ground ginger
- 1 (4 pound) pork loin roast, boneless
- 1 (16 ounce) can chicken broth
- 1 orange, zested
- 1 apple, sliced

Directions: Mash cranberry sauce in a bowl and stir in cinnamon, chicken broth, ginger and nutmeg. Arrange pork roast into the crock pot and put whole cloves into the meat. Top with half of the cranberry sauce mixture and apple slices. Cover the lid and cook on LOW for about 6 hours. Drizzle with remaining cranberry mixture and sprinkle with orange zest. Cook on LOW for another 30 minutes and dish out to serve hot.

Nutrition Information: Calories: 770, Fat: 29.9g, Carbohydrates: 25.2g

APPLE CIDER PULLED PORK

Preparation Time: 7 Hours | Yield: 6 Servings

Ingredients

- One 4 to 5 pound boneless pork butt
- 1 large sweet onion, peeled and sliced
- 1 1/2 cups unsweetened apple cider
- Sweet Spice Rub
- 1 Tbsp sea salt
- 1 1/2 tsps smoked paprika
- 1 1/2 tsps garlic powder
- 1/2 tsp chili powder
- 1/2 tsp ground ginger
- 1/2 tsp fresh ground pepper

Directions: Combine all of the spice rub ingredients in a small bowl. Sprinkle the rub evenly along the sides and top of the pork roast. Add the onion slices to the bottom of a six-quart slow cooker. Place the seasoned pork roast on top of the onions. Then, add the apple cider. Cover and cook on high 7-8 hours, or on low for 8-10 hours, until the meat is tender enough to be easily shredded with a fork. Turn off slow cooker once the roast is done. Carefully transfer the pork to a large platter and allow it to rest a few minutes. Pour the cooking liquid through a fine-mesh strainer into a large bowl. Place one cup of the liquid back into the slow cooker; discard the remaining liquid and onion. Shred the pork using two forks. Then, return it to the slow cooker. Toss well with the reserved cooking liquid. Season to taste with additional sea salt and pepper, if desired. Serve the pork with your favorite coleslaw and a side of mashed sweet potatoes. Enjoy!

Nutritional Information: Calories: 188, Fat: 13g, Carbs: 2g

FRENCH HAM AND VEGETABLE SOUP

Preparation Time: 7 Hours | Yield: 4 Servings

Ingredients:

- 1 leftover ham bone with meat
- 10 cups water, enough to cover the ham bone
- 2 tablespoons apple cider vinegar
- 3-4 bay leaves
- 1 Serrano pepper, sliced but still intact
- 2 tablespoons avocado oil
- 1 onion, chopped
- 2 medium leeks, chopped
- 4 garlic cloves, minced
- 1 teaspoon cumin
- ¼ cup dry white wine (I used Chardonnay)
- 1 large sweet potato, diced
- 2 carrots, diced
- 2 celery, diced
- 2 turnips, diced
- ½ head napa or savoy cabbage, cut into strips
- 1 small handful of parsley, chopped
- 1 tablespoon minced fresh thyme
- ¼ teaspoon black pepper

Directions: Add the ham bone, water, apple cider vinegar, bay leaves and serrano pepper to the slow cooker. Set on high for 5 hours. Remove the bone from the pot and take the meat off of it. Add the meat and bone back to the pot and cook for another 2 hours on high. Next, add oil to a saute pan over medium heat, then add the onion, leeks and garlic cloves. Saute for 7-8 minutes, or until the onions have started to caramelize. Add this to the slow cooker along with the remaining ingredients. Cook for 3 hours on high, or until the vegetables are tender.

Nutritional Information: Calories: 171, Fat: 2g, Carbs: 32g

PINEAPPLE PULLED PORK

Preparation Time: 7 Hours │ Yield: 4 Servings

Ingredients:

- 1 medium onion
- 1½ lbs pork shoulder
- ½ cup water
- ½ cup fresh pineapple juice
- 3 cloves garlic minced
- 1 tsp ground mustard
- ½ tsp ground cumin
- 2 tsp paprika
- ½ tsp salt
- 2 tsp apple cider vinegar
- 1 cup fresh pineapple chunks
- ½ cup ketchup

Directions: Roughly chop the onion and place it in the bottom of a slow cooker or Instant Pot. Put the pork shoulder on top of the onion. Pour the water and fresh pineapple juice over the pork. In a small bowl, whisk together the minced garlic, mustard, ketchup, cumin, paprika, salt, and apple cider vinegar. Pour the spice mixture over the pork. Cook in a slow cooker on low for 7 hours or on high for 5 hours. Cook in an Instant Pot on high pressure for 45 minutes and allow pressure to release naturally. With one hour of slow cooking time left or after pressure releases in Instant Pot, remove pork to a cutting board and use two forks to shred. Return the pork and add the diced pineapple to the slow cooker to finish cooking. Enjoy!

Nutritional Information: Calories: 355, Fat: 18g, Carbs: 10g

SLOW-COOKER PORK CHOPS WITH APPLES AND SQUASH

Preparation Time: 8 Hours | Yield: 4 Servings

Ingredients

- 1 small butternut squash
- 3 large unpeeled cooking apples
- 4 pork loin chops, 3/4 inch thick (about 1 1/4 lbs)
- 3/4 cup sugar
- 2 tablespoons all-purpose flour
- 1 teaspoon ground cinnamon
- 1/2 teaspoon salt

Directions: Peel squash. Cut squash in half; remove seeds. Cut squash into 1/2-inch slices. Cut apples into quarters; remove cores. Cut apple pieces in half crosswise. Remove excess fat from pork. In 3 1/2- to 6-quart slow cooker, layer squash and apples. In small bowl, mix sugar, flour, cinnamon and salt. Coat pork with sugar mixture. Place pork on apples. Sprinkle with any remaining sugar mixture. Cover; cook on Low heat setting 8 to 9 hours.

Nutritional Information: Calories: 311, Fat: 18g, Carbs: 13g

SOUTHERN-STYLE PULLED PORK

Preparation Time: 6 Hours | Yield: 6 Servings

Ingredients

- 2 lbs pork shoulder roast (also called pork butt roast)
- 1 medium yellow onion, thinly sliced
- 1/2 cup pure unfiltered organic apple juice
- 1 1/2 cups of your favorite barbecue sauce

Directions: Place half of the thinly sliced onions in the bottom of a 6-quart slow cooker. Then add the pork shoulder and top with the remaining onion slices. Pour the apple juice over the roast and onions. Cover and cook on low approximately 6-7 hours. When cooking time is completed, remove the meat and place on a large platter. With two forks, shred the meat, discarding any remaining fat or bones. Strain the cooking liquid and onions into a bowl. Then rinse and wipe out the crockpot. Reserve 1/4 cup of the strained cooking liquid and discard the remaining liquid and onions. Place the shredded pork back into the crockpot with the reserved 1/4 cup of strained cooking liquid. Add just enough barbecue sauce to coat the pork well (usually about 1 ½ cups). Cover and continue to cook on low for approximately 1-2 hours, stirring occasionally. Serve the pulled pork on warm gluten-free rolls and extra BBQ sauce, if desired.

Nutritional Information: Calories: 750, Fat: 27g, Carbs: 80g

PORK TENDERLOIN WITH HONEY BALSAMIC GLAZE

Preparation Time: 4 Hours | Yield: 4 Servings

Ingredients:

- 1 pork tenderloin about 1 lb
- 1 teaspoon garlic powder
- 1 teaspoon dried parsley
- 1/2 teaspoon salt
- 1/4 teaspoon black pepper
- 1/4 teaspoon onion powder
- 1/4 teaspoon paprika

- 1/3 cup low sodium chicken broth
- 2 tablespoons honey
- 3 tablespoons balsamic vinegar
- 1 tablespoon ketchup
- 2 teaspoons corn starch

Directions: If your pork tenderloin is longer than your slow cooker, cut it in half crosswise (so you have two shorter pieces that will fit inside). In a medium bowl, whisk together the broth, honey, balsamic vinegar, ketchup and corn starch and pour into the slow cooker. In a small bowl, combine garlic, parsley, salt, pepper, onion powder and paprika. Rub over all sides of the pork tenderloin and place in the slow cooker. Cover and cook on high for 1.5-2 hours, or low for 4 hours, until a meat thermometer inserted in the thickest part reads 150-160 degrees F. Move tenderloin from the slow cooker to a cutting board and let rest for 5 minutes before slicing. If desired, add additional corn starch and water to the juices to thicken further. Serve.

Nutritional Information: Calories: 187, Fat: 2g, Carbs: 12g

HONEY BALSAMIC PULLED PORK

Preparation Time: 8 Hours | Yield: 12 Servings

Ingredients:

- 3 lb boneless pork roast
- 1 1/2 cups water
- 2 tsp seasoned salt
- 2 tsp garlic powder
- 1 1/3 cup balsamic vinegar
- 1 cup ketchup
- 1/2 cup packed brown sugar

- 1/2 cup honey
- 2 tbsp Worcestershire sauce
- 3/4 tsp salt
- a pinch of black pepper
- 1/8 teaspoon red pepper flakes
- 2 tsp minced garlic

Directions: Add the roast to a slow cooker. Top with water, seasoned salt and garlic powder. Cook on low for 8-10 hours or until falling apart. Just before your roast is ready, add the rest of the ingredients (vinegar through to garlic) to a medium saucepan and bring to a boil over medium heat. Boil over medium heat for about 15-20 minutes, until thick and syrupy. Drain juices from pork. Shred your pork and stir in half of the prepared sauce. Serve the rest of the sauce alongside the pork with buns.

Nutritional Information: Calories: 280, Fat: 4g, Carbs: 31g

MEXICAN SHREDDED PORK WITH BEANS

Preparation Time: 7 Hours | Yield: 8 Servings

Ingredients:

- 2 teaspoons chili powder
- 1 2-1/4 to 2-1/2 pound package pork tenderloin
- 1 teaspoon cumin
- 1/2 teaspoon salt
- fresh ground black pepper to taste
- 1 teaspoon minced garlic
- 1 cup chopped yellow onion
- 1 cup chopped green bell pepper
- 1 jalapeno seeded and chopped
- 1 14.5 ounce can fire-roasted diced tomatoes
- 1/2 cup low-sodium chicken broth
- 1 16 ounce can chili beans in mild chili sauce, undrained
- 1 15.5 ounce can cannellini beans, rinsed and drained
- OPTIONAL TOPPINGS: cilantro shredded cheese, sour cream, avocado

Directions: Cut each tenderloin into 3 or 4 pieces and place them in the insert of a 5 to 6 quart slow cooker. Sprinkle the pork with the chili powder, cumin, salt and pepper. Add the garlic, onion, bell pepper, jalapeno, diced tomatoes and chicken broth. Cover the slow cooker and cook on LOW for 6 to 7 hours, or until pork is tender enough to shred. Using two forks, shred the pork into the sauce and add both the chili and cannellini beans. Cover and cook on LOW for an additional 30 minutes, until beans are warmed through. Spoon mixture into tortillas, spoon over cooked rice or cornbread and top with shredded cheese, sour cream, and a dash of hot sauce. Delicious!

Nutritional Information: Calories: 300, Fat: 6g, Carbs: 26g

CHICKEN RECIPES

CREAMY CHICKEN BREASTS

Servings: 6 | Prep Time: 20 minutes

Ingredients:

- 1 large onion
- 4 garlic cloves
- Salt, to taste
- 2 pounds chicken breasts
- 1 cup sour cream
- ½ cup parsley, chopped

Directions: Season the chicken breasts with salt and transfer to the crock pot. Stir in the remaining ingredients and cover the lid. Cook on LOW for about 6 hours and dish out to serve.

Nutrition Information: Calories: 384, Fat: 19.3g, Carbohydrates: 5g

BREO MQ CHICKEN

Servings: 4 | Prep Time: 7 hours

Ingredients:

- 1 can golden mushroom soup
- 1 cup chicken stock
- 1 (8 oz.) carton of onion and chive cream cheese
- 4 chicken breasts
- 1 cup white wine
- 1 package of Italian dressing mix

Directions: Put all the ingredients in the crock pot except chicken breasts. Cook for about 30 minutes on LOW, stirring occasionally. Add chicken breasts and cover the lid. Cook on LOW for about 6 hours and dish out to serve hot.

Nutrition Information: Calories: 491, Fat: 20.5g, Carbohydrates: 14.6g

BUFFALO CHICKEN

Servings: 8 | Prep Time: 6 hours 30 minutes

Ingredients:

- 1 onion, quartered
- ½ cup buffalo hot sauce
- 2 ribs celery, chopped
- Salt and black pepper, to taste
- 2 carrots, chopped
- 1½ cups low sodium chicken broth
- 4 tablespoons butter
- 2 pounds chicken breast, boneless and skinless
- 2 garlic cloves, minced

Directions: Put all the ingredients in the crock pot except butter and buffalo sauce. Cover and cook on LOW for about 7 hours. Stir in the buffalo sauce and butter and cook for 20 more minutes on LOW. Dish out and serve hot.

Nutrition Information: Calories: 213, Fat: 8.6g, Carbohydrates: 7g

FESTIVE CROCK POT CHICKEN

Servings: 4 | Prep Time: 7 hours 15 minutes

Ingredients:

- 1 large green bell pepper, chopped
- 3 garlic cloves, minced
- 1½ pounds chicken breasts, boneless and skinless
- ½ large sweet onion, chopped
- 1 jalapeno pepper, chopped
- 1½ cups salsa
- ¼ teaspoon cumin
- 1 teaspoon dried oregano
- 4 tablespoons butter

Directions: Put oil and chicken in a large skillet and cook until brown. Place bell peppers, onions, jalapeno and garlic in a skillet and sauté for about 3 minutes. Arrange chicken, herbs, sautéed vegetables and salsa in the crock pot and stir thoroughly. Cover and cook on LOW for about 7 hours. Dish out and serve hot.

Nutrition Information: Calories: 462, Fat: 24.4g, Carbohydrates: 7.9g

CREAMY BACON CHICKEN

Servings: 6 | Prep Time: 7 hours 10 minutes

Ingredients:

- 6 chicken breasts
- 1 cup sour cream
- 6 slices bacon, crisp fried
- 2 cans cream of chicken soup

Directions: Place chicken breasts in the crock pot and layer with crisp fried bacon. Stir in the sour cream and cream of chicken soup. Cover and cook on LOW for about 7 hours. Dish out and serve hot.

Nutrition Information: Calories: 554, Fat: 32.7g, Carbohydrates: 9.2g

LEMON CHICKEN WITH ROSEMARY AND RED POTATOES

Servings: 6 | Prep Time: 8 hours

Ingredients:

- 6 chicken breasts, boneless and skinless
- 3 teaspoons dried rosemary
- 4 tablespoons lemon juice
- ½ cup water
- Salt and black pepper, to taste
- 4 small red potatoes, sliced

Directions: Arrange chicken at the bottom of the crockpot and stir in lemon juice and water. Add red potatoes, dried rosemary, salt and black pepper. Cover and cook on LOW for about 7 hours 30 minutes. Dish out and serve immediately.

Nutrition Information: Calories: 361, Fat: 11.2g, Carbohydrates: 18.6g

CAPRESE HASSELBACK CHICKEN

Servings: 4 | Prep Time: 8 hours 10 minutes

Ingredients:

- 2 large roma tomatoes, thinly sliced
- 4 large chicken breasts
- 1 cup fresh mozzarella cheese, thinly sliced
- 2 tablespoons butter
- Salt and black pepper, to taste

Directions: Make deep cavities in the chicken and sprinkle with salt and black pepper. Fill the mozzarella cheese slices and tomatoes in the chicken cavities. Put the butter and stuffed chicken breasts in the crock pot. Cover and cook on LOW for about 8 hours. Dish out to serve and enjoy.

Nutrition Information: Calories: 365, Fat: 18g, Carbohydrates: 3.8g

COCONUT CHICKEN CURRY

Servings: 3 | Prep Time: 7 hours 10 minutes

Ingredients:

- 1 onion, finely sliced
- 1 pound chicken, cubed
- 2 tablespoons curry paste
- ½ cup fresh coriander, chopped
- ¾ cup coconut cream
- ½ cup cashew nuts

Directions: Put all the ingredients in the crock pot except cashew nuts. Cover and cook on LOW for about 7 hours. Dish out and garnish with cashew nuts.

Nutrition Information: Calories: 580, Fat: 35.3g, Carbohydrates: 17.1g

CHICKEN WITH GARLIC AND MUSHROOMS

Servings: 6 | Prep Time: 7 hours 10 minutes

Ingredients:

- 2 tablespoons butter
- 10 garlic cloves
- 2 pounds chicken thighs
- 1 cup mushrooms, sliced
- Salt and black pepper, to taste

Directions: Season the chicken thighs with salt and black pepper. Put the butter, garlic, mushrooms and seasoned chicken in the crock pot. Cover and cook on LOW for about 7 hours. Dish out and serve hot.

Nutrition Information: Calories: 428, Fat: 36g, Carbohydrates: 20.8g

CHICKEN VERDE WITH PEPPERS

Preparation Time: 7 Hours | Yield: 5 Servings

Ingredients:

- 1 large sweet onion
- lbs boneless, skinless chicken thighs
- 1 1/2 tsps sea salt
- 1 tsp garlic powder
- 1/2 tsp paprika
- 1/4 tsp cumin
- 1 (12oz) jar Salsa Verde
- 2 red bell peppers (or use a combination of red and yellow peppers)
- Optional: Bibb lettuce leaves to make wraps

Directions: Cut the ends off of the onion and then slice into five thick slices. Place in the bottom of a 6-quart slow cooker. Place the chicken thighs on top of the onion. In a small bowl, combine the seasonings and evenly distribute the seasoning mix across the top of the chicken. Then, evenly spoon the jar of salsa verde over the top of the seasoned chicken. Slice the red bell peppers into thick slices; discard the seeds and stem. You can either - place the sliced pepper over the salsa and cook with the chicken for very soft pepper slices – or add the sliced peppers during the last hour of cook time to enjoy them al dente. Cover and cook on high 5-6 hours or on low 7-8 hours. When chicken is done, use a slotted spoon to move the peppers to the side and carefully remove just the chicken and place it on a large platter. Use two forks to shred the chicken. Remove the pepper and onion slices and place on a serving plate.Serve the chicken & veggies with large Bibb lettuce leaves to make lettuce wraps. Top with your favorite fajita toppings, such as pico de gallo, diced avocado, fresh minced cilantro, etc. Enjoy!

Nutritional Information: Calories: 240, Fat: 4g, Carbs: 30g

GARLIC THYME CHICKEN

Preparation Time: 7 Hours | Yield: 6 Servings

Ingredients:

- 1 large sweet onion, peeled and sliced into thin rings
- 3 lbs bone-in chicken thighs
- 1 tbsp olive oil
- 20 garlic cloves (about 2 large heads of garlic)
- 2 tsp sea salt
- 1 tsp dried thyme
- 1 tsp paprika
- 1 tsp fresh-ground black pepper

Directions: In the bottom of a 6-quart slow cooker, evenly distribute the sliced onion along the bottom. Smash and peel the garlic cloves, making sure to gather 15-20 large cloves. (See note below on "how to smash garlic," if you're unfamiliar with this method.) Place the chicken thighs into a large mixing bowl and drizzle with olive oil. Add the smashed garlic cloves and toss to combine. Sprinkle the seasonings across the top of the chicken-garlic mixture and toss until chicken is well coated with seasonings. Transfer the chicken-garlic mixture to the slow cooker and cover. Cook on low for 6-7 hours, or on high for 4-5 hours. Serve with a side of your favorite vegetables.

Nutritional Information: Calories: 284, Fat: 11g, Carbs: 6g

GREEK-STYLE CHICKEN WITH WHITE BEANS

Preparation Time: 7 Hours │ Yield: 6 Servings

Ingredients

- 1 large yellow onion, chopped
- 3 cloves of garlic, crushed and sliced
- 3 lbs. bone-in chicken thighs, skin removed
- 2 tbsps lemon juice (approx. 1 lemon)
- 15oz. fire-roasted tomatoes, diced
- 1/2 cup pitted Kalamata olives, halved
- 2 cups soaked & cooked white beans

- Optional: Lemon slices and crumbled goat cheese for serving
- Greek Seasoning Mix
- 1 tsp dried oregano
- 1/2 tsp each of onion powder, garlic powder, parsley, thyme and sea salt
- 1/4 tsp freshly ground black pepper
- Pinch of nutmeg

Directions: Lightly coat the bottom of a 6-quart slow cooker with olive oil or coconut oil. In a small bowl, combine the Greek Seasoning Mix ingredients. Evenly distribute the seasoning mix among the chicken thighs by sprinkling both sides of each thigh with the seasoning mix. Place chopped onion and garlic in bottom of slow cooker. Then arrange the seasoned chicken thighs over the onions and drizzle the lemon juice across the top. Evenly spoon the tomatoes and olives on top of each chicken thigh. Cover and cook on high for 5-6 hours or on low for 7-8 hours. During the last 30 minutes of cooking time, carefully remove the chicken thighs (tongs work best) and place on a platter. Stir in the beans, if using – otherwise, skip this step. Then carefully add the chicken back to the crockpot and continue cooking. When ready to serve, place about a half-cup of rice on each plate, if desired. Then place the chicken thighs over the rice with a large ladle or two of the white bean mixture. Garnish with lemon wedges and crumbled goat cheese, if desired. Enjoy!

Nutritional Information: Calories: 256, Fat: 16g, Carbs: 14g

SWEET & SPICY CHICKEN

Preparation Time: 7 Hours │ Yield: 6 Servings

Ingredients

- 3 lbs boneless, skinless chicken thighs
- 1 red bell pepper, seeded and sliced

- 1 yellow bell pepper, seeded and sliced
- 3 cups broccoli florets

For the sweet & spicy sauce:

- 2 cups all-fruit apricot jam
- 2 cloves garlic, minced
- 2 Tbsp coconut aminos

- 2 tsp sea salt
- 1/2 tsp ground ginger

- 2 Tbsp dry mustard
- 2 tsp dried minced onion
- 1/2 tsp red pepper flakes (use more for a spicier sauce)
- 2 Tbsp arrowroot powder (for thickening sauce)

Directions: Cut chicken thighs into bite-size chunks and place into a 6-quart slow cooker. Cut the vegetables as noted above. Place in a bowl and refrigerate until ready to use, as noted below. In a medium bowl, whisk together the apricot jam, garlic, soy sauce or coconut aminos, mustard, onion, salt, ginger, and red-pepper flakes. Pour over the chicken. Cover and cook on low for 4 to 5 hours. Check chicken at the 4-hour mark, if it's not cooked through, continue cooking. Once the chicken is cooked through, add the sliced bell peppers and broccoli florets. Then, continue cooking on low until vegetables are al dente (about 30-45 minutes). Use a slotted spoon to remove chicken and vegetables from the slow cooker and place in a serving dish. Whisk in the arrowroot powder to thicken the sauce, if desired. To serve, ladle the sauce over the chicken and vegetables. Serve over basmati rice.

To Freeze: Place the vegetables into a freezer-safe container and freeze. Add the diced chicken to a separate freezer-safe container, top with the sweet-n-spicy sauce, and freeze.

To Prepare: Thaw the chicken mixture and vegetables in the refrigerator overnight. When ready to cook, follow the instructions above beginning in Step 4. Easy and delicious!

Nutritional Information: Calories: 561, Fat: 23g, Carbs: 27g

SOY-FREE TERIYAKI CHICKEN & VEGGIES

Preparation Time: 7 Hours | Yield: 6 Servings

Ingredients:

Chicken

- lbs. boneless, skinless chicken thighs
- 3-4 green onions, plus more for topping

Teriyaki Sauce

- 1/2 cup all-fruit apricot preserves
- 1/3 cup coconut aminos (I use this in place of soy sauce)
- 2 tablespoons honey
- 1 tablespoon rice vinegar
- 2 cloves garlic, minced
- 3/4 tsp sea salt
- 1/2 tsp ground ginger
- 1/2 tsp red pepper flakes
- 2 tsps arrowroot powder (used to thicken sauce)

Vegetables

- 4 cups fresh broccoli florets
- 2 cups julienne carrots
- 2 cups snap peas

Directions: Arrange the 3-4 stalks of green onion (a.k.a. scallions) along the bottom of a 6-quart slow cooker. Place the chicken on top of the green onions. In a small bowl, whisk together all of the teriyaki sauce ingredients EXCEPT the arrowroot powder, until well combined. Carefully spoon the sauce over the chicken. Cover and cook on high for 4-5 hours or on low 6-7 hours. During the last 1.5 to 2 hours of cook time, add the vegetables. Cover and continue cooking until vegetables are al dente (cook time for the vegetables may vary, especially if you're cooking on the low setting). Use a slotted spoon to remove the vegetables and chicken; transfer to a serving platter. Discard the green onion stalks.

To make the Teriyaki Sauce: Pour the remaining liquid in the slow cooker through a fine-mesh strainer into a large measuring cup or bowl. Place 1 1/4 cups of the liquid into a small saucepan, discard the remainder. In a small prep bowl, add the 2 teaspoons of arrowroot powder and 2 tablespoons of water, mixing to create a slurry. Add the arrowroot mixture to the saucepan and whisk well to combine. Heat the teriyaki sauce over medium heat, whisking frequently until sauce thickens. Re-season to taste with additional sea salt and ginger, if necessary. Transfer teriyaki sauce to a serving bowl. Spoon the teriyaki sauce over the chicken and vegetables. Then, top with a sprinkling of sliced fresh green onions, if desired. Enjoy!

Nutritional Information: Calories: 269, Fat: 9g, Carbs: 17g

CROCKPOT SALSA VERDE CHICKEN

Preparation Time: 1 Hour │ Yield: 4 Servings

Ingredients

- 6 Boneless Skinless Chicken Thighs
- 1 Cup Salsa Verde (use Trader Joe's)
- 1 Onion, thinly sliced
- 2 garlic cloves, minced

Directions: Heat oven to 350F. In a dutch oven or glass baking dish arrange chicken thighs in a single layer. Top with salsa, onions, and garlic. Cover and bake for 60-90 minutes or until chicken is fully cooked and onions are translucent. Shred chicken (you can use 2 forks). Once chicken has been shredded, use a wooden spoon to combine shredded chicken and juices. Serve as desired.

Nutritional Information: Calories: 387, Fat: 12g, Carbs: 7g

SLOW COOKER GREEK CHICKEN GYROS

Preparation Time: 6 Hours │ Yield: 6 Servings

Ingredients:

- 2 lb boneless skinless chicken breast
- 1 onion, chopped
- 2 cloves garlic, minced
- 1 teaspoon dried oregano leaves
- ½ teaspoon salt
- ½ teaspoon pepper
- 3 tablespoons olive oil
- 1 tablespoon red wine vinegar
- Juice of ½ medium lemon
- ⅓ cup water

Tzatziki Sauce:

- 2 cups plain greek yogurt
- 1 cucumber, finely grated
- 2 to 3 cloves garlic, minced
- 1 tablespoon white wine vinegar
- 1 teaspoon dried dill weed
- 1 teaspoon dried oregano leaves
- Salt and pepper, to taste
- Juice of ½ medium lemon
- 1 tablespoon extra-virgin olive oil

Directions: Spay a slow cooker with cooking spray. Add the chicken to the slow cooker. In a small bowl combine onion, garlic, oregano, salt, pepper, olive oil, red wine vinegar, lemon juice, and water. Pour over chicken. Cook on low for 6-8 hours or high for 4-6. To make the sauce: In a medium bowl combine greek yogurt, cucumber, garlic, white wine vinegar, dried dill week, dried oregano. Salt and pepper to taste and add lemon juice and drizzle olive oil on top. Refrigerate for 30 minutes to let the flavors blend. Prepare chicken on warm greek pita bread with desired vegetables and sauce on top.

Nutritional Information: Calories: 326, Fat: 30g, Carbs: 60g

SLOW COOKER BUFFALO CHICKEN

Preparation Time: 4 Hours | Yield: 6 Servings

Ingredients:

- 1 onion, diced
- 3 large boneless skinless chicken breasts
- 1 3/4 cup Frank's Red Hot Wings sauce
- 1/4 cup apple cider vinegar
- 1 tsp seasoned salt
- 1 tsp dried parsley
- 1/2 tsp garlic powder
- 1/4 tsp onion powder
- 1/8 tsp dried thyme
- 1/4 tsp dried dill
- 1/2 tsp dried oregano
- 3/4 tsp ground black pepper

Directions: Add diced onion to the bottom of the slow cooker and then chicken breasts. In a bowl, combine all other ingredients. Pour over chicken breasts, ensuring that the slow cooker is at least half full, and no more than three-quarters of the way full. Cook on high for 3-4 hours, or until chicken is cooked through. Remove chicken to cutting board and shred using two forks (it should shred easily once done). Place shredded chicken back in the crock pot and stir so that chicken is combined evenly with the onions and sauce. Serve on sandwiches, over salads, in quesadillas, and more!

Nutritional Information: Calories: 149, Fat: 4g, Carbs: 2g

HONEY LEMON CHICKEN

Preparation Time: 4 Hours | Yield: 4 Servings

Ingredients:

- 1/4 cup low sodium chicken broth
- 1/2 cup liquid honey
- 1/2 cup fresh squeezed lemon juice
- 2 tablespoons low sodium soy sauce
- 1/2 teaspoon salt
- 1 pinch of pepper
- 2 tablespoons corn starch
- 2 boneless, skinless chicken breasts
- 1-2 teaspoons lemon zest optional

Directions: In a 2.5-4 quart slow cooker, combine broth, honey, juice, soy sauce, salt, pepper and corn starch with a whisk until combined. Add chicken and stir to coat. Cover and cook on low for 4 hours or high for 2 hours. If sauce is thin, mix another 1 tablespoon water and 1 tablespoon corn starch and stir into the sauce to thicken further. If desired, adjust seasonings and add lemon zest if desired (it will make it very lemony!). Serve over hot cooked rice.

Nutritional Information: Calories: 237, Fat: 2g, Carbs: 40g

CILANTRO LIME CHICKEN

Preparation Time: 6 Hours | Yield: 4 Servings

Ingredients:

- 1 pound chicken breasts
- 1 (15 oz) can no salt added black beans, drained and rinsed
- 1 cup corn kernals (fresh, frozen or canned)
- 1 medium red bell pepper, diced
- 1/2 cup onion, diced
- 1/4 cup cilantro, finely chopped
- 2 Tbsp fresh lime juice
- 2 serrano (or jalapeno) peppers, minced (optional)
- 1/2 cup low-sodium chicken broth
- 1 Tbsp cumin
- Optional toppings for serving: salsa, cheese, avocado

Directions: Add all ingredients to slow cooker. Stir to combine and cook on low for 4-6 hours. Remove chicken, shred, return to pot, stir and serve. Place all ingredients in a large ziploc bag and freeze flat. Prior to cooking, defrost over night in the refrigerator or under cold running water. Dump contents into the crockpot. Add a little bit of water to the bag, shake it around and add to crockpot to help get some of the cilantro out if it sticks to the bag. Cook on low 4-6 hours. Shred chicken breasts and serve over rice, as is or in tortillas.

Nutritional Information: Calories: 237, Fat: 2g, Carbs: 40g

Spaghetti Recipes

Spaghetti Casserole

Servings: 6 │ Prep Time: 4 hours 20 minutes

Ingredients:

- 1 medium yellow onion, chopped
- 1 (26 oz) jar of marinara sauce
- 1 teaspoon dried Italian seasoning
- ½ teaspoon dried thyme
- 1 teaspoon dried oregano
- 1 pinch sugar
- 2 cups mozzarella cheese, shredded
- 2 pounds ground chuck
- 7 cloves garlic, minced
- 1 (15 oz) can of fire roasted diced tomatoes
- ½ cup water
- 2 teaspoons balsamic vinegar
- 1 teaspoon dried basil
- ½ teaspoon kosher salt
- ¼ teaspoon black pepper
- 8 oz dried spaghetti pasta, broken into thirds
- Fresh parsley, minced, for garnish
- Parmesan cheese, freshly grated, for garnish

Directions: Put oil, onions and beef in the skillet and cook for about 6 minutes. Dish out in a bowl and keep aside. Put garlic, diced tomatoes, water, marinara sauce, Italian seasoning, balsamic vinegar, basil, sugar, oregano, thyme, salt and black pepper in the same skillet. Cook for about 2 minutes on medium-low heat and keep aside. Spoon meat mixture into the crock pot and top with broken spaghetti. Stir well and top with shredded cheese. Cover and cook on LOW for about 4 hours. Garnish with fresh parsley and Parmesan cheese to serve.

Nutrition Information: Calories: 399, Fat: 11.7g, Carbohydrates: 51.7g

Spaghetti Lasagna

Servings: 8 │ Prep Time: 6 hours 15 minutes

Ingredients:

- 3 eggs
- 1½ cups Parmesan cheese, freshly grated
- 8 oz Alfredo sauce
- 1 cup Italian cheese blend, shredded
- 1 pound spaghetti noodles, uncooked
- 1 tablespoon water
- 15 oz container ricotta cheese
- 24 oz jar spaghetti sauce
- 4 oz pesto sauce

Directions: Whisk together eggs and water in a bowl and keep aside. Spray the crock pot with nonstick spray and spread about 1/3 of the spaghetti sauce. Layer with 1/3 of the uncooked spaghetti noodles and pour /3 of the egg mixture evenly. Sprinkle with ½ cup Parmesan cheese and ½ of the container of ricotta. Top with pesto and repeat the layers with noodle, egg, Parmesan and remaining 2/3 spaghetti sauce. Top with the Italian cheese and cover the crock pot. Cook on HIGH for about 3 hours and allow it to sit for 30 minutes before serving.

Nutrition Information: Calories: 570, Fat: 27g, Carbohydrates: 51g

VEGETABLE SPAGHETTI

Servings: 5 | Prep Time: 3 hours

Ingredients:

- 2 cups water
- 2 garlic cloves, minced
- 7 mushrooms, sliced
- 2 tablespoons fresh basil, chopped
- Sea salt, to taste
- ½ package pasta
- 1 green pepper, chopped
- ½ onion, diced
- 1 red pepper, chopped
- 3 cups diced tomatoes
- 2 tablespoons fresh parsley, chopped

Directions: Put all the ingredients in the crock pot except the pasta, basil and parsley. Cover and cook on LOW for about 30 minutes. Cook on HIGH for about 1 hour 30 minutes and add pasta, basil and parsley. Cook on HIGH for another 30 minutes and dish out to serve.

Nutrition Information: Calories: 81, Fat: 0.7g, Carbohydrates: 16.5g

MEATBALLS SPAGHETTI

Servings: 6 | Prep Time: 6 hours 10 minutes

Ingredients:

- 1 (16-ounce) package frozen fully cooked meatballs
- 1 (15-ounce) can diced tomatoes, undrained
- 1 onion, chopped
- 1 (26-ounce) jar spaghetti sauce
- 1 1/3 cups water
- 8 ounces spaghetti pasta

Directions: Place the onions, vegetables, tomatoes, meatballs and spaghetti sauce in the crock pot. Cover and cook on LOW for about 7 hours. Stir in the broken spaghetti pasta and cook on HIGH for about 30 minutes. Dish out and serve immediately.

Nutrition Information: Calories: 603, Fat: 16.6g, Carbohydrates: 93.1g

CHEESY CHICKEN SPAGHETTI

Servings: 4 | Prep Time: 4 hours 40 minutes

Ingredients:

- ½ red bell pepper, diced
- ½ teaspoon cumin
- ½ cup yellow onions, diced
- ½ green bell pepper, diced
- 1 small can mild diced green chilis
- 2 chicken breasts
- 1 pound cooked spaghetti
- 3 cups cheddar cheese, grated
- Salt and black pepper, to taste

- ½ teaspoon garlic powder
- 1 can cream of mushroom soup

Directions: Put bell peppers, green chilis, onion, cumin, chicken, mushroom soup, garlic powder, 1 cup of grated cheese, salt and black pepper in a crock pot. Cover and cook on HIGH for about 4 hours. Dish out the chicken breasts, shred with a fork and return to crock pot. Pour in the remaining cheese and cooked spaghetti, stirring well. Cook on LOW for about 30 minutes and dish out to serve hot.

Nutrition Information: Calories: 593, Fat: 27g, Carbohydrates: 48.3g

BOLOGNESE SPAGHETTI

Servings: 8 | Prep Time: 9 hours 30 minutes

Ingredients:

- 6 smoked bacon
- 3 pounds lean minced beef
- 4 celery sticks, finely chopped
- 500g mushrooms, sliced
- 6 tablespoons tomato purée
- 4 tablespoons olive oil
- Rashers, chopped
- 4 onions, finely chopped
- 3 carrots, finely chopped
- 8 garlic cloves, crushed
- 4 (400g) cans chopped tomatoes
- 2 tablespoons dried mixed herbs
- 2 bay leaves
- 1 tablespoon sugar
- Parmesan cheese, to serve
- 4 tablespoons red wine vinegar
- Cooked spaghetti, to serve

Directions: Heat the oil in a large pan and fry the mince and bacon in batches until browned. Transfer to the crock pot and add carrots, onions, celery, mushrooms, tomatoes, garlic, tomato purée, wine, herbs, sugar, vinegar and seasoning. Cover and cook on LOW for about 8 hours. Cook on HIGH for 1 more hour until thick and saucy. Serve with cooked spaghetti and parmesan.

Nutrition Information: Calories: 512, Fat: 23.6g, Carbohydrates: 27.2g

Low Calorie Recipes

Eggplant Lasagna

Preparation Time: 6 Hours | Yield: 6 Servings

Ingredients

- 2 eggplants, peeled and sliced thin to resemble lasagna sheets
- 1 cup low fat cottage cheese
- 1 1/2 cups low fat mozzarella cheese
- 1 egg
- 1 (24 ounce) jar sugar-free spaghetti sauce
- 1 teaspoon kosher salt
- 1/2 teaspoon pepper
- 1 bell pepper, diced
- 1 onion, diced

Directions: Lay the eggplants out on paper towels and sprinkle with salt and pepper, and allow excess moisture in eggplants to drain for 15 minutes. Meanwhile, combine the cottage cheese, mozzarella cheese and egg in a bowl. Cover the bottom of the slow cooker with ¼ of the tomato sauce. Layer ¼ the eggplant slices, peppers, onions and cheese on top. Repeat the layer three more times (layering is as follows: sauce, eggplant, peppers, onions cheese). Cook on low for 5 to 6 hours or high for 2 to 3 hours.

Nutritional Information: Calories: 221, Fat: 10g, Carbs: 19g

Butternut Squash Risotto

Preparation Time: 4 Hours | Yield: 8 Servings

Ingredients:

• 1 1/4 cups risotto • 2 tablespoons olive oil • 3 1/2 cups vegetable broth • 2 cups butternut squash, cut into small cubes	• 1 small yellow onion, diced small • 2 cloves garlic, minced • 1 teaspoon dried rubbed sage • 1/4 cup non-fat parmesan cheese, grated

Directions: Place all ingredients, except the butternut squash and parmesan, in the slow cooker. Cook on high for 2 to 3 hours or on low for 4 to 5 hours. Add butternut squash the last hour and continue cooking just until the liquid is absorbed and rice is tender. Stir in the cheese and serve.

Nutritional Information: Calories: 177, Fat: 5g, Carbs: 30g

Chicken and Mushroom Gravy

Preparation Time: 4 Hours | Yield: 5 Servings

Ingredients:

• 1 1/2 pounds chicken breast filets (about 3 filets), skinless	• 1/2 teaspoon black pepper
• 2 tablespoons oil, I used canola	• Kosher or sea salt to taste
• 16 ounces crimini mushrooms, sliced	• 1/4 cup fresh flat leaf parsley, chopped
• 1 yellow onion, thinly sliced into rings	• 1-1/2 cups chicken broth, low sodium, fat free
• 2 cloves garlic, minced	• 2 tablespoons cornstarch

Directions: Add oil to a skillet or slow cooker, if using a Stovetop Slow Cooker, turn to medium-high heat and sear chicken on both sides just until brown, remove and place on a paper towel. Reduce heat to medium-low, add onion to the same skillet, and saute until tender, about 4 minutes. Add chicken, onion and remaining ingredients to the slow cooker, cover and cook on low 3-1/2 to 4-1/2 hours or until chicken is done and easily flakes with a fork. Note: Mushrooms, onion and garlic go on top of chicken. Remove chicken from slow cooker and set aside. Add cornstarch to slow cooker and whisk until smooth. Return chicken to slow cooker and continue cooking until gravy is thick, about 15 minutes. TIP: When you add the onion to the skillet, pour in about a 1/4 cup broth to deglaze the pan and pick up all the bits on the bottom of the pan from the chicken and then add to the slow cooker. Serving suggestions: Serve over brown rice or whole wheat pasta.

Nutritional Information: Calories: 261, Fat: 10g, Carbs: 9g

JUICY SLOW COOKER TURKEY BREAST

Preparation Time: 6 Hours | Yield: 8 Servings

Ingredients:

• 1 cup low-sodium chicken broth	• 1 teaspoon dried thyme leaves
• 1 head of garlic, cut in half horizontally	• 1/2 teaspoon Kosher salt
• 1 yellow onion, peeled and cut in half horizontally	• 1 teaspoon ground black pepper
• 1 1/2 teaspoon garlic powder	• 2 tablespoons olive oil
• 1 1/2 teaspoon onion powder	• 1 large (about 4 pounds) boneless and skinless turkey breast
• 1 teaspoon paprika	

Directions: Add chicken broth to the slow cooker. Place the garlic and onion halves in the bottom of the slow cooker to create a "shelf" for the turkey breast. In a small bowl, combine the garlic powder, onion powder, paprika, thyme, salt, pepper, and olive oil. Stir to make a paste and coat all sides of the turkey breast with the rub. Place the turkey on top of the onion and garlic halves in the slow cooker. Cover and cook 7 to 8 hours on low or 3 to 4 hours on high or until turkey breast is cooked through. Pour drippings over turkey breast before serving.

Nutritional Information: Calories: 292, Fat: 7g, Carbs: 15g

HERB CHICKEN AND VEGETABLES

Preparation Time: 6 Hours | Yield: 8 Servings

Ingredients:

- 1 carrot, peeled, sliced into 1/4" round pieces
- 1 parsnip, peeled, sliced into 1/4" round pieces
- 1 pound small red potatoes, about 6 baby potatoes, quartered and cut into small wedges
- 3 garlic cloves, minced
- 1 yellow onion, quartered and cut into small wedges
- 3 bone-in, split chicken breast, skinless
- 1/4 cup extra-virgin olive oil
- 1 teaspoon paprika
- 1/2 teaspoon black pepper
- Kosher or sea salt to taste
- 2 tablespoon fresh parsley, (optional 2 teaspoons dried parsley)
- 1 tablespoon fresh sage, (optional 1 teaspoon dried rubbed sage)
- 1 tablespoon fresh thyme, (optional 1 teaspoon dried thyme)
- 1 tablespoon fresh rosemary, (optional 1 teaspoon dried rosemary)

Directions: Add carrots, parsnips, potatoes onion and garlic to a medium mixing bowl. In a small bowl, combine oil, paprika, herbs, salt and pepper. Add half oil & herb mixture to vegetables, toss to coat and add to slow cooker. Rinse and pat chicken dry, add to the mixing bowl and pour remaining oil & herb mixture over chicken, being sure to thoroughly coat. In a large skillet, turn to medium-high heat, add chicken and lightly brown on both sides. Place chicken over vegetables, cover and cook on low 5-6 hours or until juices run clear when pierced with a fork, or chicken has reached an internal temperature of 165 degrees and vegetables are tender.

Nutritional Information: Calories: 207, Fat: 10g, Carbs: 23g

SLOW COOKER POLYNESIAN CHICKEN

Preparation Time: 5 Hours | Yield: 6 Servings

Ingredients:

- 4 chicken breasts, boneless, skinless (about 1.5 pounds), cut into 2" cubes
- 1 red bell pepper, cored and seeded, sliced into 1-inch strips
- 1 (20 ounce) can pineapple chunks in natural juice
- 2 tablespoons Tamari, optional Bragg Liquid Aminos
- 2 cloves garlic, minced
- 2 teaspoons freshly grated ginger
- 1/3 cup honey
- 2 tablespoons cornstarch or arrow root

Directions: A 4-7 quart slow-cooker is recommended. Pour juice from canned pineapple chunks into a small mixing bowl. Add to juice, Bragg Liquid Aminos (or soy sauce), garlic, ginger and honey, whisk to combine. Add cornstarch and stir until combined.Place chicken in slow cooker, add pineapple chunks. Pour pineapple mixture over chicken, cover and cook on low 4-5 hours. Add bell peppers the last 15 minutes of cook time. Serve chicken over a bed of quinoa or brown rice.

Nutritional Information: Calories: 255, Fat: 7g, Carbs: 31g

CHICKEN NOODLE SOUP

Preparation Time: 6 Hours | Yield: 8 Servings

Ingredients:

Slow Cooker Ingredients

- 1 cup sliced celery
- 4 carrots, sliced
- 1 small onion, diced
- 2 cloves garlic, minced
- 2 pounds uncooked skinless, boneless chicken breasts or thighs, cut into 2" pieces (note that breast meat tends to get dryer than thigh meat when cooked in the slow cooker)

- 1/2 teaspoon crushed red pepper flakes, more or less to taste
- 3 teaspoons dried thyme
- 1 teaspoon dried oregano
- 1 teaspoon kosher or sea salt
- 1/2 teaspoon black pepper
- 6 cups low-sodium chicken broth, fat free preferred
- 1 bay leaf

Add when it is done

- 8 ounces whole wheat spaghetti, broken into small pieces
- 1/4 cup fresh, chopped, Italian parsley, to serve

- 1-2 tablespoons fresh squeezed lemon juice, to taste

Directions: Add the vegetables and garlic to the bottom of the slow cooker, and the chicken on top, sprinkle in the thyme, oregano, chili flakes, and salt and pepper. Pour in the stock and add in the bay leaf. Cook for 6-8 hours on low in the slow cooker, or until carrots are tender. If necessary, skim off any foam that has floated to the top of the soup and discard. Around 15 minutes before ready to serve, cook the broken up pasta separately on the stovetop according to package directions and drain. Stir in the noodles and chopped parsley just before serving. Then stir in one tablespoon of the lemon juice last. Taste and add in more lemon juice, if desired. Enjoy!

Nutritional Information: Calories: 346, Fat: 12g, Carbs: 31g

SLOW COOKER SWEET POTATO MASH

Preparation Time: 4 Hours | Yield: 4 Servings

Ingredients:

- 2 pounds sweet potatoes, peeled and cut into 1/2 inch slices
- 1 cup apple juice, no sugar added, 100% juice
- 1 tablespoon. ground cinnamon

- 1 1/2 teaspoons ground nutmeg
- 1 teaspoon allspice
- 1/2 teaspoon ground cloves

Directions: Prepare your sweet potatoes and place in slow cooker. Add 1/2 cup of the apple juice (NOT the full cup) and half of the spices spices. Cook on low 4-5 hours, until potatoes are tender.

Recommend 3-4 quart slow cooker. When potatoes are fully cooked through, using a hand blender, blend the sweet potatoes inside your slow cooker insert, adding the second 1/2 cup of juice and remaining spices. Top with pecans and enjoy.

Nutritional Information: Calories: 141, Fat: 3g, Carbs: 28g

DESSERT RECIPES

RASPBERRY YOGURT

Servings: 3 | Prep Time: 12 hours 20 minutes

Ingredients:

- 8 cups whole milk, pasteurized
- ½ cup natural, plain yogurt
- ½ cup raspberries
- Thick bath towel

Directions: Pour milk in the crockpot and cook, covered on LOW for about 2 hours. Allow it to sit for about 3 hours. Ladle out 2 cups of the warm milk into a bowl. Add yogurt and return to the one pot crock pot, stirring well. Cover the lid and wrap it with a heavy bath towel. Let it sit for about 7 hours and transfer to an immersion blender along with the raspberries. Transfer to a plastic container in the refrigerator and serve after set.

Nutrition Information: Calories: 421, Fat: 21g, Carbohydrates: 32g

BANANA BREAD

Servings: 5 | Prep Time: 3 hours 30 minutes

Ingredients:

- 1 teaspoon baking soda
- ½ cup pecans, chopped and lightly toasted
- 2 cups flour
- 1 teaspoon salt
- ½ cup butter, softened
- 1 cup sugar
- 4 small bananas, ripe and mashed
- 1 teaspoon vanilla
- 2 eggs
- 2 tablespoons plus 2 teaspoons milk

Directions: Mix baking soda, flour and salt in a bowl and add nuts. Mix butter, eggs, sugar, vanilla, milk and bananas in another bowl. Add the flour mixture gradually and mix well. Place insert into crock pot and add batter. Cover and cook on HIGH for about 3 hours.

Nutrition Information: Calories: 618, Fat: 23.1g, Carbohydrates: 97.7g

RICE PUDDING WITH MIXED BERRIES

Servings: 6 | Prep Time: 2 hours 40 minutes

Ingredients:

- 1 package (4 ounces) dried blueberries
- 1½ cups water
- 1 cup heavy cream
- 8 ounces frozen orange juice concentrate
- ¾ cup sugar
- A dash of salt

- 1 package (6 ounces) dried cranberries
- 1 can (12 ounces) evaporated milk
- 1 cup short-grain Arborio rice
- ¼ teaspoon ground cinnamon

Directions: Grease the one pot of the crock pot with nonstick cooking spray. Mix together all the ingredients and pour into the crock pot. Cover and cook on LOW for about 5 hours. Stir the mixture after 2 hours 30 minutes and dish out after complete time.

Nutrition Information: Calories: 349, Fat: 12.3g, Carbohydrates: 56.6g

BANANA RAISIN BREAD PUDDING

Servings: 8 | Prep Time: 4 hours 15 minutes

Ingredients:

- 2 tablespoons ground cinnamon
- 5 eggs, beaten
- ¾ cup packed brown sugar
- 3½ cups milk
- 6 cups plain breadcrumbs
- 1 tablespoon butter, melted
- 2 teaspoons vanilla
- ½ teaspoon salt
- ½ cup raisins
- 1 mashed banana

Directions: Mix together all ingredients until the mixture is smooth like thick oatmeal. Place mixture in a greased crock pot and cover the lid. Cook on high for about 5 hours and dish out.

Nutrition Information: Calories: 525, Fat: 10.8g, Carbohydrates: 89.1g

CHOCOLATE PEANUT BUTTER CUPS

Servings: 6 | Prep Time: 5 hours 15 minutes

Ingredients:

- ¼ cup heavy cream
- ½ cup sugar
- 1 cup butter
- ¼ cup peanut butter, separated
- 2 ounces milk chocolate

Directions: Melt the butter and peanut butter, and add milk chocolate, heavy cream and sugar. Stir thoroughly and put the mixture in a baking mold. Put the baking mold in the crock pot and cover the lid. Cook on LOW for about 5 hours and dish out to serve hot.

Nutrition Information: Calories: 465, Fat: 40.7g, Carbohydrates: 24.6g

FLOURLESS CHOCOLATE BROWNIES

Servings: 6 | Prep Time: 5 hours 20 minutes

Ingredients:

- ¼ cup sugar
- 1 teaspoon vanilla extract
- ½ cup butter
- 3 eggs

- ½ cup sugar-free chocolate chips

Directions: Put eggs, sugar and vanilla extract in the blender and blend until frothy. Melt butter and chocolate in a bowl and combine with the egg mixture. Pour it in the baking mold and place the mold in the crock pot. Cover and cook on LOW for about 5 hours. Dish out to serve hot.

Nutrition Information: Calories: 210, Fat: 18.1g, Carbohydrates: 10.1g

CRÈME BRÛLÉE

Servings: 4 | Prep Time: 4 hours 15 minutes

Ingredients:

- 3 egg yolks
- ½ tablespoon vanilla extract
- ¼ cup sugar
- 1 cup heavy cream
- 1 pinch salt

Directions: Put all the ingredients except sugar in a bowl and beat until well combined. Divide the mixture in the ramekins evenly and transfer to the crock pot. Cover and cook on LOW for about 4 hours. Cover the ramekins with a plastic wrap and refrigerate to chill before serving.

Nutrition Information: Calories: 195, Fat: 14.5g, Carbohydrates: 14g

CHOCOLATE CHEESE CAKE

Servings: 4 | Prep Time: 6 hours 15 minutes

Ingredients:

- 2 cups cream cheese, softened
- 2 eggs
- ½ cup sugar
- 1 teaspoon pure vanilla extract
- 2 tablespoons cocoa powder

Directions: Put eggs and cream cheese in a blender and blend until smooth. Add remaining ingredients and pulse until well combined. Transfer the mixture into 2 (8-ounce) mason jars evenly. Put the mason jars in the crock pot. Set the crock pot on low and cook for about 6 hours. Refrigerate to chill for at least 6 hours before serving.

Nutrition Information: Calories: 539, Fat: 43g, Carbohydrates: 29.9g

PEANUT BUTTER PUDDING

Servings: 4 | Prep Time: 6 hours 15 minutes

Ingredients:

- ½ cup sugar
- 2 cups cashew milk
- ½ cup cold water
- 2 teaspoons gelatin
- ¼ cup natural peanut butter

Directions: Put cashew milk, peanut butter and sugar in the crock pot and stir well. Cover and cook on LOW for about 2 hours. Mix the gelatin in cold water and transfer to the crock pot. Stir for 5 minutes and allow the pudding to sit for 1 hour. Pour into ramekins and refrigerate for 3 hours.

Nutrition Information: Calories: 270, Fat: 11g, Carbohydrates: 36.5g

COCONUT YOGURT

Servings: 6 | Prep Time: 12 hours

Ingredients:

- 1 small container yogurt
- 3 cups coconut milk
- 3 tablespoons sugar
- 1 tablespoon coconut, shredded
- 3 teaspoons gelatin

Directions: Preheat the crock pot on HIGH and add coconut milk. Cover and cook on LOW for about 2 hours. Turn off the heat and add gelatin, yogurt, shredded coconut and sugar. Wrap the entire crock pot in beach towels and allow it to sit for 10 hours while the yogurt cultures.

Nutrition Information: Calories: 332, Fat: 28.9g, Carbohydrates: 16g

PUMPKIN PIE CAKE

Preparation Time: 3 Hours | Yield: 12 Servings

Ingredients:

- ½ cup unsalted butter, softened
- 2 cups brown sugar, packed
- 3 eggs, room temperature
- 15 oz pure pumpkin puree
- 1½ cups all-purpose four
- 1½ tsp baking powder
- 1½ tsp baking soda
- ½ tsp ground cinnamon
- ½ tsp pumpkin pie spice
- ⅛ tsp ground cloves
- ½ tsp salt

Directions: Line slow cooker with foil collar and sling. Spray with cooking spray. Cream together brown sugar and butter. Beat in eggs one at a time until thoroughly combined. Beat in pumpkin. Combine flour, baking powder, baking soda, spices, and salt. Gradually stir in flour mixture. Pour into prepared slow cooker. Cover and cook on high for 3 hours or until a toothpick inserted into the center comes out clean. Check at 2 hours and rotate if necessary. Use the sling to lift cake from the slow cooker and let cool for 15 minutes before serving. Top with whipped cream or serve with ice cream.

Nutritional Information: Calories: 188, Fat: 3g, Carbs: 33g

BANANA UPSIDE DOWN CAKE

Preparation Time: 3 Hours | Yield: 8 Servings

Ingredients:

Banana:

- 5 T. unsalted butter, in small pieces, plus more for the cooker
- 3/4 c. firmly packed dark brown sugar, plus for lining the cooker

- 3 T. dark rum
- 2 lbs. ripe medium bananas (about 6), peeled and halved lengthwise

Cake:

- 3/4 c. cake flour
- 3/4 tsp. baking powder
- 1/2 tsp. ground cinnamon
- 1/4 tsp. ground nutmeg
- 1/4 tsp. fine salt
- 4 T. unsalted butter, softened (1/2 stick)

- 2/3 c. sugar
- 1 large egg, at room temperature
- 1 large egg yolk, at room temperature
- 2 T. whole milk, at room temperature
- Ice cream for serving

Directions:

Bananas: Butter the inside of a slow cooker, line completely with foil, and then butter the foil. Slow cooker on to HIGH. Sprinkle butter, brown sugar and rum over the foil on the bottom of the slow cooker. Place the banana halves on the bottom with the cut side down, in a slightly overlapping pattern. Press the bananas into the sugar.

Cake: Sift the flour, baking powder, cinnamon, nutmeg, and salt into a large bowl; then whisk to combine evenly. In another bowl, slowly beat the butter and sugar with an electric mixer until just blended. Raise the speed to high and beat until light and fluffy, scraping the sides of the bowl occasionally, about 10 minutes. Beat in the egg and then the yolk, allowing each to be fully incorporated before adding the next. While mixing slowly, add the flour mixture to the butter in 3 parts, alternating with the milk in 2 parts, beginning and ending with the flour. Mix briefly at medium speed to make a smooth batter. Pour the batter over the bananas and smooth with a spatula to even it out. Lay a doubled length of paper towel from end to end over the top of the crock pot, to line the lid and create a tighter seal. Cover the cake tightly with the lid and continue to cook on HIGH, until the cake begins to brown slightly on the sides and springs back when touched in the middle, about 3 1/2 hours. Turn off the crock pot and let the cake set, about 20 minutes more. Using the foil, lift the cake from the slow cooker; set on the counter to cool, about 30 minutes more. Fold back the foil, and carefully invert cake onto a platter so you can see the caramelized bananas.Slice or spoon cake into bowls and serve with ice cream or whipped topping, if desired.

Nutritional Information: Calories: 403, Fat: 15g, Carbs: 65g

ORANGE PUDDING CAKE

Preparation Time: 2 Hours | Yield: 8 Servings

Ingredients:

Cake

- 1 cup all-purpose flour

- 1/4 teaspoon salt

- 1/3 cup sugar
- 1 teaspoon baking powder
- 1/2 teaspoon cinnamon

- 1/2 cup milk
- 2 tablespoons butter, melted
- 1/2 cup chopped pecans or walnuts
- 1/4 cup currants or raisins

Sauce

- 2/3 cup packed brown sugar
- 3/4 cup orange juice
- 3/4 cup water

- 1 tablespoon butter
- 1 teaspoon finely chopped orange zest
- heavy cream or ice cream, for serving

Directions: To make the cake batter, combine the flour, sugar, baking powder, cinnamon, and salt in a mixing bowl. Stir in the milk and melted butter until combined. Stir in the pecans and currants and spread the batter in the bottom of a slow cooker. Combine the ingredients for the sauce in a small saucepan and bring to a boil, stirring occasionally, over moderate heat. Boil for 2 minutes and carefully pour the sauce over the batter. Cook covered on high heat for 2 1/2 hours. The center may still be soft but will set upon cooling. Cool for at least 30 minutes before serving. Serve with heavy cream or ice cream if desired.

Nutritional Information: Calories: 175, Fat: 2g, Carbs: 37g

CRANBERRY ORANGE CAKE

Preparation Time: 3 Hours | Yield: 10 Servings

Ingredients:

- 1 cup butter
- 2 cups sugar
- 4 eggs, room temperature
- 1½ teaspoons vanilla
- Zest from 1 orange
- 3 cups flour, divided

- 1 teaspoon baking powder
- ½ teaspoon salt
- 1 12-oz. pkg. fresh cranberries
- Glaze: 2 tablespoons orange juice and 1 cup powdered sugar

Directions: In a large bowl, use a mixer to cream butter and sugar. Add eggs, one at a time, vanilla, and orange zest. In a separate bowl, sift 2¾ cups flour, baking powder, and salt. Blend with creamed mixture. Fold in remaining ¼ cup flour and the cranberries. Cut waxed or parchment paper in an oval shape to fit 6-quart oval slow-cooker; put in bottom of slow-cooker. Pour batter into slow-cooker. Cover and cook on HIGH for 3 hours, until toothpick inserted in the middle comes out clean. When cool, place large oval plate on top of slow-cooker insert. Flip over slow-cooker so that the cake comes out onto the plate. Remove waxed paper. Make glaze by whisking the orange juice and powdered sugar until smooth. Drizzle glaze over the top of the cake.

Nutritional Information: Calories: 190, Fat: 9g, Carbs: 29g

MIXED BERRY PUDDING CAKE

Preparation Time: 3 Hours | Yield: 8 Servings

Ingredients:

- 1 1/2 cups loose-pack frozen blueberries
- 1 1/2 cups loose-pack frozen red raspberries
- 1/2 cup fresh cranberries
- 1 cup all-purpose flour
- 2/3 cup sugar
- 1 1/2 teaspoons baking powder
- 1/2 teaspoon ground cinnamon
- 1/4 teaspoon salt
- 1/2 cup milk
- 2 tablespoons butter, melted
- 1 teaspoon vanilla
- 3/4 cup boiling water
- 1/3 cup sugar
- 1/2 cup sliced almonds, toasted (optional)

Directions: Lightly coat a 3-1/2- or 4-quart slow cooker with nonstick cooking spray. In the prepared slow cooker combine frozen blueberries, frozen raspberries, and cranberries; set aside. In a medium bowl combine flour, the 2/3 cup sugar, the baking powder, cinnamon, and salt. Stir in milk, melted butter, and vanilla just until combined. Spoon and carefully spread batter over berries in slow cooker. In a small bowl combine the boiling water and the 1/3 cup sugar; stir to dissolve sugar. Pour evenly over mixture in slow cooker. Cover and cook on high-heat setting for 2-1/2 to 3 hours or until a toothpick inserted near center of cake comes out clean. Remove crockery liner from slow cooker, if possible, or turn off slow cooker. Cool, uncovered, for 1 hour. To serve, spoon warm pudding cake into dessert dishes. If desired, sprinkle each serving with almonds.

Nutritional Information: Calories: 220, Fat: 4g, Carbs: 45g

DOUBLE APPLE CAKE

Preparation Time: 3 Hours | Yield: 8 Servings

Ingredients:

- 1/3 cup packed dark brown sugar
  - ounces all-purpose flour (about 1 1/2 cups)
- 1 teaspoon baking soda
- 1 1/2 teaspoons ground cinnamon
- 1/2 teaspoon baking powder
- 1/4 teaspoon salt
- 1/4 teaspoon ground nutmeg
- 1/8 teaspoon ground cloves
- 1 cup unsweetened applesauce
- 1/3 cup low-fat buttermilk
- 1/4 cup butter, melted
- 1 tablespoon vanilla extract
- 1 large egg
- 1 cup dried apple slices, coarsely chopped
- 1 teaspoon powdered sugar (optional)

Directions: Coat a 5-quart round electric slow cooker with cooking spray. Line bottom of slow cooker with parchment paper. Place 2 (30-inch-long) strips of parchment paper in an X pattern under parchment paper liner in slow cooker. Coat parchment with cooking spray. Weigh or lightly spoon flour into dry measuring cups; level with a knife. Combine flour, brown sugar, and next 6 ingredients (through to cloves) in a medium bowl, stirring with a whisk. Combine applesauce and next 4 ingredients (through to egg) in a small bowl. Add applesauce mixture to flour mixture, stirring until smooth. Stir in dried apple. Pour batter into prepared slow cooker, spreading into an even layer. Cover and cook on HIGH for 1 to 1 1/2 hours or until puffed and a wooden pick inserted into center comes out clean. Cut into wedges. Sprinkle with powdered sugar, if desired.

Nutritional Information: Calories: 235, Fat: 7g, Carbs: 40g

BLACKBERRY APPLE CRISP

Preparation Time: 3 Hours | Yield: 4 Servings

Ingredients:

- 2 cups organic oats use certified organic
- 1/2 cup cold butter diced into small pieces or coconut oil
- optional 1/2 cup nuts of your choice like pecans, walnuts, or almonds
- 2 T cinnamon
- 1 T Chia Seeds
- 1 t of each wheat germ, wheat bran, & oat bran (omit for gluten free)
- 2 to 3 cups Blackberries/Apples or as much as you like/have

Directions: In a medium bowl mix all of the ingredients together except the fruit. Fill a 9x5x3 greased loaf pan with the prepared fruit (if your fruit is on the tart side you can sprinkle a couple of tablespoons of organic sugar over the fruit). Optional: you could also just place your fruit in a greased slow cooker. Top fruit with the oat mixture. Place the pan in the slow cooker with no water on the bottom. Slow cook for 1.5 to 2.5 hours on high or 4 hours on low, or until the butter/oil has melted and the fruit is bubbly.

Nutritional Information: Calories: 208, Fat: 7g, Carbs: 42g

CARAMEL APPLE CRUMBLE

Preparation Time: 3 Hours | Yield: 4 Servings

Ingredients:

- 1 cup brown sugar
- 1/2 cup granulated sugar
- 5 large apples, cut into chunks
- 1/4 teaspoon salt
- 1 teaspoon cinnamon

Topping:

- 2/3 cup oats
- 2/3 cup loosely packed brown sugar
- 1/4 cup flour
- 1/2 teaspoon cinnamon
- 3-4 tablespoons softened butter
- 1 teaspoon vanilla extract

Directions: Toss apple chunks with salt and cinnamon. In the bottom of your slow-cooker, mix brown and granulated sugars, then spread evenly to cover. Layer apples on top, keeping them in a single layer as much as possible, then adding the rest of top. Mix the crumble topping together in a bowl, using your fingers to distribute the butter evenly and thoroughly and clump it together. Sprinkle it over top of the apples. Cook apples on low for 4 hours, or high for 2 hours. Turn off heat, unplug, and let sit, covered, for one hour. During this time the caramel will thicken a bit more. Serve with vanilla ice cream.

Nutritional Information: Calories: 190, Fat: 7g, Carbs: 32g

STRAWBERRY COBBLER

Preparation Time: 3 Hours | Yield: 6 Servings

Ingredients:

- 2 1/2 – 3 lbs strawberries, sliced
- 1/2 cup sugar
- 2 tablespoons cornstarch
- 2 tablespoons water
- 3/4 cup brown sugar
- 3/4 cup quick cooking oats
- 1/2 cup flour
- 1/2 cup butter

Directions: In a saucepan combine strawberries and regular sugar. Let sit for 30 minutes. After sitting 30 minutes, cook over medium heat for 5 minutes. In a bowl combine cornstarch and water. Stir into berry mixture and bring to a boil. Boil 1 minute or until mixture is thickened. Spoon mixture into slow cooker. In a bowl combine brown sugar, oats, and flour. Cut in butter to form a crumbly mixture. Spread evenly over strawberry mixture. Cook on low for 2-3 hours. Best served warm with ice cream.

Nutritional Information: Calories: 208, Fat: 7g, Carbs: 42g

TRIPLE CHOCOLATE BROWNIES

Preparation Time: 3 Hours | Yield: 6 Servings

Ingredients:

• 1 1/4 cups all-purpose flour (spooned and leveled) • 1/4 cup unsweetened cocoa powder • 3/4 teaspoon baking powder • 1/2 teaspoon coarse salt • 1/2 cup (1 stick) unsalted butter, cut into pieces	• 8 ounces bittersweet chocolate, chopped • 1 cup of sugar • 3 large eggs, lightly beaten • 1 cup of walnut halves, coarsely chopped • 1 cup of semisweet chocolate chips (6 ounces)

Directions: Lightly coat a 5-quart slow-cooker insert with cooking spray. Line bottom with parchment paper and lightly coat with spray. In a small bowl, whisk together flour, cocoa, baking powder, and salt. Place butter and chocolate in a medium microwave-safe bowl and microwave in 30-second increments, stirring after each, until chocolate is melted. Add sugar; stir to combine. Stir in eggs. Add flour mixture, walnuts, and chocolate chips and stir just until moistened (do not overmix). Transfer to slow cooker and smooth top. Cover and cook on low, 3 1/2 hours. Uncover and cook 30 minutes. Remove insert from slow cooker and run a knife around edge to loosen brownies. Let cool completely in insert on a wire rack, about 2 hours. Turn out onto a work surface and cut into 14 brownies. Store in an airtight container, up to 2 days.

Nutritional Information: Calories: 334, Fat: 10g, Carbs: 54g

Low-Carb Breakfast Recipes

Delicious Breakfast Quiche

Preparation Time: 10 minutes │ Cooking Time: 3 hours 30 minutes │ Serves: 6

Ingredients:

- 5 eggs, lightly beaten
- 1/8 tsp nutmeg
- 1 cup green onions, sliced
- 1 cup cheddar cheese, grated
- 2 cups broccoli florets
- Pepper
- Salt

Directions: Spray the inside of a crock pot with cooking spray. In a mixing bowl, beat eggs with pepper, nutmeg, and salt. Add cheese and broccoli to the egg mixture and stir well. Pour egg mixture into the crock pot. Cover and cook on high for 3 hours. Add green onions to the top of the quiche, cover and cook on low for 30 minutes longer. Serve and enjoy.

Nutritional Value (Amount per Serving): Calories 144, Fat 10 g, Carbohydrates 3.8 g

Egg Sausage Breakfast Casserole

Preparation Time: 10 minutes │ Cooking Time: 4 hours │ Serves: 8

Ingredients:

- 10 eggs
- 3 garlic cloves, minced
- 3/4 cup whipping cream
- 1 cup cheddar cheese, shredded
- 12 oz sausage, cooked and sliced
- 2 cups broccoli, chopped
- 1/4 tsp pepper
- 1/2 tsp salt

Directions: Spray the inside of a crock pot with cooking spray. Layer half the sausage, half the broccoli, and half the shredded cheese in a crock pot. Repeat with remaining sausage, broccoli, and cheese. In a mixing bowl, whisk eggs, garlic, whipping cream, pepper, and salt until combined. Pour egg mixture over layered mixture. Cover and cook on low for 4 hours or until center is set. Serve and enjoy.

Nutritional Value (Amount per Serving): Calories 322, Fat 25.8 g, Carbohydrates 2.9 g

Spinach Frittata

Preparation Time: 10 minutes │ Cooking Time: 1 hour 30 minutes │ Serves: 6

Ingredients:

- 3 eggs
- 3 extra egg whites
- 1 tomato, diced
- 1 cup spinach, chopped
- 2 Tbsp almond milk
- 1 cup mozzarella cheese, shredded
- 1 garlic clove, minced
- 1/2 cup onion, diced
- 1 Tbsp olive oil
- 1/4 tsp pepper
- Salt

Directions: Heat the oil in a pan over medium heat. Add onion to the pan and sauté for 4–5 minutes. Spray a crock pot inside with cooking spray. In a bowl, whisk together the sautéed onion, 3/4 cup mozzarella cheese, and remaining ingredients and pour into the crock pot. Top with remaining cheese. Cover and cook on low for 1 hour 30 minutes or until eggs are set. Serve and enjoy.

Nutritional Value (Amount per Serving): Calories 93, Fat 6.6 g, Carbohydrates 2.4 g

HEALTHY ARTICHOKE FRITTATA

Preparation Time: 10 minutes | Cooking Time: 2 hours 5 minutes | Serves: 4

Ingredients:

- 6 large eggs, lightly beaten
- 1/4 cup cheddar cheese, grated
- 1/4 cup green onion, chopped
- 1/4 cup bell pepper, chopped
- 1/2 tomato, chopped
- 3/4 cup artichoke hearts, chopped
- Pepper
- Salt

Directions: Spray a crock pot inside with cooking spray. In a bowl, whisk together eggs and vegetables and pour into the crock pot. Cover and cook on low for 2 hours or until eggs are set. Sprinkle grated cheese on top. Cover crock pot with the lid for 5 minutes or until cheese is melted. Slice and serve.

Nutritional Value (Amount per Serving): Calories 153, Fat 9.9 g, Carbohydrates 4.5 g

VEGETABLE PESTO FRITTATA

Preparation Time: 10 minutes | Cooking Time: 3 hours | Serves: 4

Ingredients:

- 10 eggs
- 2 Tbsp commercial pesto
- 2 Tbsp fresh basil, chopped
- 2 cups kale, chopped
- 1/2 cup fennel, chopped
- 1 cup red pepper, chopped
- 1 cup broccoli, chopped
- 1 cup zucchini, shredded
- 1/4 tsp red pepper flakes
- 1 tsp dried oregano
- 1 tsp garlic powder
- 1/2 cup feta cheese
- 1/4 cup coconut milk
- 1/2 tsp black pepper
- 1/2 tsp salt

Directions: In a large mixing bowl, whisk eggs, feta cheese, coconut milk, and spices. Spray a crock pot inside with cooking spray. Pour egg mixture into the crock pot. Add chopped vegetables and stir to combine. Sprinkle with fresh herbs. Top with pesto. Cover and cook on low for 3 hours or until eggs are set. Serve and enjoy.

Nutritional Value (Amount per Serving): Calories 321, Fat 22.1 g, Carbohydrates 13 g

CREAMY GREEN BEAN CASSEROLE

Preparation Time: 10 minutes | Cooking Time: 2 hours 30 minutes | Serves: 10

Ingredients:

- 2 lb green beans, trimmed and cut into 1-inch pieces
- 1 Tbsp Dijon mustard
- 8 oz can water chestnuts, drained and sliced
- 1/4 cup coconut milk
- 10.5 oz can cream of mushroom soup
- 1 1/2 cups gouda cheese, shredded
- 1 cup leeks, sliced

Directions: In a crock pot stir together green beans, mustard, chestnuts, leeks, coconut milk, and cheddar cheese. Cover and cook on high for 2 1/2 hours. Serve and enjoy.

Nutritional Value (Amount per Serving): Calories 138, Fat 7.8 g, Carbohydrates 12 g

HEALTHY VEGETABLE OMELET

Preparation Time: 10 minutes | Cooking Time: 1 hour 30 minutes | Serves: 4

Ingredients:

- 6 eggs
- 1/2 cup onion, sliced
- 1 cup spinach
- 1/2 cup unsweetened almond milk
- 1 tsp parsley, dried
- 1 tsp garlic powder
- 1 bell pepper, diced
- 4 additional egg whites
- Pepper
- Salt

Directions: Spray a crock pot inside with cooking spray. In a large bowl, whisk together egg whites, eggs, parsley, garlic powder, almond milk, pepper, and salt. Stir in bell peppers, spinach, and onion. Pour egg mixture into the crock pot. Cover and cook on high for 1 1/2 hours or until eggs are set. Slice and serve.

Nutritional Value (Amount per Serving): Calories 200, Fat 13.9 g, Carbohydrates 6.8 g

HAM AND CHEESE BREAKFAST OMELET

Preparation Time: 10 minutes | Cooking Time: 2 hours 30 minutes | Serves: 4

Ingredients:

- 6 eggs
- 1 small onion, chopped
- 1 red bell pepper, sliced
- 1 garlic clove, minced
- 1 cup mozzarella cheese, shredded
- 3/4 cup ham, chopped
- 1/2 cup unsweetened almond milk
- Pepper
- Salt

Directions: Spray a crock pot inside with cooking spray. In a large bowl, whisk together eggs, garlic, pepper, salt, and milk. Pour egg mixture into the crock pot. Add ham, onions, and bell peppers to the crock pot. Cover and cook on high for 2 1/2 hours. Top with cheese, cover and cook until cheese is melted. Serve and enjoy.

Nutritional Value (Amount per Serving): Calories 242, Fat 17.2 g, Carbohydrates 7.5 g

SAUSAGE STUFFED BELL PEPPERS

Preparation Time: 10 minutes | Cooking Time: 4 hours 10 minutes | Serves: 4

Ingredients:

- 6 large eggs
- 1/2 lb ground breakfast sausage
- 4 bell peppers, tops cut off and seeded
- 4 oz green chilies, chopped
- 4 oz Jack cheese, shredded
- 1/8 tsp black pepper
- 1/4 tsp salt

Directions: Brown sausage in a pan over medium-high heat and drain excess oil. Pour 1/2 cup water into a crock pot. In a bowl, whisk eggs until smooth. Stir green chilies, cheese, black pepper, and salt into the eggs. Spoon egg mixture and brown sausage into each bell pepper. Place the stuffed bell peppers into the crock pot. Cover and cook for 4 hours. Serve and enjoy.

Nutritional Value (Amount per Serving): Calories 354, Fat 21.9 g, Carbohydrates 12 g

CREAMY CAULIFLOWER MASH

Preparation Time: 10 minutes | Cooking Time: 6 hours | Serves: 4

Ingredients:

- 1 medium cauliflower head, cut into florets
- 1 1/2 cups vegetable stock
- Pepper
- Salt
- 3 garlic cloves, minced

Directions: Add cauliflower florets, garlic, and stock to a crock pot. Cover and cook on low for 6 hours. Drain cauliflower well and transfer into a large bowl. Mash cauliflower using a potato masher until smooth and creamy. Season with pepper and salt. Stir well and serve.

Nutritional Value (Amount per Serving): Calories 38, Fat 0.2 g, Carbohydrates 8.1 g

ARUGULA HERB FRITTATA

Preparation Time: 10 minutes | Cooking Time: 3 hours | Serves: 6

Ingredients:

- 8 eggs
- 1 1/2 cups red peppers, roasted and chopped
- 4 cups baby arugula
- 3/4 cup goat cheese, crumbled
- 1/2 cup onion, sliced
- 1/3 cup unsweetened almond milk
- Pepper
- Salt
- 1 tsp oregano, dried

Directions: Spray a crock pot inside with cooking spray. In a mixing bowl, whisk together eggs, oregano, and almond milk. Season with pepper and salt. Arrange red peppers, onion, arugula, and cheese in the crock pot. Pour egg mixture into the crock pot over the vegetables. Cover and cook on low for 3 hours. Serve and enjoy.

Nutritional Value (Amount per Serving): Calories 178, Fat 12.8 g, Carbohydrates 6 g

ITALIAN FRITTATA

Preparation Time: 10 minutes | Cooking Time: 4 hours | Serves: 4

Ingredients:

- 6 eggs
- 1/4 cup cherry tomatoes, sliced
- 4 oz mushrooms, sliced
- 2 tsp Italian seasoning
- 1/2 cup cheddar cheese, shredded
- Pepper
- Salt

Directions: Spray a crock pot inside with cooking spray. Spray a pan with cooking spray and heat over medium heat. Add mushrooms and cherry tomatoes to the pan and cook until softened. Transfer vegetables to the crock pot. In a bowl, whisk together eggs, cheese, pepper, and salt. Pour egg mixture in the crock pot. Cover and cook on low for 4 hours. Slice and serve.

Nutritional Value (Amount per Serving): Calories 167, Fat 12 g, Carbohydrates 2.3 g

ZUCCHINI BREAD

Preparation Time: 10 minutes | Cooking Time: 3 hours | Serves: 12

Ingredients:

- 3 eggs
- 1/2 tsp baking soda
- 1 1/2 tsp baking powder
- 2 tsp cinnamon
- 1/2 cup walnuts, chopped
- 2 tsp vanilla
- 1/2 cup Pyure all purpose sweetener
- 1/3 cup coconut oil, softened
- 1/3 cup coconut flour
- 1 cup almond flour

- 2 cups zucchini, shredded
- 1/2 tsp salt

Directions: In a bowl combine almond flour, baking soda, baking powder, cinnamon, coconut flour, and salt. Set aside. In another bowl, whisk together eggs, vanilla, sweetener, and oil. Add dry mixture to the wet mixture and fold well. Add walnuts and zucchini and fold well. Pour batter into a bread loaf pan. Place bread pan into the crock pot on a rack. Cover and cook on high for 3 hours. Cut bread loaf into slices and serve.

Nutritional Value (Amount per Serving): Calories 174, Fat 15.4 g, Carbohydrates 5.8 g

CAULIFLOWER CASSEROLE

Preparation Time: 10 minutes | Cooking Time: 6 hours | Serves: 8

Ingredients:

- 12 eggs
- 1/2 cup unsweetened almond milk
- 1 lb sausage, cooked and crumbled
- 1 cauliflower head, shredded
- 2 cups cheddar cheese, shredded
- Pepper
- Salt

Directions: Spray a crock pot inside with cooking spray. In a bowl, whisk together eggs, almond milk, pepper, and salt. Add about a third of the shredded cauliflower into the bottom of the crock pot. Season with pepper and salt. Top with about a third of the sausage and a third of the cheese. Repeat the same layers 2 more times. Pour egg mixture into the crock pot. Cover and cook on low for 6 hours. Serve and enjoy.

Nutritional Value (Amount per Serving): Calories 443, Fat 35.6 g, Carbohydrates 3.5 g

LEMON CINNAMON APPLES

Preparation Time: 10 minutes | Cooking Time: 3 hours | Serves: 10

Ingredients:

- 9 cups apple, peeled, cored, diced
- 2 Tbsp fresh lemon juice
- 1/2 tsp nutmeg
- 2 tsp ground cinnamon
- 1 1/2 cups water

Directions: Add all ingredients to a crock pot and stir well. Cover and cook on high for 3 hours. Stir well and serve.

Nutritional Value (Amount per Serving): Calories 50, Fat 0.2 g, Carbohydrates 13.1 g

LOW-CARB POULTRY RECIPES

EASY MEXICAN CHICKEN

Preparation Time: 10 minutes | Cooking Time: 5 hours | Serves: 4

Ingredients:

- 8 chicken thighs, bone- in and skin-on
- 1/4 tsp red pepper flakes
- 1/4 cup green onion, sliced
- 1 packet taco seasoning
- 1 cup chicken stock

Directions: Add stock and half the taco seasoning to a crock pot. Stir well to blend. Place chicken thighs in the crock pot and sprinkle remaining seasoning on top of chicken. Cover and cook on low for 5 hours. Garnish with red pepper flakes and green onions. Serve and enjoy.

Nutritional Value (Amount per Serving): Calories 565, Fat 21.8 g, Carbohydrates 1.7 g

SUPER DELICIOUS RANCH CHICKEN

Preparation Time: 10 minutes | Cooking Time: 6 hours | Serves: 6

Ingredients:

- 2 lb chicken breasts, boneless
- 1 packet ranch dressing mix
- 4 oz cream cheese
- 3 Tbsp butter

Directions: Place chicken in a crock pot. Add cream cheese and butter on top of the chicken. Sprinkle ranch dressing on top of the chicken. Cover and cook on low for 6 hours. Shred the chicken using forks and serve.

Nutritional Value (Amount per Serving): Calories 404, Fat 23.6 g, Carbohydrates 0.5 g

BALSAMIC CHICKEN

Preparation Time: 10 minutes | Cooking Time: 3 hours | Serves: 8

Ingredients:

- 3 lb chicken breasts, sliced in half
- 3/4 cup balsamic vinegar
- 2 tsp dried onion, minced
- 2 tsp dried basil
- 3 garlic cloves, minced
- 1 Tbsp olive oil
- 1/4 tsp pepper
- 1/2 tsp salt

Directions: Add garlic and olive oil to a crock pot. In a small bowl, mix together the dry seasonings. Rub chicken breasts with the seasonings and place them in the crock pot. Pour balsamic vinegar over chicken breasts. Cover and cook on low for 3 hours. Slice and serve.

Nutritional Value (Amount per Serving): Calories 345, Fat 14.4 g, Carbohydrates 0.7 g

PARMESAN CHICKEN WINGS

Preparation Time: 10 minutes | Cooking Time: 3 hours 10 minutes | Serves: 8

Ingredients:

- 4 lb chicken wings
- 1 cup Parmesan cheese, shredded
- 5 garlic cloves, minced
- 1/2 cup butter, melted
- 1/4 tsp pepper
- 1 tsp salt

Directions: Place chicken wings in a crock pot and season with pepper and salt. In a small bowl, mix together garlic and butter. Pour garlic butter mixture over the chicken wings and stir well to coat. Cover and cook on high for 3 hours. Arrange chicken wings on a baking tray and broil for 5 minutes on each side. Remove chicken wings from oven and top with shredded cheese. Return chicken wings to the oven for 1–2 minutes until the cheese has melted. Serve and enjoy.

Nutritional Value (Amount per Serving): Calories 577, Fat 31.1 g, Carbohydrates 1 g

DELICIOUS CREAMY CHICKEN

Preparation Time: 10 minutes | Cooking Time: 6 hours | Serves: 6

Ingredients:

- 2 lb chicken breasts, skinless and boneless, cut into 6 pieces.
- 3 Tbsp Parmesan cheese, grated
- 4 oz cream cheese, cut in pieces
- 1/2 cup chicken stock
- 1 packet dry ranch seasoning mix
- 1 can (10.5 oz) cream of chicken soup
- 1/4 cup bell pepper, diced

Directions: Mix ranch seasoning and cream of chicken soup in a crock pot. Slowly add stock and stir well. Add bell pepper and stir well. Add chicken and stir well. Cover and cook on low for 6 hours. About a half hour before cooking time is up add the parmesan cheese and the cream cheese. Cover and continue cooking for 30 minutes. Stir well and serve.

Nutritional Value (Amount per Serving): Calories 420, Fat 21.8 g, Carbohydrates 4.5 g

MUSTARD CHICKEN

Preparation Time: 10 minutes | Cooking Time: 8 hours | Serves: 4

Ingredients:

- 4 chicken thighs
- 2 Tbsp olive oil
- 1/4 cup Dijon mustard
- 2 Tbsp honey
- 1 tsp fresh rosemary, chopped
- 1/4 tsp pepper
- 1/2 tsp sea salt

Directions: Place chicken in a crock pot. In a small bowl, mix together oil, mustard, honey, pepper, rosemary, and salt. Pour over chicken. Cover and cook on low for 8 hours. Serve and enjoy.

Nutritional Value (Amount per Serving): Calories 381, Fat 18.5 g, Carbohydrates 9.8 g

CHICKEN TOMATILLO DRUMSTICKS

Preparation Time: 10 minutes | Cooking Time: 6 hours | Serves: 4

Ingredients:

- 4 chicken drumsticks, bone-in, and skin removed
- 1 Tbsp apple cider vinegar
- 1 cup tomatillo salsa
- 1 tsp olive oil
- 1 tsp dried oregano
- Pepper
- Salt

Directions: Add all ingredients to a crock pot and stir well to combine. Cover and cook on low for 6 hours. Serve and enjoy.

Nutritional Value (Amount per Serving): Calories 100, Fat 4.2 g, Carbohydrates 2.2 g

JUICY SHREDDED TURKEY

Preparation Time: 10 minutes | Cooking Time: 8 hours | Serves: 10

Ingredients:

- 4 lb turkey breast, skinless, boneless, and halved
- 12 oz chicken stock
- 1 packet onion soup mix
- 1/2 cup butter, cubed

Directions: Place turkey in a crock pot. Combine together butter, chicken stock, and onion soup mix and pour over the turkey. Cover and cook on low for 8 hours. Shred turkey using forks and serve.

Nutritional Value (Amount per Serving): Calories 274, Fat 12.3 g, Carbohydrates 8.2 g

TENDER AND MOIST TURKEY BREAST

Preparation Time: 10 minutes | Cooking Time: 4 hours | Serves: 12

Ingredients:

- 6 lb turkey breast, bone-in
- 3 fresh rosemary sprigs
- 1/2 cup chicken stock
- 3 garlic cloves, peeled
- Pepper
- Salt

Directions: Place turkey breast in a crock pot. Add stock, garlic, and rosemary on top. Season with pepper and salt. Cover and cook on low for 4 hours or until meat is tender. Serve and enjoy.

Nutritional Value (Amount per Serving): Calories 237, Fat 3.8 g, Carbohydrates 9.9 g

PESTO CHICKEN

Preparation Time: 10 minutes | Cooking Time: 7 hours | Serves: 4

Ingredients:

- 4 chicken breasts, skinless and boneless
- 3 garlic cloves, minced
- 1/2 small onion, diced
- 1 cup frozen spinach, thawed and drained
- 1/2 cup Parmesan cheese, grated
- 2/3 cup commercial pesto
- 2 Tbsp chicken stock
- Pepper
- Salt

Directions: Place the chicken in a crock pot and season with pepper and salt. In a bowl, combine the chicken stock, pesto, onion, and spinach. Pour bowl mixture over the chicken. Cover and cook on low for 7 hours. Top with Parmesan cheese. Cover for 5 minutes and cook until the cheese has melted. Serve and enjoy.

Nutritional Value (Amount per Serving): Calories 541, Fat 32.7 g, Carbohydrates 4.5 g

BALSAMIC CHICKEN

Preparation Time: 10 minutes | Cooking Time: 4 hours | Serves: 10

Ingredients:

- 6 chicken breasts, skinless and boneless
- 1/2 tsp thyme
- 1 tsp dried oregano
- 1/2 cup balsamic vinegar
- 3 garlic cloves
- 1 onion, sliced
- 1 tsp dried basil
- 1 tsp dried rosemary
- 1 Tbsp olive oil
- 14 oz can tomatoes, diced
- Pepper
- Salt

Directions: Add all ingredients to a crock pot and stir well. Cover and cook on high for 4 hours. Stir well and serve.

Nutritional Value (Amount per Serving): Calories 197, Fat 8 g, Carbohydrates 3.8 g

MEXICAN SALSA CHICKEN

Preparation Time: 10 minutes | Cooking Time: 8 hours | Serves: 8

Ingredients:

- 3 1/2 lb chicken
- 1 tsp cumin
- 2 garlic cloves
- 1 cup onion, chopped
- 1 fresh lime juice
- 1 tsp oregano
- 1 can (4 oz) chilies
- 1 tsp salt

- 14 oz can tomatoes, diced

Directions: Add all ingredients to a crock pot and stir well. Cover and cook on low for 8 hours. Remove chicken from the crock pot and place in a bowl. Shred the chicken using forks. Blend the mixture left in the crock pot using a blender or immersion blender until smooth. Return the shredded chicken to the crock pot and stir well. Cover and cook for 5 minutes longer. Serve and enjoy.

Nutritional Value (Amount per Serving): Calories 324, Fat 6.2 g, Carbohydrates 5.6 g

TURKEY WITH MUSHROOMS

Preparation Time: 10 minutes | Cooking Time: 6 hours | Serves: 6

Ingredients:

- 1 1/2 lb turkey breast cutlets
- 1 tsp sage, minced
- 8 oz mushrooms, sliced
- 1 medium onion, sliced
- 1/4 cup water
- 1 Tbsp butter
- 1/4 tsp pepper
- 1/8 Tsp salt

Directions: Heat butter in a pan over medium heat. Add mushrooms and onion to the pan and sauté until softened. Add half the mushroom and onion mixture to a crock pot. Add turkey to the crock pot and sprinkle with pepper, sage, and salt. Pour remaining mushroom and onion mixture over the turkey. Pour the water into the crock pot. Cover and cook on low for 6 hours. Serve and enjoy.

Nutritional Value (Amount per Serving): Calories 142, Fat 1.2 g, Carbohydrates 3.1 g

CURRIED CHICKEN WINGS

Preparation Time: 10 minutes | Cooking Time: 6 hours | Serves: 6

Ingredients:

- 3 lb chicken wings
- 2 oz Thai basil, minced
- 8 oz green curry paste
- 1 Tbsp fresh cilantro, minced
- 1 Tbsp fresh ginger, minced
- 1 Tbsp coconut milk

Directions: Add chicken wings to a crock pot. In a bowl, whisk together coconut milk, cilantro, ginger, basil, and curry paste. Pour coconut milk mixture over the chicken wings and toss well. Cover and cook on low for 6 hours. Stir well and serve.

Nutritional Value (Amount per Serving): Calories 322, Fat 14.3 g, Carbohydrates 6.3 g

BACON HERB CHICKEN

Preparation Time: 10 minutes | Cooking Time: 8 hours | Serves: 4

Ingredients:

- 5 chicken breasts, skinless and boneless
- 10 bacon slices, chopped

- 1 Tbsp oregano, dried
- 2 Tbsp thyme, dried
- 5 Tbsp olive oil
- 1 Tbsp rosemary, dried
- 1 Tbsp salt

Directions: Add all ingredients to a crock pot and mix well. Cover and cook on low for 8 hours. Shred the chicken using forks and serve.

Nutritional Value (Amount per Serving): Calories 619, Fat 28.6 g, Carbohydrates 2.1 g

Low-Carb Beef, Pork And Lamb Recipes

Simple Garlic Pork Tenderloin

Preparation Time: 10 minutes | Cooking Time: 6 hours | Serves: 8

Ingredients:

- 2 lb pork tenderloin
- 1/2 tsp red pepper flakes
- 1 Tbsp Worcestershire sauce
- 1/2 cup balsamic vinegar
- 3 garlic cloves, minced
- 1 1/2 Tbsp coconut aminos
- 1 Tbsp extra-virgin olive oil
- 1/2 tsp sea salt

Directions: Place pork tenderloin in a crock pot. Drizzle olive oil over the pork tenderloin and sprinkle with garlic. In a small bowl, mix together remaining ingredients and pour over the pork tenderloin. Cover and cook on low for 6 hours. Serve and enjoy.

Nutritional Value (Amount per Serving): Calories 184, Fat 5.8 g, Carbohydrates 1 g

Flavorful Lamb Rogan Josh

Preparation Time: 15 minutes | Cooking Time: 6 hours 15 minutes | Serves: 6

Ingredients:

- 2 lb leg of lamb, cubed
- 14 oz can tomatoes, crushed
- 1 Tbsp olive oil
- 1 tsp garam masala
- 1 tsp turmeric
- 1/2 tsp ground cloves
- 1 1/2 tsp ground cardamom
- 1 1/2 tsp ground cumin
- 1 Tbsp ground coriander
- 1 Tbsp tomato paste
- 1 tsp chili powder
- 2 tsp garlic, minced
- 1 Tbsp ginger, crushed
- 1 onion, diced

Directions: Spray a pan with cooking spray and heat over high heat. Brown the meat in the hot pan. Remove meat from the pan and set aside. Heat oil in the same pan. Add onion, ginger, and garlic and sauté until onion is softened. Add chili powder, garam masala, turmeric, cloves, cardamom, cumin, coriander, and tomato paste to the pan and stir until fragrant. Transfer pan mixture to a crock pot along with the meat and crushed tomatoes, and stir well. Cover and cook on low for 6 hours. Serve and enjoy.

Nutritional Value (Amount per Serving): Calories 316, Fat 11.5 g, Carbohydrates 7.7 g

Dijon Lamb Chops

Preparation Time: 10 minutes | Cooking Time: 5 hours | Serves: 4

Ingredients:

- 4 lean lamb chops
- 1/2 tsp paprika
- 1 Tbsp fresh rosemary, minced
- 1 1/2 tbsp mustard seeds
- 2 garlic cloves, minced
- 1/2 cup Dijon mustard
- 1/4 tsp pepper

Directions: In a small bowl, mix together Dijon mustard, pepper, rosemary, mustard seeds, and garlic. Coat lamb chops with the mustard mixture and place them in a crock pot. Cover and cook on low for 5 hours. Serve and enjoy.

Nutritional Value (Amount per Serving): Calories 230, Fat 10.6 g, Carbohydrates 4.4 g

SPINACH LAMB CURRY

Preparation Time: 15 minutes | Cooking Time: 6 hours 5 minutes | Serves: 6

Ingredients:

- 2 lb lamb stew meat
- 1/3 cup plain yogurt
- 4 cups spinach, chopped
- 2 cups chicken stock
- 1/4 tsp cinnamon
- 1/2 tsp red pepper flakes
- 1/4 tsp turmeric
- 1/8 tsp ground cloves
- 2 tsp ground coriander
- 1 Tbsp ground cumin
- 1 Tbsp fresh ginger, grated
- 5 garlic cloves, minced
- 1 Tbsp olive oil
- 1 onion, diced
- 1 tsp salt
- 1/2 tsp paprika

Directions: Heat oil in a pan over medium heat. Add onion and sauté for 4 minutes. Add ginger and garlic and sauté for 1–2 minutes. Transfer pan mixture to a crock pot. Add remaining ingredients to the crock pot except for the yogurt and spinach. Stir everything well. Cover and cook on low for 6 hours. Just before serving add the yogurt and spinach and stir until spinach is wilted. Serve and enjoy.

Nutritional Value (Amount per Serving): Calories 338, Fat 14.2 g, Carbohydrates 5.9 g

PERFECT SHREDDED PORK

Preparation Time: 10 minutes | Cooking Time: 8 hours | Serves: 12

Ingredients:

- 4 lb pork shoulder
- 3/4 cup water
- 1/4 cup apple cider vinegar
- 1 tsp onion powder
- 1 tsp garlic powder
- 1 tsp cayenne pepper
- 1 tsp pepper
- 2 Tbsp paprika
- 1 tsp kosher salt

Directions: In a small bowl, mix together all dry spices and rub onto all sides of the meat. Add water and apple cider vinegar to a crock pot. Place meat in the crock pot. Cover and cook on low for 8 hours. Remove meat from the pot and shred using forks. Serve and enjoy.

Nutritional Value (Amount per Serving): Calories 448, Fat 32.5 g, Carbohydrates 1.2 g

EASY RANCH PORK CHOPS

Preparation Time: 10 minutes | Cooking Time: 8 hours | Serves: 4

Ingredients:

- 4 pork chops, boneless
- 3/4 cup chicken stock
- 10.5 oz can cream of chicken soup
- 4 oz cream cheese
- 1 packet ranch dressing mix

Directions: Place pork chops in a crock pot. Combine stock, cream of chicken soup, cream cheese, and ranch dressing mix and pour over the pork chops. Cover and cook on low for 8 hours. Serve and enjoy.

Nutritional Value (Amount per Serving): Calories 425, Fat 34.2 g, Carbohydrates 6.5 g

TASTY PORK ROAST

Preparation Time: 10 minutes Cooking Time: 6 hours | Serves: 6

Ingredients:

- 3 lb pork roast
- 2 tsp garlic, minced
- 2 Tbsp honey
- 2 Tbsp soy sauce
- 1/4 cup balsamic vinegar
- 1 cup chicken stock

Directions: Place pork roast in a crock pot. Combine the remaining ingredients and pour over the pork roast. Cover and cook on high for 6 hours. Remove meat from the crock pot and shred using forks. Pour crock pot liquid over shredded meat and serve.

Nutritional Value (Amount per Serving): Calories 499, Fat 21.5 g, Carbohydrates 6.7 g

TASTY AND SPICY BEEF CHILI

Preparation Time: 10 minutes | Cooking Time: 10 hours | Serves: 4

Ingredients:

- 1 lb lean beef, cubed
- 1/2 tsp white pepper
- 1/2 tsp black pepper
- 1/2 tsp oregano
- 1 Tbsp paprika
- 8 oz can tomato sauce
- 1/2 tsp ground chipotle
- 1/2 tsp cayenne pepper
- 2 Tbsp chili powder
- 1 Tbsp garlic powder
- 2 Tbsp onion powder

Directions: Heat a pan over medium-high heat. Place meat in the pan and sauté until brown. Drain the beef on paper towels to remove any excess grease. Place browned meat in a crock pot. Add remaining ingredients over the meat. Cover and cook on low for 10 hours. Serve and enjoy.

Nutritional Value (Amount per Serving): Calories 263, Fat 8.2 g, Carbohydrates 11 g

FLAVORFUL SHREDDED PORK

Preparation Time: 10 minutes | Cooking Time: 8 hours | Serves: 10

Ingredients:

- 3 lb pork shoulder roast, boneless and cut into 4 pieces
- 1/2 Tbsp cumin
- 1/2 Tbsp fresh oregano
- 2/3 cup orange juice
- 5 garlic cloves
- Pepper
- Salt

Directions: Add pork roast to a crock pot. Season with pepper and salt. Add garlic, cumin, oregano, and orange juice to a blender and blend until smooth. Pour blended mixture over the pork and stir well. Cover and cook on low for 8 hours. Remove pork from the crock pot and shred using forks. Return shredded pork to the crock pot and stir well. Serve warm and enjoy.

Nutritional Value (Amount per Serving): Calories 359, Fat 27.8 g, Carbohydrates 2.1 g

STEAK FAJITAS

Preparation Time: 10 minutes | Cooking Time: 6 hours | Serves: 6

Ingredients:

• 2 lb beef, sliced • 1 1/2 Tbsp fajita seasoning • 20 oz chunky salsa	• 1 bell pepper, sliced • 1 onion, sliced

Directions: Add salsa to a crock pot. Add remaining ingredients to the crock pot and stir to mix. Cover the crock pot with its lid and cook on low for 6 hours. Stir well and serve.

Nutritional Value (Amount per Serving): Calories 333, Fat 9.7 g, Carbohydrates 11.9 g

SIMPLE SEASONED PORK CHOPS

Preparation Time: 10 minutes | Cooking Time: 6 hours | Serves: 4

Ingredients:

- 4 pork chops
- 2 garlic cloves, minced
- 2 Tbsp butter, melted
- 3/4 tsp poultry seasoning
- 1 onion, chopped
- 1 1/2 cups chicken stock
- 1/2 tsp salt

Directions: In a large bowl, mix together butter, broth, poultry seasoning and salt. Pour the mixture into a crock pot. Add pork chops, onion, and garlic to the crock pot. Cover and cook on low for 6 hours. Serve and enjoy.

Nutritional Value (Amount per Serving): Calories 337, Fat 26.2 g, Carbohydrates 3.8 g

SPICY BEEF BRISKET

Preparation Time: 10 minutes | Cooking Time: 7 hours | Serves: 6

Ingredients:

- 3 lb beef brisket
- 1 Tbsp Worcestershire sauce
- 1 Tbsp chili powder
- 3 garlic cloves, chopped
- 1/2 onion, chopped
- 1 tsp cumin
- 3 Tbsp chili sauce
- 1/4 cup beef broth
- 1 1/2 tsp liquid smoke
- 1/2 tsp black pepper

Directions: In a small bowl, mix together chili powder, pepper, cumin, Worcestershire sauce, and garlic. Rub this mixture over the brisket. Place beef brisket in the crock pot. Mix together broth, chili sauce, onion, and liquid smoke and pour it over the brisket. Cover and cook on low for 7 hours. Remove brisket from the crock pot and cut into slices. Serve and enjoy.

Nutritional Value (Amount per Serving): Calories 439, Fat 14.5 g, Carbohydrates 3.1 g

DELICIOUS PORK CARNITAS

Preparation Time: 10 minutes | Cooking Time: 6 hours | Serves: 6

Ingredients:

- 2 lb pork tenderloin
- 1 jalapeño pepper, seeded, chopped
- 3 garlic cloves, minced
- 1/2 onion, chopped
- 1 Tbsp olive oil
- 1 orange juice
- 1 lime juice
- 2 tsp ground cumin
- 1 Tbsp oregano, dried

Directions: Combine olive oil, ground cumin, and oregano. Rub this well over the pork tenderloin. Place tenderloin in a crock pot. Top with remaining ingredients. Cover and cook on low for 6 hours. Remove meat from the crock pot and shred it using forks. Serve and enjoy.

Nutritional Value (Amount per Serving): Calories 256, Fat 7.9 g, Carbohydrates 4.4 g

CREAMY BEEF STROGANOFF

Preparation Time: 10 minutes | Cooking Time: 8 hours | Serves: 2

Ingredients:

- 1/2 lb beef stew meat
- 1/2 cup sour cream
- 3 oz mushrooms, sliced
- 10 oz can cream of mushroom soup
- 1 onion, chopped
- Pepper
- salt

Directions: Add all ingredients except sour cream to a crock pot and mix well. Cover and cook on low for 8 hours. Add sour cream and stir well. Serve and enjoy.

Nutritional Value (Amount per Serving): Calories 425, Fat 23.4 g, Carbohydrates 13.7 g

TENDER BEEF CARNITAS

Preparation Time: 10 minutes | Cooking Time: 8 hours | Serves: 4

Ingredients:

- 2 lb flank steak
- 1 green bell pepper, chopped
- 1 onion, chopped
- 1 jalapeño, seeded and chopped
- 1 red bell pepper, chopped
- For the rub:
- 1/4 tsp cayenne pepper
- 1 tsp cumin
- 2 tsp chili powder
- 1/4 tsp garlic powder
- 1/4 tsp onion powder
- 1/2 tsp black pepper
- 1 tsp salt

Directions: In a small bowl, mix together all spice ingredients and rub them over the flank steak. Place the flank steak in a crock pot. Add jalapeño pepper, bell peppers, and onion over the steak. Cover and cook on low for 8 hours. Remove meat from crock pot and shred using forks. Return shredded meat to the crock pot. Stir well and serve.

Nutritional Value (Amount per Serving): Calories 476, Fat 19.4 g, Carbohydrates 7.8 g

LOW-CARB FISH AND SEAFOOD RECIPES

COCONUT SHRIMP CURRY

Preparation Time: 10 minutes | Cooking Time: 2 hours 30 minutes | Serves: 4

Ingredients:

- 1 lb shrimp
- 1/4 cup fresh cilantro, chopped
- 2 tsp lemon garlic seasoning
- 1 Tbsp curry paste
- 15 oz water
- 30 oz coconut milk

Directions: Add coconut milk, cilantro, lemon garlic seasoning, curry paste, and water to a crock pot and stir well. Cover and cook on high for 2 hours. Add shrimp, cover and cook for 30 minutes longer. Serve and enjoy.

Nutritional Value (Amount per Serving): Calories 200, Fat 7.7 g, Carbohydrates 4.6 g

DELICIOUS FISH CURRY

Preparation Time: 10 minutes | Cooking Time: 2 hours | Serves: 4

Ingredients:

- 1 lb cod fish fillets
- 12 oz carrots, cut into julienne strips
- 1 bell pepper, sliced
- 1 tsp garlic powder
- 1 tsp ground ginger
- 1 Tbsp curry powder
- 3 Tbsp red curry paste
- 15 oz coconut milk
- Pepper
- Salt

Directions: Add coconut milk to a crock pot and whisk in curry powder, garlic powder, ground ginger, and curry paste. Stir in carrots and bell peppers. Place cod fillets in the sauce. Cover and cook on low for 2 hours. Season with pepper and salt. Serve and enjoy.

Nutritional Value (Amount per Serving): Calories 232, Fat 6.5 g, Carbohydrates 14.1 g

LEMON DILL SALMON

Preparation Time: 10 minutes | Cooking Time: 2 hours | Serves: 4

Ingredients:

- 1 lb salmon fillet, skin-on
- 2 Tbsp fresh dill, chopped
- 1/2 lemon juice
- 1 1/2 cups vegetable stock
- 1 lemon, sliced
- Pepper
- Salt

Directions: Line a crock pot with parchment paper. Place lemon slices on the bottom of the crock pot and then place the salmon on top of the slices Season salmon with pepper and salt. Add lemon juice and stock to the crock pot.Cover and cook on low for 2 hours. Serve and enjoy.

Nutritional Value (Amount per Serving): Calories 162, Fat 7.7 g, Carbohydrates 2.9 g

CREAMY SHRIMP

Preparation Time: 10 minutes │ Cooking Time: 2 hours 10 minutes │ Serves: 4

Ingredients:

- 1 lb cooked shrimp
- 1 cup sour cream
- 10.5 oz can cream of mushroom soup
- 1 tsp curry powder
- 1 onion, chopped

Directions: Spray a medium pan with cooking spray and heat over medium heat. Add onion to the hot pan and sauté until onion is soft. Transfer sautéed onion to a crock pot along with the shrimp, curry powder, and cream of mushroom soup. Cover and cook on low for 2 hours. Stir in sour cream and serve.

Nutritional Value (Amount per Serving): Calories 302, Fat 16.2 g, Carbohydrates 9.5 g

SPICY COCONUT FISH STEW

Preparation Time: 10 minutes │ Cooking Time: 6 hours 20 minutes │ Serves: 6

Ingredients:

- 1 ½ lb white fish fillets
- 14 oz coconut milk
- 14 oz can tomatoes, crushed
- 1 green bell pepper, chopped
- 1 red bell pepper, chopped
- 2 garlic cloves, minced
- 1 onion, chopped
- 1 Tbsp butter
- Pepper
- Salt

Directions: In a crock pot combine the butter, coconut milk, tomatoes, peppers, garlic, and onion. Cover and cook on low for 6 hours. A half hour before the time is up, open and add the fish fillets to the crock pot. Season with pepper and salt. Cover and cook on high for 30 minutes longer. Serve and enjoy.

Nutritional Value (Amount per Serving): Calories 398, Fat 26.3 g, Carbohydrates 11.6 g

ROSEMARY SALMON

Preparation Time: 10 minutes │ Cooking Time: 2 hours │ Serves: 2

Ingredients:

- 8 oz salmon
- 1/3 cup water

- 1/4 tsp fresh rosemary, minced
- 2 Tbsp fresh lemon juice
- 1 Tbsp capers
- 1 fresh lemon, sliced

Directions: Place salmon into a crock pot. Pour lemon juice and water over the salmon. Arrange lemon slices on top of the salmon. Sprinkle with rosemary and capers. Cover and cook on low for 2 hours. Serve and enjoy.

Nutritional Value (Amount per Serving): Calories 164, Fat 7.3 g, Carbohydrates 3.3 g

PAPRIKA GARLIC SHRIMP

Preparation Time: 10 minutes | Cooking Time: 50 minutes | Serves: 8

Ingredients:

- 2 lb shrimp, peeled and deveined
- 1 tsp paprika
- 5 garlic cloves, sliced
- 3/4 cup olive oil
- 1/4 tsp red pepper flakes, crushed
- 1/4 tsp black pepper
- 1 tsp kosher salt

Directions: Combine oil, red pepper flakes, black pepper, paprika, garlic, and salt in a crock pot. Cover and cook on high for 30 minutes. Open and add the shrimp; cover and cook on high for 10 minutes. Open again and stir well. Cover and cook for 10 more minutes. Serve and enjoy.

Nutritional Value (Amount per Serving): Calories 301, Fat 20.9 g, Carbohydrates 2.6 g

SIMPLE LEMON HALIBUT

Preparation Time: 10 minutes | Cooking Time: 1 hour 30 minutes | Serves: 2

Ingredients:

- 12 oz halibut fish fillet
- 1 Tbsp fresh lemon juice
- 1 Tbsp fresh dill
- 1 Tbsp olive oil
- Pepper
- Salt

Directions: Place fish fillet in the middle of a large sheet of aluminum foil. Season with pepper and salt. In a small bowl, whisk together dill, oil, and lemon juice. Pour over the fish fillet. Wrap foil around the fish fillet and make a packet. Place the foil packet in a crock pot. Cover and cook on high for 1 hour 30 minutes. Serve and enjoy.

Nutritional Value (Amount per Serving): Calories 289, Fat 11.2 g, Carbohydrates 1.1 g

CRAB DIP

Preparation Time: 10 minutes | Cooking Time: 3 hours | Serves: 24

Ingredients:

- 8 oz imitation crab meat
- 1 tsp paprika
- 2 Tbsp onion, chopped
- 8 oz cream cheese
- 1/4 cup walnuts, chopped
- 1 tsp hot sauce

Directions: Place all ingredients, except paprika and walnuts, in a crock pot and stir well. Sprinkle over the paprika and walnuts. Cover and cook on low for 3 hours. Stir well and serve.

Nutritional Value (Amount per Serving): Calories 53, Fat 4.2 g, Carbohydrates 2.4 g

LEMON BUTTER TILAPIA

Preparation Time: 10 minutes | Cooking Time: 2 hours | Serves: 4

Ingredients:

- 4 tilapia fillets
- 1/4 tsp lemon pepper seasoning
- 3/4 cup fresh lemon juice
- 12 asparagus spear
- 2 Tbsp butter, divided

Directions: Prepare four large sheets of aluminum foil. Place a fish fillet on each sheet. Sprinkle lemon pepper seasoning and lemon juice on top of fish fillets. Add 1/2 tablespoon of butter on top of each fillet. Arrange three asparagus spears on each fish fillet. Fold foil around the fish fillet and make a packet. Repeat with the remaining fish fillets. Place fish fillet packets in a crock pot. Cover and cook on high for 2 hours. Serve and enjoy.

Nutritional Value (Amount per Serving): Calories 112, Fat 6.7 g, Carbohydrates 3.8 g

Low-Carb Soup, Stew And Chili Recipes

Delicious Chicken Soup

Preparation Time: 10 minutes | Cooking Time: 4 hours 30 minutes | Serves: 4

Ingredients:

- 1 lb chicken breasts, boneless and skinless
- 2 Tbsp fresh basil, chopped
- 1 1/2 cups mozzarella cheese, shredded
- 2 garlic cloves, minced
- 1 Tbsp Parmesan cheese, grated
- 2 Tbsp dried basil
- 2 cups chicken stock
- 28 oz tomatoes, diced
- 1/4 tsp pepper
- 1/2 tsp salt

Directions: Add chicken, Parmesan cheese, dried basil, tomatoes, garlic, pepper, and salt to a crock pot and stir well to combine. Cover and cook on low for 4 hours. Add fresh basil and mozzarella cheese and stir well. Cover again and cook for 30 more minutes or until cheese is melted. Remove chicken from the crock pot and shred using forks. Return shredded chicken to the crock pot and stir to mix. Serve and enjoy.

Nutritional Value (Amount per Serving): Calories 299, Fat 11.6 g, Carbohydrates 9.3 g

Flavorful Broccoli Soup

Preparation Time: 10 minutes | Cooking Time: 4 hours 15 minutes | Serves: 6

Ingredients:

- 20 oz broccoli florets
- 4 oz cream cheese
- 8 oz cheddar cheese, shredded
- 1/2 tsp paprika
- 1/2 tsp ground mustard
- 3 cups chicken stock
- 2 garlic cloves, chopped
- 1 onion, diced
- 1 cup carrots, shredded
- 1/4 tsp baking soda
- 1/4 tsp salt

Directions: Add all ingredients except cream cheese and cheddar cheese to a crock pot and stir well. Cover and cook on low for 4 hours. Purée the soup using an immersion blender until smooth. Stir in the cream cheese and cheddar cheese. Cover and cook on low for 15 minutes longer. Season with pepper and salt. Serve and enjoy.

Nutritional Value (Amount per Serving): Calories 275, Fat 19.9 g, Carbohydrates 11.9 g

Healthy Chicken Kale Soup

Preparation Time: 10 minutes | Cooking Time: 6 hours 15 minutes | Serves: 6

Ingredients:

- 2 lb chicken breasts, skinless and boneless
- 1/4 cup fresh lemon juice
- 5 oz baby kale
- 32 oz chicken stock
- 1/2 cup olive oil
- 1 large onion, sliced
- 14 oz chicken broth
- 1 Tbsp extra-virgin olive oil
- Salt

Directions: Heat the extra-virgin olive oil in a pan over medium heat. Season chicken with salt and place in the hot pan. Cover pan and cook chicken for 15 minutes. Remove chicken from the pan and shred it using forks. Add shredded chicken to a crock pot. Add sliced onion, olive oil, and broth to a blender and blend until combined. Pour blended mixture into the crock pot. Add remaining ingredients to the crock pot and stir well. Cover and cook on low for 6 hours. Stir well and serve.

Nutritional Value (Amount per Serving): Calories 493, Fat 31.3 g, Carbohydrates 5.8 g

SPICY CHICKEN PEPPER STEW

Preparation Time: 10 minutes | Cooking Time: 6 hours | Serves: 6

Ingredients:

- 3 chicken breasts, skinless and boneless, cut into small pieces
- 1 tsp garlic, minced
- 1 tsp ground ginger
- 2 tsp olive oil
- 2 tsp soy sauce
- 1 Tbsp fresh lemon juice
- 1/2 cup green onions, sliced
- 1 Tbsp crushed red pepper
- 8 oz chicken stock
- 1 bell pepper, chopped
- 1 green chili pepper, sliced
- 2 jalapeño peppers, sliced
- 1/2 tsp black pepper
- 1/4 tsp sea salt

Directions: Add all ingredients to a large mixing bowl and mix well. Place in the refrigerator overnight. Pour marinated chicken mixture into a crock pot. Cover and cook on low for 6 hours. Stir well and serve.

Nutritional Value (Amount per Serving): Calories 171, Fat 7.4 g, Carbohydrates 3.7 g

BEEF CHILI

Preparation Time: 10 minutes | Cooking Time: 8 hours | Serves: 6

Ingredients:

- 1 lb ground beef
- 1 tsp garlic powder
- 1 tsp paprika
- 3 tsp chili powder
- 1 tsp onion powder
- 25 oz tomatoes, chopped
- 4 carrots, chopped
- 1 onion, diced

- 1 Tbsp Worcestershire sauce
- 1 Tbsp fresh parsley, chopped
- 1 bell pepper, diced
- 1/2 tsp sea salt

Directions: Brown the ground meat in a pan over high heat until meat is no longer pink. Transfer meat to a crock pot. Add bell pepper, tomatoes, carrots, and onion to the crock pot and stir well. Add remaining ingredients and stir well. Cover and cook on low for 8 hours. Serve and enjoy.

Nutritional Value (Amount per Serving): Calories 152, Fat 4 g, Carbohydrates 10.4 g

TASTY BASIL TOMATO SOUP

Preparation Time: 10 minutes | Cooking Time: 6 hours | Serves: 6

Ingredients:

- 28 oz can whole peeled tomatoes
- 1/2 cup fresh basil leaves
- 4 cups chicken stock
- 1 tsp red pepper flakes
- 3 garlic cloves, peeled
- 2 onions, diced
- 3 carrots, peeled and diced
- 3 Tbsp olive oil
- 1 tsp salt

Directions: Add all ingredients to a crock pot and stir well. Cover and cook on low for 6 hours. Purée the soup until smooth using an immersion blender. Season soup with pepper and salt. Serve and enjoy.

Nutritional Value (Amount per Serving): Calories 126, Fat 7.5 g, Carbohydrates 13.3 g

HEALTHY SPINACH SOUP

Preparation Time: 10 minutes | Cooking Time: 3 hours | Serves: 8

Ingredients:

- 3 cups frozen spinach, chopped, thawed and drained
- 8 oz cheddar cheese, shredded
- 10 oz can cream of chicken soup
- 8 oz cream cheese, softened
- 1 egg, lightly beaten

Directions: Add spinach to a large bowl. Purée the spinach. Add egg, chicken soup, cream cheese, and pepper to the spinach purée and mix well. Transfer spinach mixture to a crock pot. Cover and cook on low for 3 hours. Stir in cheddar cheese and serve.

Nutritional Value (Amount per Serving): Calories 256, Fat 21.9 g, Carbohydrates 4.1 g

MEXICAN CHICKEN SOUP

Preparation Time: 10 minutes | Cooking Time: 4 hours | Serves: 6

Ingredients:

- 1 1/2 lb chicken thighs, skinless and boneless
- 14 oz chicken stock
- 14 oz salsa
- 8 oz Monterey Jack cheese, shredded

Directions: Place chicken into a crock pot. Pour remaining ingredients over the chicken. Cover and cook on high for 4 hours. Remove chicken from crock pot and shred using forks. Return shredded chicken to the crock pot and stir well. Serve and enjoy.

Nutritional Value (Amount per Serving): Calories 371, Fat 19.5 g, Carbohydrates 5.7 g

BEEF STEW

Preparation Time: 10 minutes | Cooking Time: 5 hours 5 minutes | Serves: 8

Ingredients:

- 3 lb beef stew meat, trimmed
- 1/2 cup red curry paste
- 1/3 cup tomato paste
- 13 oz can coconut milk
- 2 tsp ginger, minced
- 2 garlic cloves, minced
- 1 medium onion, sliced
- 2 Tbsp olive oil
- 2 cups carrots, julienned
- 2 cups broccoli florets
- 2 tsp fresh lime juice
- 2 Tbsp fish sauce
- 2 tsp sea salt

Directions: Heat 1 tablespoon of oil in a pan over medium heat. Brown the meat on all sides in the pan. Add brown meat to a crock pot. Add remaining oil to the same pan and sauté the ginger, garlic, and onion over medium-high heat for 5 minutes. Add coconut milk and stir well. Transfer pan mixture to the crock pot. Add remaining ingredients except for carrots and broccoli. Cover and cook on high for 5 hours. Add carrots and broccoli during the last 30 minutes of cooking. Serve and enjoy.

Nutritional Value (Amount per Serving): Calories 537, Fat 28.6 g, Carbohydrates 13 g

CREAMY BROCCOLI CAULIFLOWER SOUP

Preparation Time: 10 minutes | Cooking Time: 6 hours | Serves: 6

Ingredients:

- 2 cups cauliflower florets, chopped
- 3 cups broccoli florets, chopped
- 3 1/2 cups chicken stock
- 1 large carrot, diced
- 1/2 cup shallots, diced
- 2 garlic cloves, minced
- 1 cup plain yogurt
- 6 oz cheddar cheese, shredded
- 1 cup coconut milk
- Pepper
- Salt

Directions: Add all ingredients except milk, cheese, and yogurt to a crock pot and stir well. Cover and cook on low for 6 hours. Purée the soup using an immersion blender until smooth. Add cheese, milk, and yogurt and blend until smooth and creamy. Season with pepper and salt. Serve and enjoy.

Nutritional Value (Amount per Serving): Calories 281, Fat 20 g, Carbohydrates 14.4 g

SQUASH SOUP

Preparation Time: 10 minutes | Cooking Time: 8 hours | Serves: 6

Ingredients:

- 2 lb butternut squash, peeled, chopped into chunks
- 1 tsp ginger, minced
- 1/4 tsp cinnamon
- 1 Tbsp curry powder
- 2 bay leaves
- 1 tsp black pepper
- 1/2 cup heavy cream
- 2 cups chicken stock
- 1 Tbsp garlic, minced
- 2 carrots, cut into chunks
- 2 apples, peeled, cored and diced
- 1 large onion, diced
- 1 tsp salt

Directions: Spray a crock pot inside with cooking spray. Add all ingredients except cream to the crock pot and stir well. Cover and cook on low for 8 hours. Purée the soup using an immersion blender until smooth and creamy. Stir in heavy cream and season soup with pepper and salt. Serve and enjoy.

Nutritional Value (Amount per Serving): Calories 170, Fat 4.4 g, Carbohydrates 34.4 g

HERB TOMATO SOUP

Preparation Time: 10 minutes | Cooking Time: 6 hours | Serves: 8

Ingredients:

- 55 oz can tomatoes, diced
- 1/2 onion, minced
- 2 cups chicken stock
- 1 cup half and half
- 4 Tbsp butter
- 1 bay leaf
- 1/2 tsp black pepper
- 1/2 tsp garlic powder
- 1 tsp oregano
- 1 tsp dried thyme
- 1 cup carrots, diced
- 1/4 tsp black pepper
- 1/2 tsp salt

Directions: Add all ingredients to a crock pot and stir well. Cover and cook on low for 6 hours. Discard bay leaf and purée the soup using an immersion blender until smooth. Serve and enjoy.

Nutritional Value (Amount per Serving): Calories 145, Fat 9.4 g, Carbohydrates 13.9 g

EASY BEEF MUSHROOM STEW

Preparation Time: 10 minutes | Cooking Time: 8 hours | Serves: 8

Ingredients:

- 2 lb stewing beef, cubed
- 1 packet dry onion soup mix
- 4 oz can mushrooms, sliced
- 14 oz can cream of mushroom soup
- 1/2 cup water
- 1/4 tsp black pepper
- 1/2 tsp salt

Directions: Spray a crock pot inside with cooking spray. Add all ingredients into the crock pot and stir well. Cover and cook on low for 8 hours. Stir well and serve.

Nutritional Value (Amount per Serving): Calories 237, Fat 8.5 g, Carbohydrates 2.7 g

LAMB STEW

Preparation Time: 10 minutes | Cooking Time: 8 hours | Serves: 2

Ingredients:

- 1/2 lb lean lamb, boneless and cubed
- 2 Tbsp lemon juice
- 1/2 onion, chopped
- 2 garlic cloves, minced
- 2 fresh thyme sprigs
- 1/4 tsp turmeric
- 1/4 cup green olives, sliced
- 1/2 tsp black pepper
- 1/4 tsp salt

Directions: Add all ingredients to a crock pot and stir well. Cover and cook on low for 8 hours. Stir well and serve.

Nutritional Value (Amount per Serving): Calories 297, Fat 20.3 g, Carbohydrates 5.4 g

VEGETABLE CHICKEN SOUP

Preparation Time: 10 minutes | Cooking Time: 6 hours | Serves: 6

Ingredients:

- 4 cups chicken, boneless, skinless, cooked and diced
- 4 tsp garlic, minced
- 2/3 cups onion, diced
- 1 1/2 cups carrot, diced
- 6 cups chicken stock
- 1/4 cup jalapeño pepper, diced
- 1/2 cup tomatoes, diced
- 1/2 cup fresh cilantro, chopped
- 1 tsp chili powder
- 1 Tbsp cumin
- 1 3/4 cups tomato juice
- 2 tsp sea salt
- 2 Tbsp lime juice

Directions: Add all ingredients to a crock pot and stir well. Cover and cook on low for 6 hours. Stir well and serve.

Nutritional Value (Amount per Serving): Calories 192, Fat 3.8 g, Carbohydrates 9.8 g

LOW-CARB VEGETABLE AND SIDES RECIPES

SQUASH AND ZUCCHINI CASSEROLE

Preparation Time: 10 minutes | Cooking Time: 6 hours | Serves: 6

Ingredients:

- 2 cups yellow squash, quartered and sliced
- 2 cups zucchini, quartered and sliced
- 1/4 cup Parmesan cheese, grated
- 1/4 cup butter, cut into pieces
- 1 tsp garlic powder
- 1 tsp Italian seasoning
- 1/4 tsp pepper
- 1/2 tsp sea salt

Directions: Add sliced yellow squash and zucchini to a crock pot. Sprinkle with garlic powder, Italian seasoning, pepper, and salt. Top with grated cheese and butter. Cover with the lid and cook on low for 6 hours. Serve and enjoy.

Nutritional Value (Amount per Serving): Calories 107, Fat 9.5 g, Carbohydrates 2.5 g

ITALIAN ZUCCHINI

Preparation Time: 10 minutes | Cooking Time: 3 hours | Serves: 3

Ingredients:

- 2 zucchini, cut in half lengthwise then cut into half moons
- 1/4 cup Parmesan cheese, grated
- 1/2 tsp Italian seasoning
- 1 Tbsp olive oil
- 1 Tbsp butter
- 2 garlic cloves, minced
- 1 onion, sliced
- 2 tomatoes, diced
- 1/2 tsp pepper
- 1/4 tsp salt

Directions: Spray a crock pot inside with cooking spray. Add all ingredients except Parmesan cheese to the crock pot and stir well. Cover and cook on low for 3 hours. Top with the Parmesan cheese and serve.

Nutritional Value (Amount per Serving): Calories 181, Fat 12.2 g, Carbohydrates 12 g

ALMOND GREEN BEANS

Preparation Time: 10 minutes | Cooking Time: 3 hours | Serves: 4

Ingredients:

- 1 lb green beans, rinsed and trimmed
- 1/2 cup almonds, sliced and toasted
- 6 oz onion, sliced
- 1 Tbsp olive oil

- 1 cup vegetable stock
- 1/4 cup butter, melted
- 1/4 tsp pepper
- 1/2 tsp salt

Directions: Heat the olive oil in a pan over medium heat. Add onion to the pan and sauté until softened. Transfer sautéed onion to a crock pot. Add remaining ingredients except for almonds to the crock pot and stir well. Cover and cook on low for 3 hours. Top with toasted almonds and serve.

Nutritional Value (Amount per Serving): Calories 253, Fat 21.6 g, Carbohydrates 14.5 g

EASY RANCH MUSHROOMS

Preparation Time: 10 minutes | Cooking Time: 3 Hours | Serves: 6

Ingredients:

- 2 lb mushrooms, rinsed, pat dry
- 2 packets ranch dressing mix
- 3/4 cup butter, melted
- 1/4 cup fresh parsley, chopped

Directions: Add all ingredients except parsley to a crock pot and stir well. Cover and cook on low for 3 hours. Garnish with parsley and serve.

Nutritional Value (Amount per Serving): Calories 237, Fat 23.5 g, Carbohydrates 5.2 g

ARTICHOKE SPINACH DIP

Preparation Time: 10 minutes | Cooking Time: 6 hours | Serves: 6

Ingredients:

- 8 oz cream cheese, softened
- 14 oz can artichoke hearts, drained and chopped
- 10 oz frozen spinach, thawed and drained
- 1/4 tsp garlic powder
- 2 Tbsp water
- 2 cups cottage cheese
- 1 tsp salt

Directions: Add spinach, cream cheese, cottage cheese, water, and artichoke hearts to a crock pot and stir well. Season with garlic powder and salt. Cover and cook on low for 6 hours. Stir well and serve.

Nutritional Value (Amount per Serving): Calories 230, Fat 14.8 g, Carbohydrates 8.9 g

YUMMY TOMATO DIP

Preparation Time: 10 minutes | Cooking Time: 1 hour | Serves: 20

Ingredients:

- 8 oz cream cheese
- 1/4 cup sun-dried tomatoes
- 1 Tbsp mayonnaise
- 3 garlic cloves
- 1/4 tsp white pepper
- 1 tsp pine nuts, toasted
- 3/4 oz fresh basil

Directions: Add all ingredients to a blender and blend until smooth. Pour mixture into a crock pot. Cover and cook on low for 1 hour. Stir well and serve.

Nutritional Value (Amount per Serving): Calories 47, Fat 4.5 g, Carbohydrates 1 g

CREAMY ONION DIP

Preparation Time: 10 minutes | Cooking Time: 4 hours 30 minutes | Serves: 12

Ingredients:

- 4 onions, sliced
- 2 Tbsp olive oil
- 2 Tbsp butter
- 1/2 cup mozzarella cheese
- 8 oz sour cream
- Pepper
- Salt

Directions: Add oil, butter, and onions to a crock pot. Cover and cook on high for 4 hours. Transfer onion mixture to a blender with the sour cream, pepper, and salt and blend until creamy. Return onion dip to the crock pot. Add mozzarella cheese and stir well. Cook on low for 30 minutes longer. Stir well and serve.

Nutritional Value (Amount per Serving): Calories 95, Fat 8.5 g, Carbohydrates 4.3 g

ITALIAN MUSHROOMS

Preparation Time: 10 minutes | Cooking Time: 4 hours | Serves: 6

Ingredients:

- 1 lb mushrooms, cleaned
- 1 onion, sliced
- 1 packet Italian dressing mix
- 1/2 cup butter, melted

Directions: Add onion and mushrooms to a crock pot and mix well. Combine butter and Italian dressing mix and pour over the onion and mushrooms. Cover and cook on low for 4 hours. Serve and enjoy.

Nutritional Value (Amount per Serving): Calories 162, Fat 15.6 g, Carbohydrates 4.8 g

GARLIC CHEESE SPINACH

Preparation Time: 10 minutes | Cooking Time: 1 hour | Serves: 4

Ingredients:

- 16 oz baby spinach
- 2 garlic cloves, minced
- 1 cup cheddar cheese, shredded
- 3 oz cream cheese

Directions: Add all ingredients to a crock pot and stir well. Cover and cook on high for 1 hour. Stir well and serve.

Nutritional Value (Amount per Serving): Calories 216, Fat 17.2 g, Carbohydrates 5.6 g

SIMPLE DILL CARROTS

Preparation Time: 10 minutes | Cooking Time: 2 hours | Serves: 6

Ingredients:

- 1 lb carrots, peeled and cut into round pieces on the diagonal
- 1 Tbsp butter
- 1 Tbsp fresh dill, minced
- 3 Tbsp water

Directions: Add all ingredients to a crock pot and stir well. Cover and cook on low for 2 hours. Stir well and serve.

Nutritional Value (Amount per Serving): Calories 49, Fat 1.9 g, Carbohydrates 7.7 g

ROSEMARY GREEN BEANS

Preparation Time: 10 minutes | Cooking Time: 1 hour 30 minutes | Serves: 4

Ingredients:

- 1 lb green beans, washed and trimmed
- 2 Tbsp fresh lemon juice
- 1 tsp fresh thyme, minced
- 2 Tbsp water
- 1 Tbsp fresh rosemary, minced

Directions: Add all ingredients to a crock pot and stir well. Cover and cook on low for 1 1/2 hours. Stir well and serve.

Nutritional Value (Amount per Serving): Calories 40, Fat 0.4 g, Carbohydrates 8.9 g

VEGETABLE STEW

Preparation Time: 10 minutes | Cooking Time: 2 hours | Serves: 12

Ingredients:

- 3 cups carrots, shredded
- 32 oz vegetable stock
- 1 cup cilantro, chopped
- 2 jalapeños, chopped
- 5 garlic cloves, minced
- 2 cups water
- 1 Tbsp cumin
- 1 Tbsp chili powder
- 2 Tbsp tomato paste
- 4 tomatoes, diced
- 1 large onion, diced
- 2 zucchini, chopped
- 1/2 head cabbage, chopped
- Pepper
- Salt

Directions: Add all ingredients to a crock pot and stir well. Cover and cook on low for 2 hours. Stir well and serve.

Nutritional Value (Amount per Serving): Calories 57, Fat 0.9 g, Carbohydrates 10.2 g

TASTY VEGETABLE FAJITAS

Preparation Time: 10 minutes | Cooking Time: 3 hours 30 minutes | Serves: 4

Ingredients:

- 1 cup cherry tomatoes, halved
- 3 bell peppers, cut into strips
- 1 onion, sliced
- 1 tsp paprika
- 1 Tbsp olive oil
- Pepper and salt

Directions: Add onion, bell peppers, oil, smoked paprika, pepper, and salt to a crock pot and stir well. Cover and cook on high for 1 1/2 hours. Add cherry tomatoes and cook for 2 hours longer. Stir well and serve.

Nutritional Value (Amount per Serving): Calories 79, Fat 3.9 g, Carbohydrates 11.4 g

SIMPLE ROASTED BROCCOLI

Preparation Time: 10 minutes | Cooking Time: 2 hours | Serves: 4

Ingredients:

- 2 lb broccoli florets
- 1 bell pepper, chopped
- 2 tsp olive oil
- Pepper and salt

Directions: Add all ingredients to a crock pot and stir well to mix. Cover and cook on high for 2 hours. Stir well and serve.

Nutritional Value (Amount per Serving): Calories 89, Fat 3.2 g, Carbohydrates 13.3 g

TOMATOES, GARLIC AND OKRA

Preparation Time: 10 minutes | Cooking Time: 2 hours | Serves: 4

Ingredients:

- 1 1/2 cups okra, diced
- 1 small onion, diced
- 2 large tomatoes, diced
- 1 tsp hot sauce
- 2 garlic cloves, minced

Directions: Add all ingredients to a crock pot and stir well. Cover and cook on low for 2 hours. Stir well and serve.

Nutritional Value (Amount per Serving): Calories 41, Fat 0.3 g, Carbohydrates 8.5 g

Low-Carb Dessert Recipes

Delicious Pumpkin Custard

Preparation Time: 10 minutes │ Cooking Time: 2 hours 30 minutes │ Serves: 6

Ingredients:

- 4 large eggs
- 4 Tbsp coconut oil, melted
- 1 tsp pumpkin pie spice
- 1/2 cup almond flour
- 1 tsp vanilla
- 1 cup pumpkin purée
- 1/2 cup erythritol
- Pinch of salt

Directions: Spray the inside of a crock pot with cooking spray. Add eggs to a large mixing bowl and blend until smooth using a hand mixer. Slowly beat in the sweetener. Add vanilla and pumpkin purée to the egg mixture and blend well. Add almond flour, pumpkin pie spice, salt, and coconut oil and blend until well combined. Pour mixture into the crock pot. Place a paper towel on the crock pot and cover. Cook on low for 2 hours 30 minutes. Cut into servings, serve and enjoy.

Nutritional Value (Amount per Serving): Calories 196, Fat 17.2 g, Carbohydrates 5.8 g

Lemon Blueberry Cake

Preparation Time: 10 minutes │ Cooking Time: 3 hours │ Serves: 12

Ingredients:

- 6 eggs, separated
- ½ cup fresh blueberries
- 2 cups heavy cream
- 1/2 cup Swerve
- 1/3 cup fresh lemon juice
- 1 tsp lemon zest
- 1/2 cup coconut flour
- 1/2 tsp salt

Directions: Add egg whites to a large mixing bowl and beat until stiff peaks form. Set aside. In another bowl, whisk egg yolks with heavy cream, Swerve, lemon juice, lemon zest, coconut flour, and salt. Slowly fold the egg whites into the egg yolk mixture until well combined. Spray the inside of a crock pot with cooking spray. Pour prepared batter into the crock pot. Sprinkle blueberries on top of batter. Cover and cook on low for 3 hours. Allow to cool completely, cut and serve.

Nutritional Value (Amount per Serving): Calories 108, Fat 9.7 g, Carbohydrates 2.2 g

Tasty Lemon Cake

Preparation Time: 10 minutes │ Cooking Time: 3 hours │ Serves: 8

Ingredients:

- 2 eggs
- Zest of 1 lemon
- 1 Tbsp lemon juice
- 1/2 cup whipping cream
- 1/2 cup butter, melted
- 2 tsp baking powder
- 6 Tbsp Swerve
- 1/2 cup coconut flour
- 1 1/2 cups almond flour

For topping:

- 2 Tbsp fresh lemon juice
- 2 Tbsp butter, melted
- 1/2 cup hot water
- 3 Tbsp Swerve

Directions: In a mixing bowl, mix together almond flour, baking powder, Swerve, and coconut flour. In a large bowl, whisk together eggs, lemon zest, 1 tablespoon lemon juice, butter, and whipping cream. Add almond flour mixture to the egg mixture and stir until well combined. Spray the inside of a crock pot with cooking spray. Pour batter into the crock pot and spread well. In a bowl, combine together all topping ingredients and pour over the cake batter. Cover and cook on high for 3 hours. Serve warm cut into squares and enjoy.

Nutritional Value (Amount per Serving): Calories 294, Fat 28.5 g, Carbohydrates 7.4 g

CHOCOLATE CAKE

Preparation Time: 10 minutes | Cooking Time: 2 hours 30 minutes | Serves: 10

Ingredients:

- 3 large eggs
- 1/2 tsp vanilla
- 2/3 cup unsweetened almond milk
- 6 Tbsp butter, melted
- 1 1/2 tsp baking powder
- 3 Tbsp whey protein powder
- 1/2 cup unsweetened cocoa powder
- 1/2 cup Swerve
- 1 cup almond flour
- Pinch of salt

Directions: Spray a crock pot inside with cooking spray. In a mixing bowl, whisk together almond flour, baking powder, protein powder, cocoa powder, Swerve, and salt. Stir in eggs, vanilla, almond milk, and butter until well combined. Pour batter into the crock pot. Cover and cook on low for 2 1/2 hours. Serve warm cut into squares and enjoy.

Nutritional Value (Amount per Serving): Calories 176, Fat 15 g, Carbohydrates 6.3 g

COCONUT RASPBERRY CAKE

Preparation Time: 10 minutes | Cooking Time: 3 hours | Serves: 10

Ingredients:

- 4 large eggs
- 1 cup raspberries
- 1/4 cup powdered egg whites
- 3/4 cup Swerve

- 1 tsp vanilla
- 3/4 cup unsweetened coconut milk
- 1/2 cup coconut oil, melted
- 2 tsp baking soda
- 1 cup unsweetened shredded coconut
- 2 cups almond flour
- Pinch of salt

Directions: Spray a crock pot inside with cooking spray. In a mixing bowl, whisk together almond flour, baking soda, powdered egg whites, Swerve, shredded coconut, and salt. Stir in eggs, vanilla, coconut milk, and coconut oil until well combined. Add raspberries and fold well. Pour batter into the crock pot and spread well. Cover and cook on low for 3 hours. Slice, serve and enjoy.

Nutritional Value (Amount per Serving): Calories 382, Fat 34.9 g, Carbohydrates 10.1 g

CHOCOLATE FUDGE

Preparation Time: 10 minutes | Cooking Time: 2 hours | Serves: 30

Ingredients:

- 2 1/2 cups unsweetened chocolate chips
- 1 tsp vanilla
- 1/3 cup unsweetened coconut milk
- Pinch of salt

Directions: Add all ingredients to a crock pot and stir well. Cover and cook on low for 2 hours. Stir until smooth. Line a baking dish with parchment paper. Spread fudge mixture in prepared baking dish and place in the refrigerator for 30 minutes. Serve chilled, cut into squares and enjoy.

Nutritional Value (Amount per Serving): Calories 134, Fat 10.7 g, Carbohydrates 5.4 g

YUMMY BROWNIE BITES

Preparation Time: 10 minutes | Cooking Time: 4 hours | Serves: 10

Ingredients:

- 2 eggs
- 2 cups almond flour
- 1/3 cup water
- 1 tsp vanilla
- 1/2 cup coconut oil, melted
- 1/2 cup unsweetened coconut milk
- 2 tsp baking soda
- 2 tsp baking powder
- 3/4 cup cocoa powder
- 1 cup Swerve
- Pinch of salt

Directions: Spray a crock pot inside with cooking spray. In a large bowl, mix together all ingredients and pour into the crock pot and spread well. Cover and cook on low for 4 hours. Allow brownie mixture to cool for 30 minutes. Scoop out brownie mixture with an ice cream scoop and form into balls. Serve and enjoy.

Nutritional Value (Amount per Serving): Calories 279, Fat 26.7 g, Carbohydrates 9.8 g

MOIST BERRY CAKE

Preparation Time: 10 minutes | Cooking Time: 3 hours | Serves: 10

Ingredients:

- 4 eggs
- 2 tsp baking soda
- 1/4 cup protein powder
- 1/2 cup Swerve
- 1 cup unsweetened shredded coconut
- 2 cups almond flour
- 1/3 cup unsweetened chocolate chips
- 1 cup blackberries
- 1/2 cup heavy cream
- 1/4 cup butter, melted
- 1/4 cup coconut oil, melted
- Pinch of salt

Directions: Spray a crock pot inside with cooking spray. In a large bowl, mix together almond flour, baking soda, protein powder, Swerve, coconut, and salt. Stir in heavy cream, butter, coconut oil, and eggs until combined. Add chocolate chips and blackberries and fold well. Pour batter into the crock pot and spread evenly. Cover and cook on low for 3 hours. Allow to cool completely and serve.

Nutritional Value (Amount per Serving): Calories 382, Fat 32.3 g, Carbohydrates 9.9 g

CHOCÓ ALMOND FUDGE

Preparation Time: 10 minutes | Cooking Time: 6 hours | Serves: 30

Ingredients:

- 2 Tbsp almonds, sliced
- 2 Tbsp Swerve
- 8 oz unsweetened chocolate chips
- 1/2 cup unsweetened coconut milk
- 1 Tbsp butter, melted

Directions: Grease an 8-inch baking dish with butter and set aside. Add chocolate chips, coconut milk, butter, and Swerve to a crock pot and mix well. Cover the crock pot with the lid and cook on low for 2 hours. Add almonds and stir fudge until smooth. Pour fudge mixture into a baking dish and spread evenly. Place in the refrigerator for 6 hours. Cut into squares and serve.

Nutritional Value (Amount per Serving): Calories 66, Fat 5.6 g, Carbohydrates 2.5 g

DELICIOUS PUMPKIN CUSTARD

Preparation Time: 10 minutes | Cooking Time: 5 hours | Serves: 6

Ingredients:

- 6 eggs
- 3 cups canned pumpkin purée
- 2 Tbsp coconut oil
- 10 drops liquid Stevia
- 1/4 cup unsweetened coconut milk

Directions: Pour 1 inch of water into a crock pot. Add all ingredients to a blender and blend until smooth. Spray six ramekins with cooking spray. Pour blended mixture into the prepared ramekins and place into the crock pot. Cover and cook on high for 5 hours. Serve warm and enjoy.

Nutritional Value (Amount per Serving): Calories 146, Fat 11.3 g, Carbohydrates 5.9 g

Low-Carb Broths, Stocks And Sauces

Mixed Berry Sauce

Preparation Time: 10 minutes | Cooking Time: 3 hours | Serves: 8

Ingredients:

- 4 oz fresh blueberries
- 6 oz fresh blackberries
- 8 oz fresh strawberries
- 1/4 cup erythritol

Directions: Add all ingredients to a crock pot and stir well. Cover and cook on low for 3 hours. Allow to cool completely and store in an air-tight container.

Nutritional Value (Amount per Serving): Calories 26, Fat 0.2 g, Carbohydrates 6.3 g

Apple Cranberry Sauce

Preparation Time: 10 minutes | Cooking Time: 2 hours | Serves: 16

Ingredients:

- 3 cups fresh cranberries
- 1/2 tsp cinnamon
- 1 Tbsp honey
- 1/2 fresh lime juice
- 1/4 cup fresh orange juice
- 1 apple, cored ,peeled and diced
- 10 strawberries
- 1 cup dried cranberries
- 1/4 tsp salt

Directions: Add all ingredients to a crock pot and stir well. Cover and cook on high for 2 hours. Purée the sauce using an immersion blender. Allow to cool completely and store in an air-tight container.

Nutritional Value (Amount per Serving): Calories 60, Fat 0.1 g, Carbohydrates 14 g

Fresh Cranberry Sauce

Preparation Time: 10 minutes | Cooking Time: 3 hours | Serves: 8

Ingredients:

- 12 oz fresh cranberries, rinsed
- 1 tsp ginger, grated
- 1 tsp orange zest
- 1/2 cup water
- 1/2 cup orange juice

Directions: Add all ingredients to a crock pot and stir well. Cover and cook on low for 3 hours. Gently mash the cranberries using a spoon until you have the desired consistency.

Nutritional Value (Amount per Serving): Calories 31, Fat 0 g, Carbohydrates 5.7 g

BONE BROTH

Preparation Time: 10 minutes | Cooking Time: 24 hours | Serves: 4

Ingredients:

- 5 lb beef bones
- 4 parsley sprigs
- 2 Tbsp peppercorns
- 2 bay leaves
- 2 celery stalks
- 2 carrots, peeled and cut in half
- 2 onions, quartered
- 2 Tbsp apple cider vinegar
- 1 tsp kosher salt

Directions: Add beef bones to a crock pot and place remaining ingredients on top of the bones. Pour enough water into the crock pot to cover everything. Cover and cook on high for 24 hours. Strain the liquid into a container and store in the refrigerator.

Nutritional Value (Amount per Serving): Calories 45, Fat 0.2 g, Carbohydrates 10.5 g

TURKEY STOCK

Preparation Time: 10 minutes | Cooking Time: 24 hours | Serves: 10

Ingredients:

- 1 whole turkey
- 1 Tbsp whole peppercorns
- 1 onion, cut in half
- 2 celery stalks, chopped
- 1 carrot, chopped
- Water

Directions: Place turkey in a crock pot. Add peppercorns and vegetables on top of the turkey. Fill crock pot with water. Cover and cook on low for 24 hours. Strain the stock into a container and store in the refrigerator.

Nutritional Value (Amount per Serving): Calories 10, Fat 0 g, Carbohydrates 2 g

APPLESAUCE

Preparation Time: 10 minutes | Cooking Time: 2 hours | Serves: 6

Ingredients:

- 3 lb apples, peeled, cored, and sliced
- 2 cinnamon sticks
- 2 Tbsp fresh lemon juice
- 1/4 cup water

Directions: Add all ingredients to a crock pot and stir well. Cover and cook on high for 2 hours. Discard cinnamon sticks and mash the apples with a potato masher until you have the desired consistency.

Nutritional Value (Amount per Serving): Calories 59, Fat 0.2 g, Carbohydrates 15 g

PEACH SAUCE

Preparation Time: 10 minutes | Cooking Time: 8 hours | Serves: 6

Ingredients:

- 4 lb frozen peaches, thawed
- 1/4 tsp ground cloves
- 1/2 tsp ground ginger
- 1 tsp fresh lemon juice
- 1/2 cup Swerve

Directions: Add peaches to a blender and blend until smooth and creamy. Transfer blended peaches to a crock pot along with Swerve and stir well. Cover and cook on low for 8 hours. Stir in cloves, ginger, and lemon juice. Allow to cool completely and store in a container in the refrigerator.

Nutritional Value (Amount per Serving): Calories 41, Fat 0.3 g, Carbohydrates 9.7 g

HAM STOCK

Preparation Time: 10 minutes | Cooking Time: 24 hours | Serves: 14

Ingredients:

- 1 large ham bone
- 1 tsp black peppercorns
- 1 bay leaf
- 1 thyme sprig
- 1 garlic clove, peeled
- 2 carrots, cut in half
- 1 celery stalk, cut in half
- 1 onion, peeled and quartered

Directions: Add all ingredients to a crock pot. Fill crock pot with cold water. Cover and cook on low for 24 hours. Strain the stock into a container and store in the refrigerator.

Nutritional Value (Amount per Serving): Calories 10, Fat 0 g, Carbohydrates 2 g

DELICIOUS STRAWBERRY SAUCE

Preparation Time: 10 minutes | Cooking Time: 2 hours | Serves: 4

Ingredients:

- 1 lb strawberries, hulled and chopped
- 1 Tbsp fresh lemon juice
- 1/4 cup Swerve
- Pinch of salt

Directions: Add strawberries, Swerve, and salt to a crock pot. Cover and cook on low for 2 hours. Add lemon juice and stir well. Once sauce has cooled completely, pour it into a container and store in the refrigerator.

Nutritional Value (Amount per Serving): Calories 38, Fat 0.4 g, Carbohydrates 8.9 g

BLUEBERRY APPLE SAUCE

Preparation Time: 10 minutes | Cooking Time: 4 hours | Serves: 4

Ingredients:

- 1 1/2 lb apples
- 1 tsp cinnamon
- 2 Tbsp water
- 4 oz blueberries

Directions: Add all ingredients to a crock pot and stir to mix. Cover and cook on low for 4 hours. Blend the sauce using an immersion blender until the desired consistency. Once sauce has cooled completely, store in a container in the refrigerator.

Nutritional Value (Amount per Serving): Calories 61, Fat 0.3 g, Carbohydrates 16.1 g

MEDITERRANEAN BREAKFAST RECIPES

MEDITERRANEAN CROCKPOT BREAKFAST

Preparation Time: 15 minutes | Cooking Time: 7 hours | Serves: 8

Ingredients:

- Eggs - 1 dozen
- Hash brown potatoes - 2 pounds
- Milk - 1 cup
- Shredded cheddar cheese - 3 cups
- Diced onions - ½ cup
- Bacon – 1 pound
- Garlic powder - ¼ teaspoon
- Dry mustard - ¼ teaspoon
- Salt - 1 teaspoon
- Pepper - ½ teaspoon
- Spring onions – for garnishing

Directions: Beat the eggs using a blender until they gets combined well with one another. Now add garlic powder, milk, salt, mustard, and pepper along with the beaten eggs and continue blending. Keep aside. Season the hash brown potatoes with pepper and salt. Place the hash brown potatoes in layer by layer and diced onions into the crockpot. Sprinkle a quarter portion of bacon and mix them well together. Add a cup of cheese to the crockpot to make it a smooth looking texture. Repeat this layering process two to three times . Now pour the blended egg mixture over the layers of hash potatoes in the crockpot. Set slow cooking for 7 hours. Garnish with finely chopped spring onions while serving.

Nutritional Value: Calories: 416, Carbohydrate: 23g

SLOW COOKER MEDITERRANEAN POTATOES

(Perfect Mediterranean Diet recipe)

Preparation Time: 5 minut | Cooking Time: 5 hours | Serves: 8

Ingredients:

- Fingerling potatoes - 3 pounds
- Dried oregano - 1 tablespoon
- Olive oil - 2 tablespoons
- Smoked paprika - 1 teaspoon
- Unsalted butter - 2 tablespoons
- Ground black pepper, fresh – 1 teaspoon
- Lemon juice - 1 teaspoon
- Minced garlic - 4 cloves
- Fresh parsley leaves, chopped - 2 tablespoons
- Kosher salt - ½ teaspoon
- Lemon - 1 zest

Directions: Peel, wash potatoes and cut into half. Keep aside. Slightly grease the inside of a 6-quart slow cooker with non-stick spray. Add olive oil, potatoes, lemon juice, butter, paprika, and oregano in the cooker. Season by using pepper and salt. Close the lid. Set it to slow cook for 5 hours. Serve hot by garnishing with chopped parsley and lemon zest.

Nutritional Value: Calories: 179.5, Carbohydrate: 28.4g, Fat: 6.5g

MEDITERRANEAN CROCKPOT BREAKFAST

Preparation Time: 15 minuts | Cooking Time: 4 hours | Serves: 8

Ingredients:

- Hash browns, frozen - 30 ounces
- Eggs - 8
- Milk - ¾ cup
- Egg whites - 4
- Garlic salt - ½ teaspoon
- Ground mustard – 2 teaspoon
- Cooked bacon - 4 strips
- Roughly chopped bell peppers - 2
- Onion chopped coarsely - ½
- Cheddar cheese - 6 ounces
- Roughly chopped broccoli head - 1 small
- Pepper - ½ teaspoon
- Salt - 1 teaspoon

Directions: Whisk eggs, milk, egg whites, garlic salt, mustard, pepper, and salt together in a medium bowl and keep aside. Slightly grease the bottom of the crockpot. Add half of the hash browns into the crockpot and set it as the bottom layer. Over this layer of hash browns, put chopped onion, bacon, broccoli, bell peppers and cheese. Now, add the remaining hash browns and make a new layer. Top this second layer with the remaining bacon, vegetables, and cheese. Pour the egg mixture on top of these layers. Cover the crockpot and slow cook for four hours. Serve hot.

Nutritional Value: Calories: 320, Carbohydrate: 29g, Fat: 13g

MEDITERRANEAN CROCKPOT QUICHE

Preparation Time: 15 minuts | Cooking Time: 6 hours | Serves: 9

Ingredients:

- Milk – 1 cup
- Eggs – 8
- Feta cheese, crumbled - 1½ cup
- Bisquick mix – 1 cup
- Spinach, fresh, chopped – 2 cups
- Red bell pepper - ½ cup
- Garlic, nicely chopped – 1 teaspoon
- Basil leaves, fresh - ¼ cup
- Sausage crumbles fully cooked – 9.6 ounces
- Feta cheese, crumbled (for garnishing) - ¼ cup

Directions: Grease a 5-quart slow cooker with cooking spray. In a large bowl, whisk eggs, Bisquick mix, milk thoroughly. Add one, and half crumbled feta cheese, garlic, basil, sausage, bell pepper and stir the entire mix thoroughly. Close the lid and set slow cooking for 6 hours. Your Quiche will be ready when the center becomes firm and sides become golden brown. Cut into pieces for serving. Garnish with feta cheese sprinkling.

Nutritional Value: Calories: 308, Carbohydrate: 13.7g, Fat: 21g

SLOW COOKER MEATLOAF

Preparation Time: 15 minuts | Cooking Time: 4 hours | Serves: 4

Ingredients:

- Minced Beef - ½ pound
- Tomato sauce – 2 cups
- Onion, diced - 1 small
- Bacon unsmoked - 4
- Red wine - ½ cup
- Mustard - 1 teaspoon
- Cheddar cheese - 1 Oz
- Oregano - 1 teaspoon
- Garlic puree - 1 teaspoon
- Thyme - 1 teaspoon
- Paprika - 1 teaspoon
- Salt - ½ teaspoon
- Pepper - ½ teaspoon
- Parsley - 1 teaspoon
- Fresh herbs – as required

Directions: In a large bowl put all the seasoning items. Add onion and minced beef to the bowl and mix well by combing with your hands. Spread the mixture on a clean worktop and press it forms like a pastry, which can roll out cleanly. In the middle portion of the meatloaf pastry, layer some chopped cheese. After adding the cheese as a layer, wrap the meat like a sausage roll. Pour little olive oil into the slow cooker for greasing and then place the roll. Mix homemade tomato sauce and red wine in a separate bowl and pour it on the sides of the meatloaf. Do not pour this mixture over the meatloaf. Now, spread the bacon over the meatloaf. Slow cook it for four hours. Serve hot along with roast vegetables and potatoes.

Nutritional Value: Calories: 385, Carbohydrate: 14g, Fat: 26g

SLOW COOKER FRITTATA

(Perfect Mediterranean Diet recipe)

Preparation Time: 30 minuts | Cooking Time: 3 hours | Serves: 6

Ingredients:

- Eggs - 8
- Oregano, dried - 1 teaspoon
- Milk - ⅓ cup
- Red peppers, chopped and roasted - 1¼ cup
- Baby arugula - 4 cups
- Ground pepper, fresh - ½ teaspoon
- Goats' cheese, grated - ¾ cup
- Red onion, finely sliced - ½ cup
- Salt - ½ teaspoon

Directions: Spray some non-stick oil into the slow cooker. In a large bowl whisk milk, eggs, and oregano together. Season it with salt and pepper as per your taste. Arrange the roasted red pepper, baby arugula, goat cheese and red onion in the slow cooker. Pour the egg mixture over the vegetables. Let it slow cook for 3 hours. Serve hot.

Nutritional Value: Calories: 164, Carbohydrate: 4g, Fat: 11g

CROCK POT CHICKEN NOODLE SOUP

(Perfect Mediterranean Diet recipe)

Ingredients:

- Chicken breasts, boneless and skinless, cut into ½" size – 3
- Chicken broth - 5½ cup
- Chopped celery stalks - 3
- Chopped carrots - 3
- Chopped onion - 1
- Bay leaf - 1
- Minced garlic cloves - 3
- Peas, frozen - 1 cup
- Egg noodles - 2½ cup
- Fresh parsley, chopped - ¼ cup
- Ground black pepper, fresh - ½ teaspoon
- Salt - ½ teaspoon

Directions: Place chicken breasts in the bottom of the slow cooker. On top of the chicken put onion, celery stalks, garlic cloves, and carrots. Pour in the chicken broth and put the bay leaf in. Add pepper and salt as per your taste. Cook on slow cook mode for 6 hours. After six hours, add egg noodles and frozen peas to the cooker. Cook further about 5-6 minutes until the egg noodles turn tender. Stir in chopped fresh parsley. Serve hot.

Nutritional Value: Calories: 527, Carbohydrate: 44g, Protein: 61g

Hash Brown & Cheddar Breakfast

Preparation Time: 30 minuts | Cooking Time: 6 hours | Serves: 12

Ingredients:

- Hash browns, frozen & shredded - 32 ounces
- Onion, green, coarsely chopped - 6
- Breakfast sausage, crumbled & cooked - 16 ounces
- Eggs - 12
- Shredded cheddar cheese - 12 ounces
- Milk - ¼ cup
- Pepper - ½ teaspoon
- Salt - 1 teaspoon
- Pepper – 1 teaspoon for seasoning
- Salt - ½ teaspoon for seasoning
- Garlic powder - ¼ teaspoon

Directions: Oil a 6-quart slow cooker with non-stick cooking spray. In the slow cooker, layer ⅓ portion of hash brown. Season this layer with pepper and salt. Now, layer ⅓ portion of the cooked and crumbled sausage over the first layer. Again layer ⅓ portion of both cheddar cheese and green onions over the sausage. Repeat both these layers twice, ending with cheese. Take a large bowl and whisk milk, egg, salt, garlic powder and pepper together. Pour this egg mixture all over the sausage, hash brown and cheese layers in the slow cooker. Slow cook it for about six to eight hours until the edges turn brown and the center become firm. Serve hot.

Nutritional Value: Calories: 431, Carbohydrate: 17g, Fat: 29g

Slow Cooker Fava Beans

Preparation Time: 10 minuts | Cooking Time: 8 hours | Serves: 12

Ingredients:

- Fava beans (dried) - 1 pound
- Red lentils – 3 tablespoons
- Uncooked rice – 3 tablespoons
- Tomato, chopped - 1

For sausage:

- Onion, finely sliced in rings - ½
- Tomato – 1 small
- Olive oil – 2 tablespoons

- Garlic, chopped – 3 cloves
- Water – as required (about 2 cups)
- Salt - ½ teaspoon

- Sausages, cut into halves – 4
- Cumin seed - ¼ teaspoon
- Lemon juice - ½ teaspoon

Directions: Soak the fava beans for about 4 hours. Wash and drain the beans. Put the drained beans in a 6-quart slow cooker. Wash the lentils, rice, and drain. Put the drained lentils and rice also into the slow cooker. Now add the chopped tomato and garlic into the slow cooker. Add water above the ingredients level. Set the slow cooking for 8 hours. When cooking over, prepare the sausages. Pour olive oil in non-stick pan and bring to heat at a medium-high temperature. When the oil becomes hot, add chopped onions and sauté on medium heat until it becomes tender. Now add chopped garlic and continue stirring until the fragrance starts to release. Add cumin seeds and continue stirring. After that add chopped tomatoes and sausages. Continue stirring for 5 minutes. Now transfer the cooked beans over the sausages. Drizzle the lemon juice over the beans. Add salt if required. Stir the mix and cook for 2-3 minutes to warm the food. Serve hot.

Nutritional Value: Calories: 99.9, Carbohydrate: 19g, Fat: 0.5g

PORK SAUSAGE BREAKFAST

Preparation Time: 15 minuts | Cooking Time: 6 hours | Serves: 12

Ingredients:

- Pork sausage - 16 ounce
- Eggs - 12
- Milk - 1 cup
- Veg oil – 2 tablespoons
- Hash brown potatoes, frozen - 26 ounces
- Ground mustard - 1 tablespoon

- Ground black pepper - as per taste required
- Cheddar cheese, shredded - 16 ounces.
- Salt - ½ teaspoon
- Pepper - ¾ teaspoon
- Cooking spray – as required

Directions: Spray some non-stick cooking oil into the bottom of your crockpot. Layer the hash brown potatoes in the crockpot. Now pour vegetable oil into a large skillet and heat on medium high temperature. When the oil becomes hot put the sausages in, stir and continue cooking for 7 minutes until it becomes brown and crumbly. Once the cooking is over, remove the sausage and discard the oil. Now, spread the sausage over the hash brown potatoes and top it with cheddar cheese. Beat milk and eggs together in a separate large bowl. Add ground mustard along with salt and pepper to this mixture and stir thoroughly. Pour this mixture on top of the cheese layer. Set on slow cook for six hours. If you wish you can further slow down the cooking to 8 hours or even more time. Serve hot.

Nutritional Value: Calories: 382, Carbohydrate: 13.1g, Fat: 30g

MEDITERRANEAN APPETIZERS AND SNACKS

SLOW COOKER CRUSTLESS MEDITERRANEAN QUICHE

Preparation Time: 15 minuts | Cooking Time: 3 hours | Serves: 9

Ingredients:

- Milk - 1 cup
- Eggs - 8
- Fresh spinach fresh - 2 cups
- Bisquick mix - 1 cup
- Red bell peppers, roasted - ½ cup
- Feta cheese, grated - 6 ounces
- Garlic, finely chopped - 1 teaspoon
- Basil leaves, fresh, chopped - ¼ cup
- Sausage crumbles (cooked) - 9.6 ounces
- Feta cheese, grated (for garnish) - ¼ cup
- Non-stick cooking spray

Directions: Lightly grease a 5-quart slow cooker with non-stick cooking spray. Whisk milk, eggs, and Bisquick mix until they get mixed well together in a medium bowl. Pour this mix to the slow cooker. Add feta cheese, spinach, basil, bell peppers, sausage, and garlic to the slow cooker and stir well. Cover the cooker and slow cook for 6 hours. Check the cooking status after 6 hours. If the center is firm, then it is ready to serve. Cut and serve hot by sprinkling feta cheese.

Nutritional Value: Calories: 226, Carbohydrate: 3.2g, Fat: 17.1g

SLOW-COOKED MEDITERRANEAN EGGPLANT SALAD

(Perfect Mediterranean Diet recipe)

Preparation Time: 15 minuts | Cooking Time: 8 hours | Serves: 6

Ingredients:

- Eggplant quartered sliced – 1 large
- Bell peppers, sliced - 2
- Red onion, sliced - 1
- Canned tomatoes - 24 ounces
- Cumin - 2 teaspoons
- Smoked paprika - 1 tablespoon
- Black pepper – 1 teaspoon
- Salt – ¾ teaspoon
- Lemon juice - 1 tablespoon

Directions: Put all ingredients in a slow cooker and combine. Slow cook for eight hours. Serve hot.

Nutritional Value: Calories: 67, Carbohydrate: 14.8g, Fat: 0.8g

CROCK POT MEDITERRANEAN MEAT BALLS

Preparation Time: 20 minuts | Cooking Time: 4 hours | Serves: 25

Ingredients:

For meatballs:

161

- Minced onion - ¼ cup
- Meat (Ground Pork or beef) - 2 pounds
- Chopped fresh parsley - 3 tablespoons
- Minced garlic - 3 cloves
- Eggs - 2
- Breadcrumbs (seasoned) - 1 cup
- Ground pepper – 1 teaspoon
- Crumbled parmesan cheese - ¾ cup
- Salt - as required

For the sauce:
- Crushed tomatoes – 48 ounces
- Bay leaf - 1 whole
- Tomato paste - 6 ounces
- Italian seasoning - 1 teaspoon
- Red pepper flakes, crushed - ½ teaspoon
- Salt - as per taste required
- Pepper – 1 teaspoon
- Oregano - 1 teaspoon

Extra for garnishing:
- Parmesan cheese, grated - ¼cup
- Fresh parsley, chopped - ¼ cup.

Directions: In a large bowl mix onion, meat, breadcrumbs, cheese, parsley, salt, eggs, and pepper by hand. Make meatballs with the mix. Keep the meatball size between 1 and 2 inches.Take a baking sheet and lightly grease it. Broil the meatballs under high heat until the balls turn brown on both sides. Make sure to turn the meatballs intermittently to have an even browning. Once the meatballs turn golden brown, transfer it to the crockpot. To prepare the sauce, take a new bowl and mix ingredients mentioned under the sauce category. Pour this mix directly all over the meatballs. Stir around the meatballs and make sure the balls coated thoroughly with the sauce. Cook on low heat about 4 hours Sprinkle grated parmesan cheese and chopped fresh parsley before serving. Serve hot.

Nutritional Value: Calories: 148, Carbohydrate: 6.9g, Fat: 8.3g

CROCK POT PIZZA DIP

Preparation Time: 5 minuts | Cooking Time: 2 hours | Serves: 20

Ingredients:

- Italian seasoning - 1 teaspoon
- Soft cream cheese - 8 0unces
- Parmesan cheese, shredded - ¾ cup
- Mozzarella cheese, grated - 1 cup
- Pepperoni pieces, cut piece - 1/4 cup
- Pizza sauce - 8 ounces

Directions: In a crock pot put all the ingredients. Set on high cooking for about 1 hour. After an hour, when the cheese starts to melt, turn the setting to low and continue cooking for one more hour. Serve hot.

Nutritional Value: Calories: 81, Carbohydrate: 1g, Fat: 6g

SLOW COOKER MEDITERRANEAN MUSHROOM

(Perfect Mediterranean Diet recipe)

Preparation Time: 10 minuts | Cooking Time: 3 hours | Serves: 6

Ingredients:

- Mushrooms (White button) - 16 ounces
- Fresh parsley, finely chopped - ¼ cup
- Virgin olive oil – 2 tablespoons
- Garlic, finely chopped – 3 cloves
- Black pepper - ¼ teaspoon
- Salt – 1 teaspoon

Directions: Wash, clean and pat dry mushrooms. Cut off the ends and cut into quarters. Pour olive oil into the slow cooker. Now put all the ingredients in the slow cooker. Slow cook for 3 hours. Serve along with ketchup.

Nutritional Value: Calories: 60, Carbohydrate: 3.2g, Fat: 4.9g

SLOW COOKER BUFFALO MEAT BALLS

(Perfect Mediterranean Diet recipe)

Preparation Time: 20 minuts │ Cooking Time: 3 hours 40 minutes │ Serves: 6

Ingredients:

- Egg - 1 large
- Ground turkey - 1 pound
- Thinly sliced green onions - 3
- Onion powder - ½ teaspoon
- Garlic powder - ½ teaspoon
- Grounded black pepper, fresh - ½ teaspoon
- Bread crumbs - ¾ cup
- Frank's Wing Sauce - ¾ cup
- Non-stick spray – as required
- Blue cheese for dressing - ¼ cup
- Scallions, chopped - ¼ cup
- Kosher salt - ½ teaspoon

Directions: Preheat the oven at 200 degrees Celsius. Prepare a baking sheet by applying non-stick spray and set it aside. Combine eggs, ground turkey, garlic, green onions and onion powder in a large bowl. Add pepper, salt, panko and season it. Stir all these ingredients either using a wooden spoon or hands. Roll the mixture into one, and a half inch sized meatballs. The mixture is enough to make 24 meatballs. Now, place the meatballs into the already prepared baking sheet and bake it for 4-5 minutes until all sides become brown. Now place the meatballs into the slow cooker. Add buffalo sauce all over the meatballs and gently toss it. Cover the cooker and slow cook for 2 hours. Spread blue cheese before serving. Before serving the meatballs, drizzle some blue cheese all over them with chopped scallions.

Nutritional Value: Calories: 548, Carbohydrate: 24g, Fat: 36g

MEDITERRANEAN LENTIL & CHICKPEAS APPETIZER

(Perfect Mediterranean Diet recipe)

Preparation: 15 minutes | Cooking: 8 hours | Servings: 8

Ingredients:

- Chickpeas, canned – 14 ounces
- Red harissa - 2 tablespoons

- Finely chopped sweet onion - 1
- Green lentils - 1½ cup
- Minced garlic - 2 cloves
- Grated fresh ginger - 1 inch
- Chopped red bell pepper - 1
- Chopped carrots - 3
- Chicken broth - 4 cups
- Diced tomatoes - 14 ounce
- Smoked paprika - 2 teaspoons

- Cinnamon - ¾ teaspoon
- Cumin - ¾ teaspoon
- Fresh lemon juice - 1 tablespoon
- Kosher salt - ½ teaspoon
- Pepper - ¾ teaspoon
- Cilantro, fresh chopped - ½ cup
- Water - ½ cup

For garnishing:
- Toasted almonds - ¼ cup

- Goat cheese, grated - ½ cup

Directions: In a crockpot, put onion, lentils, garlic, ginger, red pepper, carrots, chicken broth, tomatoes, harissa, half a cup of water, cumin, paprika, salt, pepper, and cinnamon. Stir all these ingredients to combine thoroughly. Cover and slow cook for 8 hours. Before serving the soup, put chickpeas, lemon juice, and cilantro and cook until it simmers. If the soup consistency is thick, add water or chicken broth. Taste and adjust the salt levels are per your taste. Garnish the soup with toasted almonds, grated goat cheese, and fresh cilantro. Serve hot.

Nutritional Value: Calories: 251, Carbohydrate: 39.2g, Fat: 5.2g

YAM & RED BEAN STEW MEDITERRANEAN STYLE

(Perfect Mediterranean Diet recipe)

Preparation Time: 30 minuts | Cooking Time: 10 hours | Serves: 8

Ingredients:

- Yam, peeled and chopped – 2 pounds
- Onion, chopped - 1 large
- Dried red beans - ½ cup
- Minced garlic - 3 cloves
- Red bell peppers, chopped - 2 large
- Fresh ginger, minced - 2 tablespoons
- Vegetable stock - 3 cups
- Jalapeno pepper, minced - 3
- Diced large tomatoes - 14 ounces

- Ground cumin - ½ teaspoon
- Salt - ½ teaspoon
- Ground cinnamon - ¼ teaspoon
- Ground coriander - ½ teaspoon
- Creamy peanut butter - ¼ cup
- Ground black pepper - ¼ teaspoon
- Lime wedges - 1
- Dry roasted peanuts - ¼ cup

Directions: Soak the beans overnight. In a crock pot, combine bell peppers, onion, ginger, garlic, stock, yams, jalapenos, tomatoes, cumin, salt, cinnamon, coriander, and black pepper. Combine it thoroughly. Later on, add the beans that have kept for soaking. Stir before you start cooking it. Cover the crockpot and cook for 10 hours. Before serving, make sure the beans and Yams have become tender. Before serving the stew, mix peanut butter with a small portion of the stew in a different bowl. Combine it thoroughly. Transfer the peanut butter mixture into the crock pot and stir with the stew. Top the stew with dry roasted peanuts and squeeze fresh lemon juice before serving.

Nutritional Value: Calories: 200**,** Carbohydrate: 44.6g**,** Fat: 0.5g

CROCK POT MEDITERRANEAN LENTIL STEW

(Perfect Mediterranean Diet recipe)

Preparation Time: 10 minuts │ Cooking Time: 6 hours │ Serves: 4

Ingredients:

- Vegetable broth - 7 cups
- Green lentils, dry - 2 cups
- Ground coriander - 1½ tablespoon
- Apple cider vinegar - 1 tablespoon
- Ground ginger - ½ teaspoon
- Ground cumin - 1½ teaspoon
- Ground cloves - ¼ teaspoon
- Ground cardamom - ⅛ teaspoon
- Ground nutmeg - ⅛ teaspoon
- Cinnamon stick - 1
- Ground cayenne pepper - ½ teaspoon
- Bay leaf - 1
- Smoked paprika - ½ teaspoon
- Salt - 1 teaspoon
- Chopped carrot - 1 large
- Minced garlic - 3 cloves
- Sweet potato - 2 cups

For seasoning:

- Plain yogurt - ½ cup
- Golden raisins - ¼ cup

Directions: Rinse the lentils under running tap water, dry and keep aside. Put apple cider vinegar, vegetable broth, ground coriander, ground cumin, ground cardamom, ground ginger, cinnamon stick, ground cloves, ground cayenne pepper, ground nutmeg, bay leaf, smoked paprika, salt, garlic, carrot, and sweet potato into a crock pot. Mix all these ingredients thoroughly. Add the lentils to the crock pot as well. Slow cook it for 6 hours. After six hours, if the lentils are undercooked, then turn the setting to high and wait until it gets finely cooked. Now, blend half portion of the lentils. Do not blend the potatoes and add back the blended lentils into the crockpot. Stir them well with the potatoes. Season the stew with raisins, plain yogurt, and cilantro**.** Serve hot.

Nutritional Value: Calories: 535**,** Carbohydrate: 85.9g**,** Fat: 4.1g

CROCK POT MEDITERRANEAN CHICKPEAS STEW

(Perfect Mediterranean Diet recipe)

Preparation Time: 10 minuts │ Cooking Time: 4 hours │ Serves: 6

Ingredients:

- Minced garlic - 3 cloves
- Chopped white onion - 1 medium
- Red bell pepper,
- Turmeric - 1 teaspoon
- Freshly grated ginger - 1 teaspoon
- Smoked paprika - 1 teaspoon

- chopped - 1
- Butternut squash, chopped – 1 small
- Drained and rinsed chickpeas - 15 ounces
- Red lentils - ¾ cup
- Tomato sauce - 15 ounces

- Cumin - 1 teaspoon
- Salt - ½ teaspoon
- Pepper - ½ teaspoon
- Cinnamon - ½ teaspoon
- Vegetable broth - 3 cups

For Serving:
- Arugula, chopped - ¼ cup
- Cooked quinoa - ¼ cup

- Coconut yogurt - ½ cup

Directions: Chop butternut squash into bite size and keep aside. Put all the ingredients into the slow cooker. Combine the ingredients thoroughly. Cover the cooker and slow cook for 7 hours. For having a thick stew, open the lid one hour before the set time of cooking and let it cook open. Before serving spread chopped quinoa, arugula over the stew and the yogurt.

Nutritional Value: Calories: 178, Carbohydrate: 37g, Protein: 8g

MEDITERRANEAN VEGETABLE RECIPES

CROCK POT MEDITERRANEAN RICE & VEGETABLES

(Perfect Mediterranean Diet recipe)

Preparation Time: 5 minuts | Cooking Time: 8 hours | Serves: 6

Ingredients:

- Diced onion - 1
- Rice - 2 cups
- Diced tomatoes - 15 ounces
- Diced green bell pepper - 1
- Garlic powder - 1½ teaspoon
- Vegetable broth - 1¾ cups
- Onion water - 1 teaspoon
- Chili powder - 2 teaspoons
- Salsa - ¼ cup

Directions: Put diced onion, rice, diced tomatoes, bell pepper, and vegetable broth into the crockpot. Combine the ingredients thoroughly. Stir in chili powder, garlic powder, salsa, and onion powder. Cover up the crockpot and slow cook for eight hours. Stir again before serving.

Nutritional Value: Calories: 271, Carbohydrate: 57, Fat: 1.2g

SLOW COOKER SPANISH CHICKPEAS

(Perfect Mediterranean Diet recipe)

Preparation Time: 12 minuts | Cooking Time: 5 hours | Serves: 6

Ingredients:

- Peeled and diced potatoes - 2 medium
- Rinsed and drained chickpeas - 15½ ounces
- Onion, chopped - 1 medium
- Diced tomatoes with juice - 28 ounces
- Garlic, grated - 2 cloves
- Smoked paprika, sweet – 2 teaspoons
- Pepper - ½ teaspoon
- Baby spinach - 4 cups
- Extra virgin olive oil - 4 tablespoons
- Salt - 1 teaspoon

Directions: In slow cooker combine potatoes, chickpeas, onion, tomatoes, paprika, garlic, and salt thoroughly. Close the lid and slow cook for five hours. Add the baby spinach and continue cooking for 10 minutes until the spinach becomes wilted. Before serving, season with pepper and salt as per your taste. Drizzle olive oil before serving.

Nutritional Value: Calories: 330, Carbohydrate: 49g, Fat: 11g

MEDITERRANEAN VEGETABLE CURRY

(Perfect Mediterranean Diet recipe)

Preparation Time: 35 minutes | Cooking Time: 6 hours | Serves: 6

Ingredients:

- Onion, finely chopped - 1 medium
- Vegetable oil - 1 tablespoon
- Ground coriander - 3 teaspoons
- Minced garlic - 4 cloves
- Ground turmeric - 1 teaspoon
- Ground ginger - 1 teaspoon
- Ground cinnamon - 1½ teaspoon
- Tomato paste - 2 tablespoons
- Cayenne pepper - ½ teaspoon
- Rinsed and drained chickpeas - 15 ounces
- Tomato paste - 2 tablespoons
- Cauliflower florets, fresh - 3 cups
- Chopped tomatoes - 2 medium
- Cut carrots, sized to ¾" pieces - 4 medium
- Seeded tomatoes, chopped – 2 medium
- Light coconut milk - 1 cup
- Chicken broth - 2 cups
- Salt - ½ teaspoon
- Pepper - ½ teaspoon
- Minced fresh cilantro - ¼ cup
- Lime wedges – 3
- Plain yogurt - ½ cup
- Peeled sweet potatoes - 3 cups

Directions: Heat a large skillet and pour oil at medium temperature. Sauté onion for 5 minutes until it turns light brown. Add spices and garlic to the skillet and keep stirring for one minute. Stir in the tomato paste and continue cooking for a minute. Transfer this mixture into a six-quart slow cooker. Mash the beans until it becomes smooth and add it to the slow cooker. Add the vegetables, beans, coconut milk, broth, salt, and pepper. Close the lid and slow cook for six hours. Sprinkle some cilantro over the dish, after cooking. Serve along with lime wedges and top with yogurt.

Nutritional Value: Calories: 304, Carbohydrate: 49g, Fat: 8g

ITALIAN CROCK POT VEGETABLE DISH

(Perfect Mediterranean Diet recipe)

Preparation Time: 15 minuts | Cooking Time: 9 hours | Serves: 5

Ingredients:

- Drained and rinsed cannellini beans - 1 can
- Olive oil - 1 teaspoon
- Diced fresh tomatoes - 1½ cup
- Drained and rinsed green beans - 1 can
- Peeled and quartered garlic - 2 cloves
- Thickly sliced zucchini - 2 small
- Ground oregano - 1 tablespoon
- Celery - 2 stalks
- Diced and peeled eggplant - 1
- Black pepper - 1 dash
- Quartered yellow onion - 1 medium

Directions: Grease the bottom of the crockpot with olive oil. Put all the ingredients into the crockpot. Combine the ingredients. Cover the crock pot and slow cook for nine hours. Once it gets thoroughly cooked, season it before serving. Serve hot.

Nutritional Value: Calories: 68, Carbohydrate: 13.5g, Fat: 1.5g

MEDITERRANEAN VEGETABLE LASAGNA

(Perfect Mediterranean Diet recipe)

Preparation Time: 25 minuts | Cooking Time: 6 hours | Serves: 9

Ingredients:

- Uncooked whole wheat lasagna noodles - 12
- Marinara sauce - 32 ounces
- Skim ricotta cheese - 24 ounces
- Chopped spinach, frozen and liquid squeezed - 16 ounces
- Mozzarella cheese - 2 pounds
- Cherry tomatoes - 3 ounces
- Chopped fresh parsley - ½ cup
- Salt - 1 teaspoon
- Mushrooms - 12 ounces

Directions: In a medium bowl put spinach, ricotta cheese, salt and combine. Spread half a cup of tomato sauce into the bottom of a 6-quart slow cooker. Break the noodles and layer a portion of it on the tomato sauce. On top of the noodles layer ricotta mixture, along with one-third portions of mushrooms, and one-third portions of mozzarella cheese, and a cup of marinara sauce. Above this layer add another portion of broken noodles. Again layer mozzarella cheese, tomato sauce, and cherry tomatoes. Repeat the layering process until you can make 3 layers. Close the lid and slow cook 6 hours. Once the cooking is over, allow it to settle for 30 minutes. Garnish it with chopped parsley while serving.

Nutritional Value: Calories: 510, Carbohydrate: 21g, Fat: 31g

CROCK POT TORTELLINI STEW

(Perfect Mediterranean Diet recipe)

Preparation Time: 15 minuts | Cooking Time: 8 hours | Serves: 8

Ingredients:

- Zucchini cut into one-inch slices - 2 medium
- Finely chopped onion - 1 small
- Diced tomatoes, undrained - 28 ounces
- Vegetable broth – 29 ounces
- Great Northern Beans - 15½ ounces
- Dried basil leaves - 1 tablespoon
- Pepper - ¼ teaspoon
- Uncooked dry cheese filled tortellini - 8 ounces
- Salt - ¼ teaspoon

Directions: Put onion, vegetable broth, zucchini, great northern beans, tomatoes, pepper and salt into a 6-quart slow cooker. Combine it thoroughly. Close the slow cooker and slow cook for 8 hours. Twenty minutes before serving, stir in tortellini and basil. Now put on high heat for 20 minutes until the tortellini becomes tender. Serve hot.

Nutritional Value: Calories: 170, Carbohydrate: 26g, Fat: 3g

Slow Cooker Spinach Lasagna

(Perfect Mediterranean Diet recipe)

Preparation Time: 30 minuts | Cooking Time: 6 hours | Serves: 8

Ingredients:

- Canned diced tomatoes, undrained - 14½ ounces
- Organic tomato basil paste sauce - 25½ ounces
- Coarsely chopped yellow bell pepper - 1
- Red pepper, crushed - ¼ teaspoon
- Uncooked lasagna noodles - 9
- Thinly sliced zucchini - 1
- Shredded skimmed mozzarella cheese - 6 ounces
- Light ricotta cheese - 1¼ cups
- Coarsely chopped fresh baby spinach - 4 ounces

Directions: Spray some cooking spray in the bottom of a 6-quart slow cooker. In a medium bowl mix tomatoes, pasta sauce, bell pepper, crushed red pepper, and zucchini. Spread a cup of tomato mixture on the bottom part of the slow cooker. Layer the three lasagna noodles over the tomato mixture. Break the noodles so that you can easily layer the noodles. Layer half portion of the ricotta cheese on top of the noodles. Sprinkle half the quantity of spinach and 1/4 cup of mozzarella cheese above the layer. Top it with one-third portion of tomato sauce mixture. Repeat the layering process of noodles, cheese, and spinach for at least three layers. Cover the slow cooker and slow cook for 6 hours until the noodles become tender. Before serving, sprinkle mozzarella all over the lasagna and let it the cheese start melting.

Nutritional Value: Calories: 440, Carbohydrate: 37g, Fat: 22g

Crock Pot Mediterranean Egg Plant Dish

(Perfect Mediterranean Diet recipe)

Preparation Time: 15 minuts | Cooking Time: 9 hours | Serves: 8

Ingredients:

- Diced onion - 1
- Peeled and cubed eggplants - 3 medium
- Diced tomatoes - 1 can
- Diced carrots - 2
- Veg oil - 3 tablespoons
- Tomato paste - 1 tablespoon
- Salt - ¼ teaspoon
- Pepper - ½ teaspoon
- Paprika – as required
- Water – as needed
- Cilantro chopped - ¼ cup

Directions: In a large bowl put cubed eggplants, add water and salt. Stir it so that it can remove the bitter taste of eggplants. Pour oil into a saucepan and bring to medium heat. Put the chopped onion and sauté until it turns light brown and keeps it aside. Now put canned tomatoes, tomato paste, and paprika into a 6-quart slow cooker. Remove the eggplants from the water and wash it under running tap water. Now put the eggplants along with the chopped carrots into the slow cooker. Transfer the sautéed onion into the slow cooker and combine all the ingredients. Add a sufficient quantity of water to cook the vegetables, or until the eggplants and carrots get entirely immersed. Add pepper and salt as per your taste required. Set slow cooker for 9 hours. Garnish with chopped cilantro before serving. Serve hot with rice and salad.

Nutritional Value: Calories: 63, Carbohydrate: 4.1g, Fat: 5.2g

SLOW COOKER RATATOUILLE

(Perfect Mediterranean Diet recipe)

Preparation Time: 25 minuts | Cooking Time: 6 hours | Serves: 6

Ingredients:

- Eggplant, cut into ¾" size - 1 medium
- Tomato paste - 2 tablespoons
- Olive oil - 3 tablespoons
- Plum tomatoes, medium dice – 1 pound
- Freshly ground black pepper - ¼ teaspoon
- Yellow bell pepper cut into ¼ inch slices - 1 large
- Yellow summer squash, cut into 3/4 inch pieces- 8 ounces
- Garlic, finely sliced - 4 large cloves
- Bay leaf - 1
- Onion sliced into half - 1 large
- Fresh thyme leaves, chopped - 1 tablespoon
- Salt - 1½ teaspoons
- Fresh basil leaves, cut in ribbon size - for garnish

Directions: In a large bowl put eggplant, one teaspoon salt and add water. Stir it and keep aside. Drain after 30 minutes. Rinse it under running tap water and place the eggplant over a paper towel. Take a new bowl and whisk tomato paste, oil and the remaining salt along with black pepper. Combine the drained eggplant, zucchini or squash, tomatoes, onion, bell pepper, thyme, garlic in a slow cooker. Add the tomato-oil paste mixture into the slow cooker and combine. Add bay leaf. Cover and slow cook for 4 hours until the vegetable becomes tender. After four hours, open up the lid and cook for one more hour to let the extra liquid evaporate. Discard the bay leaf before serving. Garnish with fresh basil leaves before serving.

Nutritional Value: Calories: 130, Carbohydrate: 15g, Fat: 8g

SLOW COOKER BEANS CHILI

(Perfect Mediterranean Diet recipe)

Preparation Time: 15 minuts | Cooking Time: 7 hours | Serves: 6

Ingredients:

- Yellow onion, chopped - 1 large1
- Baked beans with liquid - 28 ounces

- Olive oil, extra virgin - 2 tablespoons
- Red sweet pepper, cored and chopped - 1 medium
- Garlic, minced - 2 large cloves
- Celery stalk, finely chopped - 1 medium
- Yellow sweet pepper, cored and chopped - 1 medium
- Chili powder - 1½ tablespoons
- Cumin - 1 teaspoon
- Carrot peeled and sliced into a ¼ inch - 1 large
- Tomatoes, drained and diced - 28 ounces
- Corn Kernels fresh or frozen - 15 ounces
- Black beans rinsed and drained - 15 ounces
- Kosher salt - ¼ teaspoons
- Unsweetened coconut milk - ¾ cup

For Garnishing:
- Lime zest - ½ teaspoon
- Fresh parsley leaves, chopped - ¼ cup
- Greek yogurt - ½ cup
- Cheddar cheese - ½ cup

Directions: Take a large skillet and heat olive oil on medium heat. Add garlic and onion to the skillet and sauté it until it becomes soft. Add celery, red and yellow sweet pepper, chili powder, cumin and stir for about 3 minutes. Now transfer all these ingredients into a 6-quart slow cooker. Stir to combine all these ingredients. Cover the lid and slow cook for 7 hours. Before serving, garnish using lime zest, fresh Italian parsley leaves, cheddar cheese, and Greek yogurt.

Nutritional Value: Calories: 720, Carbohydrate: 94g, Fat: 22g

MEDITERRANEAN SOUP RECIPES

SLOW COOKER LENTIL & HAM SOUP

Preparation Time: 20 minuts | Cooking Time: 11 hours | Serves: 6

Ingredients:

- Chopped celery - 1 cup
- Dried lentils - 1 cup
- Chopped onion - 1 cup
- Chopped carrots - 1 cup
- Cooked ham, chopped - 1½ cups
- Minced garlic - 2 cloves
- Dried thyme - ¼ teaspoon
- Dried basil - ½ teaspoon
- Bay leaf - 1
- Dried oregano - 1/2 teaspoon
- Chicken broth - 32 ounces
- Black pepper - ¼ teaspoon
- Tomato sauce - 8 teaspoons
- Water - 1 cup

Directions: Put celery, lentils, onion, carrots, ham, and garlic in a 4-quart slow cooker and combine thoroughly. Season the ingredients with thyme, basil, bay leaf, oregano, and pepper. Pour chicken broth and stir well. Now add the tomato sauce and water into the slow cooker. Close the lid and slow cook for 11 hours. Remove bay leaf before serving. Serve hot.

Nutritional Value: Calories: 222, Carbohydrate: 26.3g, Fat: 6.1g

BEEF BARLEY VEGETABLE SOUP

Preparation Time: 20 minuts | Cooking Time: 5 hours 30 minutes | Serves: 10

Ingredients:

- Barley - ½ cup
- Beef chuck roast - 3 pounds
- Oil - 2 tablespoons
- Bay leaf - 1
- Chopped celery - 3 stalks
- Chopped carrots - 3
- Mixed vegetables - 16 ounces
- Beef bouillon - 4 cubes
- Water - 4 cups
- Ground black pepper - ¼ teaspoon
- White sugar - 1 tablespoon
- Salt - ¼ teaspoon
- Stewed tomatoes, diced - 28 ounces
- Chopped onion - 1

Directions: Take a slow cooker and Cook chuck roast in the slow cooker at high heat for 5 until it becomes soft. Add a bay leaf and barley into the slow cooker one hour before the end of cooking. Remove the meat and chop it into small pieces. Discard the bay leaf as well. Set the broth, beef and the barley aside. Pour oil in a large cooking pot and bring it on medium heat. Sauté celery, onion, frozen mixed vegetables, and carrots until they become soft. Add beef bouillon cubes, water, pepper, sugar, beef or barley mixture, tomatoes. Boil the mix and reduce the heat and let it simmer for about ten to twenty minutes. Season it with salt and pepper before serving.

Nutritional Value: Calories: 321, Carbohydrate: 22.4g, Fat: 17.3g

SLOW COOKER CORN CHOWDER

Preparation Time: 15 minuts | Cooking Time: 4 hours | Serves: 8

Ingredients:

- Cream style corn - 14¾ ounces
- Milk - 3 cups
- Chopped green chilies - 4 ounces
- Condensed mushroom cream soup - 10¾ ounces
- Hash brown potatoes, frozen & shredded - 2 cups
- Frozen corn - 2 cups
- Hot sauce - 2 tablespoons
- Butter - 2 tablespoons
- Chili powder - 1 teaspoon
- Dried parsley - 2 teaspoons
- Salt - ¼ teaspoon
- Ground black pepper - ½ teaspoon
- Chopped onion - 1 large
- Cooked ham, cubed - 2 cups

Directions: Stir in cream-style corn, milk, chopped green chilies, cream of mushroom soup, hash brown potatoes, frozen corn, ham, butter, onion, parsley, chili powder and hot sauce in a slow cooker. Season the soup with black pepper and salt as per your taste. Cover the cooker and slow cook for 6 hours. Serve hot.

Nutritional Value: Calories: 376, Carbohydrate: 47.1g, Fat: 18.7g

SLOW COOKER CHICKEN POSOLE

(Perfect Mediterranean Diet recipe)

Preparation Time: 120 minuts | Cooking Time: 6 hours 40 minutes | Serves: 6

Ingredients:

- Skinless, boneless chicken breasts - 3
- Chicken broth, low sodium - 4 cups
- Chopped white onion - 1
- Chopped poblano peppers - 2
- Cumin - 1 tablespoon
- Minced garlic - 2 cloves
- Chili powder - 2 teaspoons
- Oregano - 1 tablespoon
- Kosher salt - 2 teaspoons
- Ground black pepper, fresh - ½ teaspoon
- Drained hominy - 15 ounces

For Garnish:

- Sliced green cabbage - ¾ cup
- Thinly sliced radish - ½ cup
- Fresh cilantro, chopped - ¼ cup

Directions: In a slow cooker combine all items, except the ingredients for garnish and hominy. Cover and slow cook for 8 hours. After cooking, take the chicken out of the slow cooker and shred it using a fork. Return it to the slow cooker along with hominy. Cook it further 30 minutes. Garnish it with cabbage, radish, and cilantro before serving.

Nutritional Value: Calories: 105, Carbohydrate: 16.6g, Fat: 2.1g

CROCK POT BUTTERNUT SQUASH SOUP

(Perfect Mediterranean Diet recipe)

Preparation Time: 40 minuts | Cooking Time: 8 hours | Serves: 6

Ingredients:

• Chicken broth, low sodium - 4 cups • Diced butternut squash - 6 cups • Halved and quartered onion - 1 medium • Peeled and diced carrots - 2 medium	• Cinnamon - 1 teaspoon • Chipotle peppers in adobo sauce - 2 • Pepper - ½ teaspoon • Salt - 1 teaspoon • Yogurt - ¼cup

Directions: Put all the ingredients in the slow cooker and combine. Close the lid and slow cook for 8 hours. After cooking, make a puree by using an immersion blender. Check salt and other seasonings as per your taste. If you want to reduce the consistency add more chicken broth. Drizzle with plain yogurt before serving.

Nutritional Value: Calories: 142, Carbohydrate, Fat: 0.6g

SLOW COOKER MEDITERRANEAN CHICKEN SOUP

(Perfect Mediterranean Diet recipe)

Preparation Time: 10 minuts | Cooking Time: 3 hours | Serves: 11

Ingredients:

- Boneless chicken breast – 1pound
- Chicken broth - 3 cups
- Lite coconut milk - 14 ounces
- Red curry paste - 4 ounces
- Peanut butter - ½ cup
- Soy sauce, low sodium - 5 tablespoons
- Fish sauce - 2 tablespoons
- Garlic, minced - 4 cloves
- Dark brown sugar - 2 tablespoons
- Ground ginger - 1 teaspoon
- Diced yellow onion - 1
- Red bell pepper, chopped - 1
- Carrots, diagonally sliced - 1 cup
- Broccoli, sliced florets - 1 head
- Sliced mushrooms - 8 ounces
- Lime juice - 3 tablespoons
- Salt - ¼ teaspoon
- Red pepper flakes - ½ teaspoon

For Garnish:

- Chopped peanuts - ¼ cup
- Chopped cilantro - ¼ cup

Directions: Slightly oil the bottom of the crockpot and stir in broth, coconut milk, curry paste, peanut butter, soy sauce, fish sauce, garlic, brown sugar, red pepper flakes, salt, and ginger. Put onion, chicken breasts, pepper, carrots, broccoli, mushrooms and mix thoroughly. Cover the lid and slow cook for 8 hours. Remove the cooked chicken into a bowl and chop into small pieces. Put it back into the soup.

Add lime juice and stir. Season with curry paste, salt and red pepper flakes as per your taste, if required. Garnish with chopped peanuts and cilantro before serving.

Nutritional Value: Calories: 239, Carbohydrate: 16g, Fat: 12g

SLOW COOKER CHICKEN & VEGETABLE SOUP

(Perfect Mediterranean Diet recipe)

Preparation Time: 15 minuts | Cooking Time: 8 hours | Serves: 8

Ingredients:

- Chicken broth, low sodium - 4 cups
- Fat trimmed and skinned chicken breasts - 1½ pounds
- Parsnips, ¼" sliced - 3 medium
- Carrots, ¼" sliced - 3 medium
- Chopped onion - 1 medium
- Peeled & finely sliced celery - 2 stalks
- Yellow curry powder - 1 teaspoon
- Parmesan rind 2" piece - ½ cup
- Frozen peas - 1 cup
- Kosher salt - ¼ teaspoon
- Ground black pepper - ½ teaspoon
- Fresh dill fronds, chopped - ½ cup loosely packed

For Garnish:

- Lemon, grated – 1 tablespoon
- Grated Parmesan - ¼ cup

Directions: Put all the ingredients, except the garnish into 6-quart slow cooker. Close the lid and slow cook for 8 hours. After cooking, take out the chicken breast and allow it to cool for some time. Shred the meat after cooling and discard the bone. Now put back the shredded chicken meat into the slow cooker. Add dill. Season the soup with pepper and salt as per your taste. While serving garnish it with lemon juice and grated parmesan.

Nutritional Value: Calories: 212, Carbohydrate: 8.5g, Fat: 7.2g

CROCK POT MEDITERRANEAN BEEF SOUP

Preparation Time: 20 minuts | Cooking Time: 9 hours | Serves: 8

Ingredients:

- Stew beef, cut to 1" size – 2 pound
- Carrots, chopped – 1 cup
- Onion, diced – 1
- Beef broth – 30 ounces
- Oregano – 1 teaspoon
- Italian diced tomatoes – 29 ounces
- Onion powder – 2 teaspoon
- Drained beans – 30 ounces
- Salt - ½ teaspoon
- Ground black pepper - ½ teaspoon
- Parmesan cheese, shredded - ¼ cup

Directions: Drain the beans. Cut the onions and carrots. Put all the ingredients in a slow cooker, except parmesan cheese. Slow cook for 9 hours. Before serving, garnish it with parmesan.

Nutritional Value: Calories: 230, Carbohydrate: 11, Fat: 7.6g

SLOW COOKER SPLIT PEA SOUP

Preparation Time: 5 minuts │ Cooking Time: 6 hours │ Serves: 6

Ingredients:

- Hambone - 1½ pounds
- Dried split peas - 16 ounces
- Diced yellow onion - 1
- Diced carrots – 3
- Diced shallot - 1
- Minced garlic - 3 cloves
- Diced celery - 2 stalks
- Dried thyme - 1 teaspoon
- Minced garlic - 3 cloves
- Bay leaf - 1
- Ground black pepper - ½ teaspoon
- Chicken broth, low sodium - 6 cups

Directions: Combine carrots, split peas, shallot, yellow onion, garlic, celery, pepper, thyme, chicken stock and bay leaf in a slow cooker. Add ham bone and stir. Cover the lid and slow cook for 6 hours. Remove the ham from the slow cooker and shred into small pieces using a fork Discard the bone. Put back ham meat back into the slow cooker. Discard the bay leaf and serve hot.

Nutritional Value: Calories: 321, Carbohydrate: 54g, Fat: 2g

SLOW COOKER FISH SOUP

(Perfect Mediterranean Diet recipe)

Preparation Time: 20 minuts │ Cooking Time: 6 hours 20 minutes │ Serves: 6

Ingredients:

- Shrimp, deveined medium – 1 pound
- Cubed cod fillets - 1 pound
- Chopped green bell pepper - ½
- Chopped onion - 1
- Drained and diced tomatoes - 14½ ounces
- Minced garlic - 2 cloves
- Tomato sauce - 8 ounces
- Chicken broth - 14 ounces
- Sliced black olives - ¼ cup
- Canned mushrooms - 2½ ounces
- Dry white wine - ½ cup
- Orange juice - ½ cup
- Dried basil - 1 teaspoon
- Bay leaves - 2
- Ground black pepper - ⅛ teaspoon
- Crushed fennel seed - ¼ teaspoon

Directions: In a slow cooker combine garlic, green bell pepper, chicken broth, tomatoes, mushrooms, tomato sauce, orange juice, olives, bay leaves, wine, fennel seeds, dried basil, and pepper. Close the lid and slow cook 4½ hours. Put cod and shrimp. Stir thoroughly. Cook it for about 30 minutes or until the shrimp become opaque. Discard the bay leaf before serving.

Nutritional Value: Calories: 222, Carbohydrate: 11.9g, Fat: 3g

Mediterranean Pizza & Pasta

Crock Pot Pizza and Pasta

Preparation Time: 10 minuts | Cooking Time: 3 hours 30 minutes | Serves: 4

Ingredients:

- Chicken broth, low sodium, divided into - 3½ cups and 1 tablespoon
- Lean ground beef - ½ pound
- Turkey pepperonis - ½ cup
- Organic pizza sauce - 1½ cups
- Chopped and cooked ham - ½ cup
- Italian seasoning - 2 teaspoons
- Gluten-free rotini pasta - 8 ounces
- Pepper - as per taste required
- Mozzarella cheese - 1 cup
- Non - GMO Cornstarch - ½ tablespoon
- Salt - ¾ teaspoon

Directions: Crush the lean ground beef into the slow cooker. Add a cup of broth to the slow cooker, reserve the rest for later use. Cook the beef on slow cook mode for three hours. After cooking, add about ¾ cups of pizza sauce, ham, pepperonis, salt, Italian seasoning and pepper into the slow cooker. Mix them well together. Next, add the pasta and the remaining two and a half cups of broth to the slow cooker. Take a small bowl and whisk the remaining chicken broth along with the cornstarch until it becomes smooth. Pour this mixture into the slow cooker. Cover the slow cooker and let it cook under high heat for an hour or until the pasta gets thoroughly cooked. Do not overcook the noodles, and it is highly recommended to check with the consistency level of the noodles by opening the slow cooker when the timer hits forty-five minutes. Once the noodles are cooked well, pour the remaining ¾ cups of pizza sauce along with cheese. Serve hot.

Nutritional Value: Calories: 282, Carbohydrate: 34.8g, Fat: 8.2g

Slow Cooker Beef Pizza

Preparation Time: 2 minuts | Cooking Time: 4 hours | Serves: 6

Ingredients:

- Rigatoni pasta - 8 ounces
- Ground beef - 1½ pounds
- Shredded mozzarella cheese - 16 ounces
- Pizza sauce - 14 ounces
- Tomato soup, condensed cream in a can - 10¾ ounces
- Sliced pepperoni sausage - 8 ounces

Directions: Boil salt water in a large pot. Cook pasta in it for about 10 minutes. Add pasta to it and let it cook for about eight to ten minutes so that it will remain firm and smooth to bite. Drain the pasta and set it aside. Now cook beef in a large skillet on medium high heat, until it becomes brown on all sides. Layer the beef in the slow cooker and on top layer mozzarella cheese, cooked pasta, and condensed cream of tomato sauce, soup and pepperoni. Slow cook the ingredients for 4 hours. Serve hot.

Nutritional Value: Calories: 820, Carbohydrate: 50.9g, Fat: 43.3g

SLOW COOKER DEEP DISH PIZZA

Preparation Time: 10 minuts | Cooking Time: 2 hours | Serves: 4

Ingredients:

- Pizza sauce - ⅓ cup
- Refrigerated Pizza crust - 11 ounces
- Cooked and crumbled sausage - ¼ pound
- Shredded mozzarella cheese – 1 cup
- Sliced pepperoni - ½ cup
- Non-stick cooking spray – as required

Directions: Drizzle non-stick cooking spray in a 4-quart slow cooker. Spread out pizza dough and fold in half crosswise and place in the slow cooker. Press the pizza to the bottom by keeping the edges one inch up. Now evenly spread the pizza sauce on the dough. Layer it with half portions of sausage, cheese, and pepperoni. Repeat the process by adding the remaining pepperoni, sausage, and cheese. Close the cooker lit and slow cook for 2 hours until the crust edges turn golden brown, and the cheese melted. Remove the pizza from the slow cooker and transfer it to a cutting board. Cut the pizza into four slices and serve hot.

Nutritional Value: Calories: 430, Carbohydrate: 39g, Fat: 22g

MEDITERRANEAN-ITALIAN STYLE PORK PIZZA

Preparation Time: 15 minuts | Cooking Time: 5 hours | Serves: 4

Ingredients:

- Thawed, frozen pizza dough – 1 pound
- Italian pork sausage, cooked ½ - pound
- Flour – 1 tablespoon
- Marinara sauce - 1½ cup
- Garlic, minced – 1 clove
- Pepperoni, sliced – 12 slices
- Italian blend cheese, grated - 1½ cup
- Parmesan cheese, grated - ¼ cup
- Parsley, chopped - ¼ cup

Directions: Place a large parchment paper in the crock pot and spread flour. Roll the thawed frozen pizza dough on the flour in an oval shape. The doughs edges should overlap the size of your crockpot and keep it aside. Now heat a skillet on medium high temperature and cook the pork sausage. While cooking, break the sausages into tiny pieces. Stir in minced garlic and continue cooking. Once cooking over keep it aside. Spread the sauce over the pizza crust. Layer over it with cheese. Stretch out the side of the pizza dough, so that the cheese will not sweep out. Now sprinkle the cooked sausage over it. Over the layer, spread the pepperoni. Stretch out the side of the pizza dough, so that the layering will stay within the pizza crust. Now place a large paper towel over the mouth of the crock pot and close the lit firmly. Slow cook for 5 hours. Serve hot by topping with grated parmesan cheese and sprinkling chopped parsley.

Nutritional Value: Calories: 635, Carbohydrate: 62g, Fat: 31g

Slow Cooker Mediterranean Pasta

(Perfect Mediterranean Diet recipe)

Preparation Time: 10 minuts | Cooking Time: 4 hours | Serves: 8

Ingredients:

- Pasta – 1 pound
- Minced garlic - 2 cloves
- Chopped onion - 1
- Salt - as per taste required
- Pepper - as per taste required
- Chicken tenders - 1¼ pounds
- Marinara sauce - 25 ounces
- Italian seasoning - 1 teaspoon
- Cream cheese - 12 ounces
- Bay leaves – 2
- Pepper - ¼ teaspoon
- Salt - ¼ teaspoon

Directions: Put garlic, onion, salt, chicken pepper, cream cheese, marinara, bay leaves, and Italian seasoning in a crockpot. Cover and slow cook for 4 hours, until the chicken becomes soft. Shred the chicken with a spoon. Add cream cheese into the sauce and let it melt. Top it with cooked hot pasta. Serve hot.

Nutritional Value: Calories: 465, Carbohydrate: 50g, Fat: 17g

Slow Cooker Chicken Parmesan Pasta

(Perfect Mediterranean Diet recipe)

Preparation Time: 15 minuts | Cooking Time: 4 hours 30 minutes | Serves: 8

Ingredients:

- Skinless, boneless chicken breasts - 4
- Dried oregano - 1 teaspoon
- Diced onion - 1
- Dried basil - 1 tablespoon
- Crushed tomatoes - 56 ounces (2 cans)
- Crushed red pepper flakes - ½ teaspoon
- Shredded mozzarella cheese - 1½ cups
- Penne - 1 pound
- Chopped fresh parsley leaves - 2 tablespoons
- Parmesan cheese, shredded - ¼ cup
- Ground black pepper, fresh - ¼ teaspoon
- Kosher salt - ¼ teaspoon
- Dried parsley - 1 teaspoon

Directions: Season the chicken breasts with pepper and salt. Place the chicken breasts into a 6-quart slow cooker. In a large bowl combine onion, crushed tomatoes, basil, parsley, oregano, and red pepper flakes. Stir in this mixture into the slow cooker and gently toss it to combine. Cover the cooker and slow cook for 4 hours. After four hours, remove the chicken breasts from the cooker and shred with a fork. Boil pasta in salted water and drain it. Put back the shredded chicken and add the cooked pasta into the slow cooker and top it up with cheese. Cover the slow cooker and slow cook for 30 minutes until the cheese melts thoroughly. Garnish with freshly chopped parsley before serving.

Nutritional Value: Calories: 455.5, Carbohydrate: 59.7g, Fat: 8.5g

SLOW COOKER PASTA MEAT SAUCE WITH GROUND TURKEY

(Perfect Mediterranean Diet recipe)

Preparation Time: 15 minuts | Cooking Time: 8 hours | Serves: 8

Ingredients:

- Turkey, grounded - 1 pound
- Diced onion - 1 medium
- Minced garlic - 6 cloves
- Diced tomatoes - 29 ounces (2 cans)
- Olive oil - 2 tablespoons
- Tomato paste - 2 tablespoons
- Tomato sauce - 14½ ounces (1 can)
- Italian herb seasoning - 2 tablespoons
- Dry red wine - 1/2 cup
- Black pepper, grounded - ¼ teaspoon
- Salt - ½ teaspoon
- Red pepper, crushed - ¼ teaspoon
- Non-stick cooking spray – as required

For Garnish:

- Fresh Italian parsley, chopped - ¼ cup
- Parmesan cheese - ¼ cup

Directions: Spray some non-stick cooking oil in the bottom of the slow cooker. Put onion, olive oil and garlic in a slow bowl and microwave for two minutes at full power. Make sure to stop the microwave at one minute and stir the mixture and then cook it for the remaining one minute. In the slow cooker, put tomato sauce or crushed tomatoes, diced tomatoes, dry red wine, tomato paste, Italian herb seasoning, ground black pepper, salt, and crushed red pepper and combine. Break the ground turkey into chunks and put into the sauce. Tap the turkey chunks with a large spoon so that they should get partially covered with the sauce. Do not stir the turkey. Close the cooker and slow cook for 8 hours. Once the turkey gets finely cooked, stir in the microwave cooked sauce. Sprinkle grated parmesan cheese and chopped parsley before serving.

Nutritional Value: Calories: 201, Carbohydrate: 11.4g, Fat: 8g

CROCK POT PIZZA CASSEROLE

Preparation Time: 15 minuts | Cooking Time: 5 hours | Serves: 6

Ingredients:

- Low-fat beef, minced - 1 pound
- Onion – 1 small
- Crushed tomatoes - 28 ounces
- Crushed garlic - 2 cloves
- Sliced pepperoni - 4 ounces
- Oregano - 2 teaspoons
- Green pepper - ½ teaspoon
- Pepper - 1 teaspoon
- Divided mozzarella cheese - 2 cups
- Chopped green pepper - ½ teaspoon
- Uncooked pasta - 2 cups
- Water - 1 cup
- Salt - 2 teaspoons

Directions: Chop half of green pepper, onion and keep aside. In a large skillet, over medium heat brown the ground beef. When the beef becomes brown add chopped onions and let it cook for 8 minutes. Stir continuously. When the onion becomes tender, add crushed garlic and stir it for a minute. In a crockpot, add water, crushed tomatoes, oregano, four ounces of sliced pepperoni, salt, pepper, salt, mozzarella cheese, and green pepper. Add the uncooked pasta into the slow cooker and mix thoroughly. Now, transfer the cooked ground beef mixture into the slow cooker. Top it up with mozzarella and twelve slices of pepperoni. Close the lid and slow cook for 5 hours or until the edges turn brown in terms of color. Serve hot.

Nutritional Value: Calories: 485, Carbohydrate: 27g, Fat: 28g

SLOW COOKER MEDITERRANEAN PASTA

Preparation Time: 15 minuts | Cooking Time: 9 hours 15 minutes | Serves: 4

Ingredients:

- Beef meat, stew type - 1 pound
- Penne pasta - 1½ cups
- Chopped onion - 1/2 cup
- Drained and sliced mushrooms - 4½ ounces
- Drained and chopped artichoke hearts - 14 ounces
- Drained capers - 1 tablespoon
- Garlic, dried minced - 1 tablespoon
- Sugar - 1 teaspoon
- Salt - 1 teaspoon
- Olive oil - 1 tablespoon
- Parmesan cheese, grated - ½ cup
- Fresh ground pepper - ¼ teaspoon
- Olive oil – as required
- Balsamic vinegar - 1 tablespoon
- Italian seasoning - 1 teaspoon

Directions: Sprinkle cooking spray into a four-quart slow cooker. Add beef stew meat, mushrooms, onion, artichoke hearts, tomatoes, drained capers, balsamic vinegar, minced garlic, salt, and Italian seasoning into the slow cooker. Cover the lid and slow cook for 9 hours. Cook the pasta 15 minutes before serving. Put the cooked pasta, oil and pepper in the beef mixture and stir. Serve hot topping with cheese.

Nutritional Value: Calories: 560, Carbohydrate: 58g, Fat: 21g

ROBUST MEDITERRANEAN SAUSAGE & PASTA

Preparation Time: 15 minuts | Cooking Time: 6 hours 30 minutes | Serves: 4

Ingredients:

- Sausage, Italian links, cut into half – 4 ounces each
- Undrained tomatoes and chilies chopped – 10 ounces
- Italian sausage spaghetti sauce – 25.6 ounces
- Green pepper, julienned – 1 large
- Italian seasoning – 1 teaspoon
- Spiral pasta, uncooked – 2 cups
- Garlic, minced – 2 cloves
- Onion, chopped – 1 medium

Directions: Brown the sausages in a large non-stick skillet. Transfer the brown sausages into a 4-quarter slow cooker. Now put tomatoes, onion, green pepper, garlic, spaghetti sauce, Italian seasoning and combine. Close the lid and slow cook for 6 hours. Add pasta. Cover and cook again high for 30 minutes to tender the pasta. Serve hot.

Nutritional Value: Calories: 529, Carbohydrate: 60g, Fat: 22g

MEDITERRANEAN BEANS & GRAINS

THREE BEAN MEDITERRANEAN SLOW COOKER CHILI

(Perfect Mediterranean Diet recipe)

Preparation Time: 10 minuts | Cooking Time: 12 hours | Serves: 10

Ingredients:

- Ground Turkey breast 99% lean – 1.3 pounds
- Diced tomatoes, drained – 28 ounces
- Onion, small, chopped – 1
- Tomato sauce – 16 ounces
- Chopped chilies in the can – 4½ ounces

- Black beans drained – 15½ ounces
- Chickpeas drained – 15 ounces
- Small red beans, drained – 15½ ounces
- Chili powder – 2 tablespoons
- Cumin – 1 teaspoon

For the topping:

- Chopped fresh cilantro for topping – ½ cup
- Red onion, chopped – ½ cup

- Shredded cheddar - ¼ cup
- Sour cream - ¼ cup
- Avocado pieces - ¼ cup

Directions: Put turkey and onion into a medium-size skillet on medium-high heat. Continue cooking until the turkey becomes brown on all sides. Now, take a slow cooker and transfer the turkey and onion into it. Add beans, tomatoes, chickpeas, chilies, tomato sauce, cumin, and chili powder into the cooker and combine. Slow cook it for 12 hours. Top it with onions, cilantro, avocado pieces, shredded cheddar, and sour cream while serving. Serve it hot.

Nutritional Value: Calories: 231, Carbohydrates: 27.5g, Fat: 5g

BEANS AND BARLEY STEW

(Perfect Mediterranean Diet recipe)

Preparation Time: 10 minuts | Cooking Time: 8 hours 10 minutes | Serves: 10

Ingredients:

- Dried bean mix, rinsed (kidney, navy, pinto) – 1 pound
- Dried barley – 8 ounces
- Low sodium chicken broth – 8 cups
- Yellow onion, chopped - 1
- Celery stalks, diced - 3
- Barley – ½ pound

- Carrots, diced - 2
- Garlic, minced – 2 cloves
- Bay leaf – 1
- Fresh thyme – few springs
- Baby spinach – 8 ounces
- Kosher salt – 2 teaspoon
- Water – 2 cups

Directions: In the slow cooker combine bean mix, pepper, carrots, celery, garlic, thyme, onions, bay leaf, and salt. Pour the broth and also 2 cups of water and stir thoroughly. Cover the cooker and slow cook for 7 hours. Now add barely. If the stew consistency is too thick, add some more water. Cover again and cook for 1 more hour. Before serving add spinach and stir. Serve hot.

Nutritional value: Calories: 262, Fat: 1.1g, Carbohydrate: 48.8g

MEDITERRANEAN LENTILS AND RICE

(Perfect Mediterranean Diet recipe)

Preparation Time: 15 minuts | Cooking Time: 8 hours | Serves: 6

Ingredients:

- Brown lentils – 1 cup
- Onion, chopped – 1
- Rice – ½ cup
- Salt – ¾ teaspoon
- Cinnamon – ½ teaspoon

- Ground cumin – 1 tablespoon
- Olive oil – 4½ teaspoons
- Water or homemade vegetable stock or chicken stock – 6 cups

Directions: Pour olive oil in the crock pot. Set the crock pot on high heat. Put onion into it and sauté. After 10-15 minutes, put all the remaining ingredients including water into the crockpot. Cover the crock pot and slow cook for 8 hours. You may stir the dish in between to check whether food is dry or moisturized. Add water if required. Serve hot.

Nutritional Value: Calories: 98, Fat: 3.8g, Carbohydrate: 14.7g

ITALIAN-MEDITERRANEAN MULTI-BEAN SOUP

(Perfect Mediterranean Diet recipe)

Preparation Time: 10 minuts | Cooking Time: 10 hours | Serves: 12

Ingredients:

- Chicken broth – 8¾ cups
- Organic tomato, diced - 14½ ounces
- Dried bean soup – 16 ounces
- Carrots, chopped – 4 medium
- Onion, chopped – 1 large

- Stalks celery, chopped – 3 medium
- Tomato paste – 2 tablespoons
- Pepper – ½ teaspoon
- Italian seasoning – 1 teaspoon
- Salt – 1 teaspoon

Directions: In a 6-quart slow cooker, combine all the ingredients, except tomatoes. Cover the slow cooker, and set low cooking for 10 hours. Add tomatoes and mix them well. Switch from low heat to high heat. Cover the cooker and cook further 15 more minutes or until it becomes hot. Serve hot.

Nutritional Value: Calories: 180, Carbohydrate: 30g, Fat: 1g

MEDITERRANEAN SLOW COOKED GREEN BEANS

(Perfect Mediterranean Diet recipe)

Preparation Time: 10 minuts | Cooking Time: 3 hours | Serves: 12

Ingredients:

- Frozen French-style green beans, thawed – 16 cups
- Brown sugar – ½ cup
- Butter, melted – ½ cup
- Garlic salt – 1½ teaspoons
- Low sodium soy sauce – ¾ teaspoon

Directions: Put beans into a 6-quart slow cooker. Stir in other ingredients including sugar, soy sauce, butter, and garlic salt. Cover the cooker and cook the beans for about 3 hours on low heat. Serve hot.

Nutritional Value: Calories: 143, Carbohydrate: 17g, Fat: 8g

SLOW COOKED GREEN BEANS

Preparation Time: 15 minuts | Cooking Time: 3 hours 30 minutes | Serves: 6

Ingredients:

- Bacon sliced crosswise into ½ inch pieces – 6 slices
- Garlic, minced – 3 cloves
- Onion, sliced lengthwise – 1
- Fresh green beans, trimmed – 2 pounds
- Tomato sauce – ¼ cup
- Cayenne pepper – 1 pinch
- Salt - ¼ teaspoon
- Black pepper ground – ¼ teaspoon
- Chicken broth – 3 cups

Directions: Heat a saucepan on medium heat. Add sliced bacon into the hot pan. Stir and cook it for about 6 minutes until it becomes brown and crispy. Now, add onion into the pan and cook it for about 5 minutes until the onion becomes mushy and golden brown. Let the brown chunks of food at the bottom gets dissolved with the onion's juices. Add tomato sauce and minced garlic into the pan and mix it well. Cook for about 1 more minute until the garlic becomes soft. Take a skillet and add green beans into it and add chicken broth into it. Heat the skillet on high heat and add black pepper, cayenne pepper, and salt into the skillet. Cook the beans until it becomes soft. Now, switch the cooker from high heat to slow cooking mode for 3 hours. Keep stirring the mixture intermittently. If the mixture appears to be dry, pour more water or broth into it. Check the salt and pepper. If required adjust its taste as needed. After adding salt and pepper, cook it further for about 30 minutes. Serve it hot along with its juice.

Nutritional Value: Calories: 124, Carbohydrate: 16g, Fat: 4.3g

SLOW COOKER MOROCCAN CHICKPEA STEW

(Perfect Mediterranean Diet recipe)

Preparation Time: 10 minuts | Cooking Time: 7 hours | Serves: 6

Ingredients:

- Medium white onion chopped – 1
- Garlic cloves minced – 3
- Red bell pepper chopped – 1
- Small butternut squash peeled and cut into bite-sized pieces – 1
- Chickpeas drained and rinsed – 15 ounces can
- Pure tomato sauce – 15 ounces can
- Grated ginger, fresh – 1 teaspoon
- Turmeric – 1 teaspoon
- Cinnamon – ½ teaspoon
- Cumin – 1 teaspoon
- Salt - ½ teaspoon
- Pepper – ½ teaspoon
- Smoked paprika – 1 teaspoon
- Vegetable broth – 3 cups
- Red lentils – ¾ cup

To serve:

- Arugula - ¼ cup
- Cooked quinoa - ¼ cup
- Coconut yogurt - ¼ cup

Directions: In a slow cooker and put all the ingredients and combine thoroughly. Cover the cooker and slow cook for 7 hours. Serve it along with arugula, quinoa, and yogurt.

Nutritional Value: Calories: 178, Carbohydrate: 37g, Protein: 8g

SLOW COOKER SPANISH RICE

(Perfect Mediterranean Diet recipe)

Preparation Time: 10 minuts ｜ Cooking Time: 4 hours 10 minutes ｜ Serves: 8

Ingredients:

- Olive oil – 2 tablespoons, extra olive oil for crockpot greasing.
- Wholegrain rice – 2 cups
- Diced tomatoes in the can – 14½ ounces
- Medium yellow onion, chopped – 1
- Garlic, minced – 3 cloves
- Low-sodium broth or stock (chicken or vegetable), or water – 2 cups
- Red bell pepper, medium cut size – ½
- Yellow bell pepper, medium dice – ½
- Ground cumin – 1 ½ teaspoon
- Chili powder – 2 teaspoons
- Kosher salt – 1½ teaspoons
- Fresh cilantro leaves, for garnishing – 2 tablespoons

Directions: Pour olive oil into a large skillet and bring it to medium heat. Add rice into the skillet and combine well so that the grains get olive oil coating. Now put the onion into the skillet and sauté for about 5 minutes, until the rice becomes pale golden brown. Slightly grease the inside of crockpot with olive oil. Transfer the browned rice to the crockpot. Add broth, bell peppers, tomatoes, garlic, cumin, chili powder, salt and combine thoroughly. Cover the crock, and slow cook for about 4 hours. Two hours later, check if the liquid is being absorbed by the rice well. Continue cooking until the rice becomes soft and all the moisture gets absorbed. Top it with cilantro leaves and serve hot.

Nutritional Value: Calories: 55, Carbohydrates: 5.36g, Fat: 3.78g

SLOW COOKER TURKISH/MEDITERRANEAN CHICKPEA STEW

(Perfect Mediterranean Diet recipe)

Preparation Time: 15 minuts | Cooking Time: 8 hours 22 minutes | Serves: 7

Ingredients:

- 93% lean ground Turkey – 1.3 pounds package
- Extra virgin olive oil, light – 1 tablespoon
- Poblano pepper, chopped – 3 tablespoons
- Yellow onion, chopped – 1
- Diced carrots – 1 cup
- Garlic cloves, chopped – 2
- Diced celery – 1 cup
- Chickpeas, drained – 30 ounces
- Finely diced tomatoes – 28 ounces can
- Low sodium, 99% fat-free chicken broth – 2 cups
- Paprika – 2 teaspoons
- Turmeric – 2 teaspoons
- Coriander – 1 teaspoon
- Crushed red pepper flakes – ½ teaspoon
- Bay leaves – 2
- Fresh Italian parsley chopped – 2 tablespoons
- Salt – 2 teaspoons
- Cooking spray – as required

Directions: Take a large skillet and spray some non-stick cooking oil in the bottom and bring to medium-high heat. Put ground Turkey in it and cook for about 12 minutes. Break the ground meat into pieces. Mix it well to ensure that it gets cooked uniformly. Transfer the ground meat into the slow cooker. Now in the same skillet pour olive oil and the oil become hot, sauté onions, carrots, pepper, and celery for about 8 minutes until the vegetables become tender and brown. Add garlic in the skillet and sauté for 2 more minutes. Now, transfer the browned vegetables into the slow cooker. Add diced tomatoes, spices, chickpeas and broth as well and mix them lightly. Cover the slow cooker, and set the timer for 8 hours. Remove the bay leaves while serving and top it with fresh herbs. Serve hot.

Nutritional Value: Calories: 342, Fat: 10g, Carbohydrates: 38g

WHOLE WHEAT CROCK POT LASAGNA

(Perfect Mediterranean Diet recipe)

Preparation Time: 10 minuts | Cooking Time: 5 hours | Serves: 8

Ingredients:

- Extra lean ground Turkey – 2 pounds
- Uncooked, whole wheat lasagna noodles – 8
- Low fat and low sugar spaghetti sauce – 28 ounces
- Sliced mushrooms – 4 ounces
- Italian seasoning – 1 teaspoon
- Shredded skim milk mozzarella cheese – 2 cups
- Water – ⅓ cup
- Ricotta cheese, fat-free – 15 ounces

Directions: Clean, rinse and drain the mushrooms. Keep them ready. Before starting the cooking, add a little olive oil in the crockpot. Place 4 lasagna noodles in the bottom of the crockpot. In a non-stick pan sauté the ground Turkey until it becomes brown. Add Italian seasoning and mix well. Place half of the browned Turkey over the noodles in the crock pot and spread it well. Spread a layer of ½ of the sauce over Turkey. Now, add another layer of ½ of the mushrooms over it. Similarly, add a layer of ½ of the ricotta and then, half of the mozzarella over it. Repeat the layering. Cover the crock pot and slow cook for 5 hours.

Nutritional Value: Calories: 469, Carbohydrates: 31.3g, Fat: 21g

MEDITERRANEAN CHICKEN RECIPES

SLOW COOKER MEDITERRANEAN CHICKEN

(Perfect Mediterranean Diet recipe)

Preparation Time: 15 minuts | Cooking Time: 4 hours 30 minutes | Serves: 4

Ingredients:

- Chicken broth, low sodium - 1 cup
- Skinless, boneless chicken breasts - 1 pound
- Juice of lemon – 1
- Sliced onion - 1 medium
- Chopped tomatoes – 2 medium
- Ground pepper - ½ teaspoon
- Black olives - 1/2 cup
- Whole wheat orzo - ¾ cup
- Chopped fresh parsley - 2 tablespoons
- Lemon zest - 4
- Herbes de Provence - 1 teaspoon
- Salt - ½ teaspoon

Directions: Cut the chicken breasts half into four different pieces. Combine broth, chicken, onion, tomatoes, lemon juice, lemon zest, salt, herbs de Provence and pepper in a six-quart slow cooker. Cook it on a slow cook mode for 4 hours. Stir in olives and orzo.Cook it further for 30 minutes. Let it cool for a few minutes, sprinkle some parsley and serve.

Nutritional Value: Calories: 278, Carbohydrate: 29g, Fat: 5g

SLOW COOKER GREEK CHICKEN

(Perfect Mediterranean Diet recipe)

Preparation Time: 20 minuts | Cooking Time: 3 hours | Serves: 4

Ingredients:

- Skinless, boneless chicken thighs or breasts - 2 pounds
- Extra virgin olive oil - 1 tablespoon
- Ground black pepper - ¼ teaspoon
- Drained and chopped roasted red peppers - 12 ounces
- Red onion, half-inch cut size - 1 medium
- Olives - 1 cup
- Red wine vinegar - 3 tablespoons
- Dried oregano - 1 teaspoon
- Honey - 1 teaspoon
- Dried thyme leaves - 1 teaspoon
- Chopped fresh herbs - thyme or parsley
- Kosher salt - ½ teaspoon
- Feta cheese - ½ cup
- Garlic, grated - 1 tablespoon

Directions: Coat with a little olive oil in a 5-quart slow cooker. Pour olive oil in large skillet and bring to medium-high heat. Season chicken with pepper, and salt. Put the seasoned chicken in the hot skillet. Let the chicken cook for three minutes until it becomes brown on both sides. After browning, transfer the chicken to the five-quart slow cooker. Arrange the olives, onions, and peppers all around the chicken. In a small bowl whisk together garlic, red wine vinegar, oregano, honey, and thyme. Pour the mixture over the vegetables and chicken. Close the lid and slow cook for 4 hours. Garnish with fresh herbs and feta cheese before serving. Serve hot.

Nutritional Value: Calories: 399, Carbohydrate: 13g, Fat: 17g

CROCK POT MEDITERRANEAN CHICKEN

(Perfect Mediterranean Diet recipe)

Preparation Time: 5 minuts | Cooking Time: 6 hours | Serves: 4

Ingredients:

- Curry powder - 1 tablespoon
- Skinless, boneless chicken breasts - 32 ounces
- Dried thyme - 2 teaspoons
- Dried basil - 2 teaspoons
- Black pepper - 1 teaspoon
- Drained and quartered artichoke hearts, two can - 28 ounces
- Chopped onion - 1 medium
- Low sodium chicken broth - 1 cup
- White wine vinegar - ¼ cup
- Pitted and chopped olives - ½ cup
- Chopped cilantro fresh - ¼ cup
- Kosher salt - 1 teaspoon
- Drained and chopped tomatoes, one can - 28 ounces

Directions: Put chicken breasts in a 6-quart slow cooker. Combine basil, curry powder, thyme, basil, pepper, and salt thoroughly. Season the chicken with half portions of this seasoning mixture. Now, add tomatoes, chicken broth, artichoke hearts, white wine vinegar, olives, and onion into the slow cooker. Add the remaining seasoning mixture into the slow cooker as well. Cover the cooker lid and slow cook for 8 hours. Once it has cooked thoroughly, remove the chicken breasts from the slow cooker. Shred the chicken breasts meat by using forks. Stir in the shredded chicken breasts back to the slow cooker and cook for about 30 minutes. Sprinkle chopped fresh cilantro while serving.

Nutritional Value: Calories: 305, Carbohydrate: 6g, Fat: 8g

CROCK POT ITALIAN CHICKEN

(Perfect Mediterranean Diet recipe)

Preparation Time: 5 minuts | Cooking Time: 4 hours | Serves: 4

Ingredients:

- Italian dressing seasoning - 1 packet
- Boneless chicken breasts chopped into small pieces - 4
- Cream of chicken soup - 2 cans
- Cream cheese - 8 ounces
- Pasta - 2 cups

Directions: Combine both the cans of soup, Italian dressing seasoning and softened cream cheese together and then transfer it into a crock pot. Place the chicken breast pieces on top of this mix. Cook it on low heat for 4 hours. Boil the pasta as per the directions on the package. Serve it over the pasta.

Nutritional Value: Calories: 388.6, Carbohydrate: 14.8g, Fat: 11.1g

SLOW COOKER ITALIAN CHICKEN

(Perfect Mediterranean Diet recipe)

Preparation Time: 15 minuts | Cooking Time: 4 hours | Serves: 6

Ingredients:

- Italian dressing - 0.6 ounces
- Skinless, boneless chicken breasts - 4
- Softened cream cheese one can - 8 ounces
- Cream of chicken soup - 10¾ ounces

Directions: Place the chicken breasts into the slow cooker. Sprinkle Italian dressing all over the chicken breasts. Combine cream of chicken soup and cream cheese in a small bowl and cook it under low heat, until it melts down completely. Pour it over the chicken breasts in the slow cooker. Cover the cooker and slow cook for 4 hours. After cooking, take out the chicken and shred it. Add back the shredded chicken into the slow cooker. Serve over pasta or rice.

Nutritional Value: Calories: 177, Carbohydrate: 4.8g, Fat: 15.3g

CROCK POT GREEK CHICKEN & SALAD

(Perfect Mediterranean Diet recipe)

Preparation Time: 15 minuts | Cooking Time: 4 hours | Serves: 4

Ingredients:

For the Chicken:

- Skinless chicken thighs with bone - 4 ounces
- Minced garlic - 4 cloves
- Lemon juice – 2 lemon
- Dried oregano - 3 teaspoons
- Pepper - ¼ teaspoon
- Salt - ¼ teaspoon
- Feta cheese, grated - 2 tablespoons

For the Salad:

- Sliced cucumbers - 2 large
- Chopped tomatoes - 4 medium
- Olive oil - 1 tablespoon
- Onion - ½ medium
- Feta cheese, grated - ¼ cup
- White wine vinegar - 1 teaspoon

Directions: Season the chicken thighs with garlic, pepper, salt, and oregano. Place the chicken thighs into the crockpot. Pour the lemon juice all over the chicken thighs. Cover the crock pot and low cook for 4 hours. While the cooking is in progress, you can prepare the salad. Combine cucumbers, onion, and tomatoes in a small bowl. Take another bowl and whisk vinegar and olive oil. Pour this dressing all over the salad mixture. Toss it well and then refrigerate until the chicken is ready to serve. While serving, dress the chicken with the Greek salad on the side. Sprinkle feta cheese on top of chicken.

Nutritional Value: Calories: 301, Carbohydrate: 18g, Fat: 16g

SLOW COOKER GREEK CHICKEN

(Perfect Mediterranean Diet recipe)

Preparation Time: 5 minuts | Cooking Time: 4 hours 30 minutes | Serves: 4

Ingredients:

- Sliced onions - 1 cup
- Olive oil – 2 tablespoons
- Skinless, boneless chicken thighs – 10
- Garlic powder - 2 tablespoons
- Lemon juice - ¼ cup
- Dried oregano - 1 tablespoon
- Smoked paprika - 1 tablespoon
- Salt - ¼ teaspoon

Directions: In 6-quart slow cooker, put chicken thighs and the sliced onions. Pour olive oil and toss it. Add garlic powder, dried oregano, smoked paprika, salt, and lemon juice into the slow cooker. Toss it until they get completely coated with the chicken thighs. Cover the slow cooker and cook on low heat for 4½ hours. Once the chicken is cooked thoroughly, remove it from the slow cooker and shred the meat. Add back the shredded chicken into the slow cooker. Give it a good mix and cook for another 30 minutes. Sprinkle some feta cheese over the chicken before serving.

Nutritional Value: Calories: 400, Carbohydrate: 7g, Fat: 29g

CROCK POT TURKISH CHICKEN

Preparation Time: 5 minuts | Cooking Time: 8 hours | Serves: 4

Ingredients:

- Green olives - 14 ounces
- Whole chicken - 1
- Tomato paste - 4 ounces
- Bottle beer - 16 ounces
- Pepper - ¼ teaspoon
- Salt - ¼ teaspoon
- Garlic powder - 1 teaspoon
- Paprika chopped - ¼ cup

Directions: Wash the chicken under running tap water and put it in a collator to drain. Now season the drained chicken with pepper, salt, garlic powder, and paprika. Put the chicken into the slow cooker. In a jar combine tomato paste, beer, olives and transfer this into the slow cooker. Make sure to dump the olives on top of the chicken. Cover the crockpot and slow cook for 8 hours. Serve hot.

Nutritional Value: Calories: 174, Carbohydrate: 19.1g, Fat: 7.8g

SLOW COOKER MEDITERRANEAN CHICKEN & CHICKPEA SOUP

(Perfect Mediterranean Diet recipe)

Preparation Time: 20 minuts | Cooking Time: 8 hours 20 minutes | Serves: 6

Ingredients:

- Overnight soaked chickpeas - 1½ cups
- Skinless chicken thighs - 2 pounds
- Tomato paste - 2 tablespoons
- Fire roasted, no-salt diced tomatoes - 15 ounces
- Finely chopped yellow onion - 1 large
- Finely chopped garlic - 4 cloves
- Tomato paste - 2 tablespoons
- Ground cumin - 4 teaspoons
- Bay leaf - 1
- Cayenne pepper - ¼ teaspoon
- Paprika - 4 teaspoons
- Ground pepper - ¼ teaspoon
- Artichoke hearts in the can - 14 ounces
- Pitted and halved oil-cured olives - ¼ cup
- Chopped cilantro - ¼ cup
- Water - 4 cups
- Salt - ½ teaspoon

Directions: Drain the soaked chickpeas. Put it into a six-quart slow cooker and pour 4 cups of water. Add tomatoes, onion, tomato paste, bay leaf, garlic, paprika, cumin, ground pepper, and cayenne. Combine it thoroughly. Now, put the chicken thighs into the slow cooker. Close the lid and low cook it for 8 eight hours. After cooking, take out the chicken and shred the meat. Discard the bones and bay leaf. Put the shredded chicken back into the slow cooker and cook for a further 20 minutes. Add olives, artichokes, and salt into the cooker. Stir it thoroughly. Top the soup with chopped cilantro. Serve hot.

Nutritional Value: Calories: 446, Carbohydrate: 43g, Fat: 15g

BASQUE CHICKEN STEW

(Perfect Mediterranean Diet recipe)

Preparation Time: 20 minuts | Cooking Time: 4 hours 30 minutes | Serves: 8

Ingredients:

- Red potatoes, large cuts - 1½ pounds
- Boneless and skinless chicken thighs, cut into large pieces - 2 pounds
- Sliced red bell pepper - 1 large
- Low sodium chicken broth - 1 cup
- Drained and diced tinned tomatoes - 28 ounces
- Chopped fresh thyme - 2 teaspoons
- Minced garlic - 4 cloves
- Ground pepper - ½ teaspoon
- Pimiento-stuffed olives - ½ cup
- Crushed dried savory - ½ teaspoon
- Salt - 1 teaspoon
- Thinly sliced onion - 1

Directions: Combine potatoes, chicken, bell pepper and onion in a six-quart slow cooker. Stir in the broth, tomatoes, thyme, garlic, pepper, savory and salt. Cover up the slow cooker and slow cook for 8 hours. Stir in the olives into the slow cooker. Serve the stew hot.

Nutritional Value: Calories: 246, Carbohydrate: 20g, Fat: 8g

MEDITERRANEAN MEAT RECIPES

SLOW COOKER MEDITERRANEAN BEEF ROAST

Preparation Time: 10 minuts | Cooking Time: 10 hours 10 minutes | Serves: 6

Ingredients:

- Chuck roast, boneless - 3 pounds
- Rosemary - 2 teaspoons
- Tomatoes, sun-dried and chopped - ½ cup
- Grated garlic - 10 cloves
- Beef stock - ½ cup
- Balsamic vinegar - 2 tablespoons
- Chopped Italian parsley, fresh - ¼ cup
- Chopped olives - ¼ cup
- Lemon zest - 1 teaspoon
- Cheese grits - ¼ cup

Directions: In the slow cooker, put garlic, sun dried tomatoes, and the beef roast. Add beef stock and Rosemary. Close the cooker and slow cook for 10 hours. After cooking is over, remove the beef, and shred the meet. Discard the fat. Add back the shredded meat to the slow cooker and simmer for 10 minutes. In a small bowl combine lemon zest, parsley, and olives. Refrigerate the mixture until you are ready to serve. Garnish using the refrigerated mix. Serve it over pasta or egg noodles. Top it with cheese grits.

Nutritional Value: Calories: 314, Carbohydrate: 1g, Fat: 19g

SLOW COOKER MEDITERRANEAN BEEF WITH ARTICHOKES

Preparation Time: 20 minuts | Cooking Time: 7 hours | Serves: 6

Ingredients:

- Beef for stew - 2 pounds
- Artichoke hearts - 14 ounces
- Grapeseed oil - 1 tablespoon
- Diced onion - 1
- Beef broth – 32 ounces
- Garlic, grated - 4 cloves
- Tinned tomatoes, diced - 14½ ounces
- Tomato sauce - 15 ounces
- Dried oregano - 1 teaspoon
- Pitted, chopped olives - ½ cup
- Dried parsley - 1 teaspoon
- Dried oregano - 1 teaspoon
- Ground cumin - ½ teaspoon
- Dried basil - 1 teaspoon
- Bay leaf – 1
- Salt - ½ teaspoon

Directions: In a large non-stick skillet pour some oil and bring to medium-high heat. Roast the beef until it turns brown on both the sides. Transfer the beef into a slow cooker. Add in beef broth, diced tomatoes, tomato sauce, salt and combine. Pour in beef broth, diced tomatoes, oregano, olives, basil, parsley, bay leaf, and cumin. Combine the mixture thoroughly. Close the slow cooker and cook on low heat for 7 hours. Discard the bay leaf at the time serving. Serve hot.

Nutritional Value: Calories: 416, Carbohydrate: 14.1g, Fat: 26.2g

SLOW COOKER MEDITERRANEAN BEEF STEW

Preparation Time: 10 minuts | Cooking Time: 10 hours | Serves: 10

Ingredients:

- Beef meat (for stew) - 3 pounds
- Beef broth – 2 cups
- Baby mushrooms - 16 ounces
- Garlic, minced - 10 cloves
- Chopped onion - 1 large
- Dried rosemary - 2 tablespoons
- Tomato sauce - 15 ounces
- Balsamic vinegar - ½ cup
- Diced tomatoes in a can - 14½ ounces
- Jar capers, drained - 2 ounces
- Drained black olives - 6 ounces
- Salt - ½ teaspoon
- Pepper - ½ teaspoon

For Garnish:

- Parmesan cheese, grated - ¼ cup
- Parsley, fresh chopped - ¼ cup

Directions: Put all the ingredients except the ingredients for garnishing in a 6-quart slow cooker and combine. Cover the cooker and slow cook for 10 hours. Add pepper and salt as required. Garnish with parmesan and chopped parsley while serving.

Nutritional Value: Calories: 273, Carbohydrate: 16g, Fat: 9g

SKINNY SLOW COOKER MEDITERRANEAN STYLE POT ROAST

Preparation Time: 30 minuts | Cooking Time: 8 hours | Serves: 10

Ingredients:

- Eye of round roast - 4 pounds
- Garlic - 4 cloves
- Olive oil - 2 teaspoons
- Freshly ground black pepper - 1 teaspoon
- Chopped onions - 1 cup
- Carrots, chopped - 4
- Dried Rosemary - 2 teaspoons
- Chopped celery stalks - 2
- Crushed tomatoes in the can - 28 ounces
- Low sodium beef broth - 1 cup
- Red wine - 1 cup
- Salt - 2 teaspoons

Directions: Season the beef roast with salt, garlic, and pepper and set aside. Pour oil in a non-stick skillet and bring to medium-high heat. Put the beef into it and roast until it becomes brown on all sides. Now, transfer the roasted beef into a 6-quart slow cooker. Add carrots, onion, rosemary, and celery into the skillet. Continue cooking until the onion and vegetable become soft. Stir in the tomatoes and wine into this vegetable mixture. Add beef broth and tomato mixture into the slow cooker along with the vegetable mixture. Cover the slow cooker and cook on low heat setting for 8 hours. Once the meat gets cooked, remove it from the slow cooker and place it on a cutting board and wrap with an aluminum foil. If you want to thicken the sauce, then transfer it into a saucepan and boil it under low heat for about ten to fifteen minutes until it reaches to the required consistency. Discard fats before serving.

Nutritional Value: Calories: 260, Carbohydrate: 8.7g, Fat: 6g

SLOW COOKER MEATLOAF RECIPE

Preparation Time: 10 minuts | Cooking Time: 6 hours 10 minutes | Serves: 8

Ingredients:

- Ground bison - 2 pounds
- Grated zucchini - 1
- Eggs – 2 large
- Olive oil cooking spray – as required
- Zucchini, shredded - 1
- Parsley, fresh, finely chopped - ½ cup
- Parmesan cheese, shredded - ½ cup

- Balsamic vinegar - 3 tablespoons
- Garlic, grated - 4 cloves
- Onion minced, dry - 2 tablespoons
- Dried oregano - 1 tablespoon
- Ground black pepper - ½ teaspoon
- Kosher salt - ½ teaspoon

For the topping:

- Shredded mozzarella cheese - ¼ cup
- Ketchup without sugar - ¼ cup

- Freshly chopped parsley - ¼ cup

Directions: Stripe line the inside of a six-quart slow cooker with aluminum foil. Spray non-stick cooking oil over it. In a large bowl combine ground bison or extra lean ground sirloin, zucchini, eggs, parsley, balsamic vinegar, garlic, dried oregano, sea or kosher salt, minced dry onion, and ground black pepper. Transfer this mixture into the slow cooker and form an oblong shaped loaf. Cover the cooker, set on a low heat and cook for 6 hours. After cooking, open the cooker and spread ketchup all over the meatloaf. Now, place the cheese above the ketchup as a new layer and close the slow cooker. Let the meatloaf sit on these two layers for about 10 minutes or until the cheese starts to melt. Garnish with fresh parsley, and shredded mozzarella cheese.

Nutritional Value: Calories: 320, Carbohydrate: 4g, Fat: 20g

SLOW COOKER MEDITERRANEAN BEEF HOAGIES

Preparation Time: 10 minuts | Cooking Time: 13 hours | Serves: 6

Ingredients:

- Beef top round roast fatless - 3 pounds
- Onion powder - ½ teaspoon
- Black pepper - ½ teaspoon
- Low sodium beef broth - 3 cups
- Salad dressing mix - 4 teaspoons
- Bay leaf - 1

- Garlic, minced - 1 tablespoon
- Red bell peppers, thin strips cut - 2
- Pepperoncino - 16 ounces
- Sargento Provolone, thin - 8 slices
- Gluten-free bread - 2 ounces
- Salt - ½ teaspoon

For seasoning:

- Onion powder - 1½ tablespoon
- Garlic powder - 1½ tablespoon
- Dried parsley - 2 tablespoon
- Stevia - 1 tablespoon
- Dried thyme - ½ teaspoon
- Dried oregano - 1 tablespoon
- Black pepper - 2 tablespoons
- Salt - 1 tablespoon
- Cheese slice - 6

Directions: Pat dry the roast with a paper towel. Combine black pepper, onion powder and salt in a small bowl and rub the mixture over the roast. Place the seasoned roast into a slow cooker. Add broth, salad dressing mix, bay leaf, and garlic to the slow cooker. Combine it gently. Cover the slow cooker and set to low cooking for 12 hours. After cooking, remove the bay leaf. Take out the cooked beef and shred the beef meet. Put back the shredded beef and add bell peppers and Add bell peppers and pepperoncino into the slow cooker. Cover the cooker and low cook for 1 hour. Before serving, top each of the bread with 3 ounces of the meat mixture. Top it with a cheese slice. The liquid gravy can be used as a dip.

Nutritional Value: Calories: 442, Carbohydrate: 37g, Fat: 11.5g

MEDITERRANEAN PORK ROAST

Preparation Time: 10 minuts | Cooking Time: 8 hours 10 minutes | Serves: 6

Ingredients:

- Olive oil - 2 tablespoons
- Pork roast - 2 pounds
- Paprika - ½ teaspoon
- Chicken broth - ¾ cup
- Dried sage - 2 teaspoons
- Garlic minced - ½ tablespoon
- Dried marjoram - ¼ teaspoon
- Dried Rosemary - ¼ teaspoon
- Oregano - 1 teaspoon
- Dried thyme - ¼ teaspoon
- Basil - 1 teaspoon
- Kosher salt - ½ teaspoon

Directions: In a small bowl mix broth, oil, salt, and spices. In a skillet pour olive oil and bring to medium-high heat. Put the pork into it and roast until all sides become brown. Take out the pork after cooking and poke the roast all over with a knife. Place the poked pork roast into a 6-quart crock pot. Now, pour the small bowl mixture liquid all over the roast. Close the crock pot and cook on low heat setting for 8 hours. After cooking, remove it from the crock pot on to a cutting board and shred into pieces. Afterward, add the shredded pork back into the crockpot. Simmer it another 10 minutes. Serve along with feta cheese, pita bread, and tomatoes.

Nutritional Value: Calories: 361, Carbohydrate: 0.7g, Fat: 10.4g

PULLED PORK WITH BOURBON-PEACH BARBECUE SAUCE

Preparation Time: 30 minuts | Cooking Time: 7 hours | Serves: 12

Ingredients:

- Pork with bone, trimmed, shoulder roast - 3½ pounds
- Spanish smoked paprika - 2 teaspoons
- Ground black pepper, fresh - 1 teaspoon
- Chicken stock, unsalted - ½ cup
- Molasses - ⅓ cup
- Balsamic vinegar - ⅓ cup
- Crushed red pepper - 1 teaspoon
- Soy sauce, low sodium - 2 teaspoons
- Onion, vertically sliced - 2 cups
- Peach preserves - ½ cup
- Bourbon - ¼ cup
- Kosher salt - 1¼ teaspoons
- Olive oil – as required
- Garlic, minced - 5 cloves
- Cornstarch - 2 teaspoons
- Cold water - 2 tablespoons

Directions: Combine salt, black pepper, and paprika in a small bowl. Apply this mixture all over the pork. Take a large skillet and coat some cooking spray and bring to medium-high heat. Add the pork to the pan and cook it for 10 minutes until it turns brown on both sides. Once the pork gets brown, transfer it into a 6-quart slow cooker. Add the stock, molasses, balsamic vinegar, red pepper, and low sodium soy sauce into the skillet. Boil these ingredients. Pour this mixture all over the pork in the slow cooker. Top it up with garlic and onion. Cover the slow cooker and low cook for 6½ hours. Once the pork is wholly cooked, transfer it to a cutting board and shred. Remove onion from the slow cooker and add it to the pork. Take a large 4-cup measuring cup glass and place a large sized top open zip plastic bag into it. Pour the cooking liquid into the bag. Let the liquid stand in the bag for about ten minutes so that the fat rises to the top. Seal the bag and carefully prick the bottom corner of the bag and let the liquid drip into the skillet until the fat layer reaches the prickled opening. Stop dripping and discard fat. Whisk the bourbon with the liquid and boil. Boil for 10 minutes or until the mixture reduces to 1½ cup. Now, combine cornstarch and cold water in a separate small bowl. Whisk it and then add it to the sauce. Keep stirring it constantly until it turns into a thick consistency. Stir in the remaining salt. Drizzle the sauce all over the pork and toss it for an even coating.

Nutritional Value: Calories: 267, Carbohydrate: 19g, Fat: 4.8g

Beef Stew with Rosemary & Balsamic Vinegar

Preparation Time: 25 minuts │ Cooking Time: 8 hours │ Serves: 6

Ingredients:

- Sliced mushrooms - 8 ounces
- Olive oil - 2 tablespoons
- Diced chuck steak - 2 pounds
- Diced onion - 1
- Tomatoes with juice, diced - 14½ ounces
- Beef stock - 1 cup
- Balsamic vinegar - ¼ cup
- Tomato sauce - ½ cup
- Garlic, coarsely chopped - ½ cup
- Half cut black olives – 2 cups
- Fresh parsley, finely chopped - 2 tablespoons
- Rosemary, fresh, chopped - 2 tablespoons
- Salt - ½ teaspoon
- Fresh ground black pepper - ½ teaspoon
- Capers - 1 tablespoon

Directions: Pour some olive oil in a non-stick pan and bring to medium-high temperature. Add mushrooms to the pan and cook for 8 minutes or until the mushrooms become brown and transfer the roasted mushrooms into the slow cooker. Add some more oil to the pan and cook the diced onions for 5 minutes or until it becomes brown. Transfer the cooked onion also to the slow cooker. Again pour some oil into the pan and put the diced beef. Continue cooking until the beef becomes brown and transfer the roasted beef to the slow cooker. Now pour a cup of beef stock into the pan and simmer on low heat. Scrap off the food items stuck to the pan and transfer the liquid to the slow cooker. Add tomato sauce, diced tomatoes with juice, olives, balsamic vinegar, rosemary, garlic, capers, black pepper and parsley to the slow cooker and combine it thoroughly. Close the slow cooker and cook on low heat for 8 hours. After cooking, season the beef with freshly grounded black pepper and salt.

Nutritional Value: Calories: 529, Carbohydrate: 14.5g, Fat: 29.8g

PLUM PORK TENDERLOIN

Preparation Time: 10 minuts | Cooking Time: 6 hours | Serves: 3

Ingredients:

- Trimmed pork tenderloins - 1 pound
- Ground allspice - 1 tablespoon
- Ground cinnamon - 1 tablespoon
- Olive oil – as required
- Water - ½ cup
- Plum sauce - 9.3 ounces
- Plums cut into 6 wedges – 2 plum

Directions: Combine allspice and cinnamon in a small bowl. Season the pork by rubbing the allspice mix over it. Coat a 5-quart slow cooker with little cooking spray and place the pork into it. Pour the plum sauce and plums over the pork. Add half a cup of water and the plum wedges to the slow cooker. Cover the cooker and slow cook for 8 hours. Serve hot.

Nutritional Value: Calories: 199, Carbohydrate: 17.6g, Fat: 2.9g

Mediterranean Fish & Seafood Recipes

Slow Cooker Mediterranean Salmon

(Perfect Mediterranean Diet recipe)

Preparation Time: 10 minuts | Cooking Time: 6 hours | Serves: 4

Ingredients:

- Salmon fillets - 1 pound
- Italian seasoning - 1 tablespoon
- Onion powder - 1 teaspoon
- Garlic powder - 1 teaspoon
- Olive oil - 1 tablespoon
- Black pepper - ½ teaspoon

- Onion, nicely chopped - ½
- Garlic, minced - 3 cloves
- Red bell pepper - 1
- Quartered and sliced zucchini - 1
- Chopped tomato – 1
- Olive oil – as required

Directions: Take an oven safe-dish that fits perfectly inside a six-quart slow cooker. Spray some cooking oil inside the oven safe dish. In a medium bowl put half portion of the garlic powder, Italian seasoning, onion powder, olive oil, and black pepper. Combine the ingredients thoroughly. Add the sliced garlic cloves, zucchini, onions, tomato, and bell pepper as well. Season the salmon fillets with the mix and place the fillets one by one into the bottom part of the oven-safe dish. Season it with the remaining herbs, olive oil, and spices. Gently toss it up with the vegetables to coat them thoroughly. Cover up the oven-safe dish using a glass lid. Place the dish correctly inside the slow cooker and cover the cooker. Now low cook it for six hours. Serve it with couscous or whole grain pasta.

Nutritional Value: Calories: 225, Carbohydrate: 8.1g, Fat: 11.8g

Mediterranean Shrimp Soup

(Perfect Mediterranean Diet recipe)

Preparation Time: 15 minuts | Cooking Time: 5 hours | Serves: 6

Ingredients:

- Peeled, veined, uncooked medium shrimp - 1 pound
- Diced tomatoes - 14 ounces
- Chicken broth, low sodium - 14 ounces
- Chopped onion - 1 medium
- Tomato sauce - 8 ounces
- Orange juice - ½ cup
- Bell pepper, green, chopped - 1 medium

- Dry white wine (optional) - ½ cup
- Garlic, minced - 2 cloves
- Sliced ripe olives - ¼ cup
- Bay leaves - 2
- Dried basil - 1 teaspoon
- Crushed fennel seeds - ¼ teaspoon
- Black pepper - ¼ teaspoon
- Sliced mushrooms - 2½ ounces

Directions: In a slow cooker and add diced tomatoes, reduced sodium chicken broth, chopped onion, tomato sauce, orange juice, chopped green bell pepper, dry white wine, orange juice, sliced ripe olives, sliced mushrooms, bay leaves, dried basil, minced garlic, black pepper, and crushed fennel seeds. Combine the ingredients thoroughly. Cover the slow cooker and slow cook for 4½ hours until the vegetables become tender. Afterward, stir in the shrimp into the slow cooker. Cover the cooker and again slow cook for 30 minutes. Discard the bay leaves before serving.

Nutritional Value: Calories: 162, Carbohydrate: 12g, Fat: 3g

SLOW COOKER SEAFOOD STEW

(Perfect Mediterranean Diet recipe)

Preparation Time: 20 minuts | Cooking Time: 5 hours 5 minutes | Serves: 8

Ingredients:

- Whitefish, cut to 1" size – 1 pound
- Shrimp, medium, shelled, uncooked, veined - ¾ pound
- Tined crab meat, drained – 6 ounces.
- Onions, sliced - 2 cups
- Tinned tomatoes, diced with liquid - 28 ounces
- Garlic, grated - 5 cloves
- Tomato paste - 6 ounces
- Clam juice - 8 ounces

- Dried Italian seasoning - 2½ teaspoons
- Olive oil - 1 tablespoon
- Crushed red pepper flakes - ¼ teaspoon
- Sugar - ¼ teaspoon
- Celery finely chopped - 2 stalks
- Bay leaf - 1
- Chopped clams with juice - 6½ ounces
- Chopped fresh parsley - 1/4 cup
- Red wine vinegar - 1 tablespoon
- Dry white wine - ½ cup

Directions: Combine celery, onions, clam juice, tomatoes, wine, tomato paste, Italian seasoning, vinegar, pepper flakes, bay leaf, and sugar in a 6-quart slow cooker. Close the slow cooker and cook on low heat for 8 hours. Stir in shrimp, fish, crabmeat, and clams with juice into the stew. Continue slow cooking for 2 hours. Remove the bay leaf before serving. For seasoning, stir in parsley. Serve hot.

Nutritional Value: Calories: 215, Carbohydrate: 15g, Fat: 4g

SLOW COOKER SPANISH SHRIMP STEW

(Perfect Mediterranean Diet recipe)

Preparation Time: 10 minuts | Cooking Time: 3 hours 30 minutes | Serves: 4

Ingredients:

- Frozen shrimp - 10 ounces
- Vegetable broth - 2 cups
- Rinsed quinoa - 1 cup
- Olive oil - 1 tablespoon

- Frozen spinach - 1 cup
- Dried coriander - 1 teaspoon
- Pepper ground - ½ teaspoon
- Goat cheese, shredded - 1 cup

- Tomatoes, tinned, fire roasted, drained – 14 ounces
- Lime juice - 1 tablespoon
- Honey - 2 tablespoons
- Cayenne pepper - ½ teaspoon
- Worcestershire sauce - 1 tablespoon
- Chopped green onion - 1 cup
- Salt - ½ teaspoon
- Fresh parsley, chopped - 1 cup
- Olive oil – as required
- Onion powder - 1 teaspoon
- Smoked paprika - ½ teaspoon

Directions: Grease the crockpot using cooking spray. Add in broth, quinoa, olive oil, tomatoes, lime juice, honey, cayenne, Worcestershire sauce, onion powder, paprika, spinach, coriander, and shrimp. Stir to combine all these ingredients. Close the crockpot and slow cook for 3½ hours. Season it with pepper and salt. Garnish with goat cheese, green onions, and parsley.

Nutritional Value: Calories: 345, Carbohydrate: 47g, Fat: 7g

CROCK POT SEAFOOD STEW

(Perfect Mediterranean Diet recipe)

Preparation Time: 10 minuts | Cooking Time: 7 hours | Serves: 6

Ingredients:

- Crab legs, extra-large shrimp and scallops, thawed - 2 pounds
- Vegetable broth - 4 cups
- Crushed tomatoes - 28 ounces
- Garlic, grated - 3 cloves
- White wine - ½ cup
- Diced onion - ½ cup
- Baby potatoes - 1 pound
- Dried thyme - 1 teaspoon
- Celery salt - ½ teaspoon
- Dried cilantro - 1 teaspoon
- Pepper ground - ½ teaspoon
- Salt - ½ teaspoon
- Cayenne pepper - ¼ teaspoon
- Red pepper flakes - ¼ teaspoon
- Dried basil - 1 teaspoon

Directions: Excluding the thawed seafood, put all the ingredients in a 6-quart slow cooker and combine thoroughly. Close the slow cooker and cook on low heat for 6 hours. After 6 hours, add the thawed seafood and cook for 1 hour on high heat. Serve hot.

Nutritional Value: Calories: 236, Carbohydrate: 31g, Fat: 1g

SLOW COOKER SALMON RISOTTO

(Perfect Mediterranean Diet recipe)

Preparation Time: 20 minuts | Cooking Time: 1 hours | Serves: 4

Ingredients:

- Salmon fillet, skinned and diced - 17.63 ounces
- Chopped shallots - 2
- Arborio rice - 1¼ cup
- Diced cucumbers - ½ cup
- White wine - 1/2 cup

- Olive oil - 2 tablespoons
- Vegetable broth - 3 cups
- Salt - ½ teaspoon
- Chopped green onions – 1
- Pepper - ½ teaspoon

Directions: Pour olive oil into a non-stick pan and bring to medium-high heat. Add cucumber and shallots to the pan and sauté it for about two to three minutes by stirring. Cover the pan and cook on a low heat for 15 minutes. Turn the heat to high and add the rice grains to the pan. Sauté it for one minute by stirring. Afterward, transfer it to a slow cooker. Stir in the wine and the hot broth. Close the slow cooker and cook on low heat for 45 minutes. After 45 minutes, open the cooker and add salmon pieces. Season it with salt and pepper. Cover the cooker and cook further 15 minutes. Once the rice and salmon cooked well, turn off the slow cooker. Let it rest for 5 minutes and stir in green onion and dill. Serve hot.

Nutritional Value: Calories: 320, Carbohydrate: 41g, Fat: 7g

SLOW COOKER MEDITERRANEAN SHRIMP SOUP

(Perfect Mediterranean Diet recipe)

Preparation Time: 10 minuts | Cooking Time: 5 hours | Serves: 6

Ingredients:

- Peeled shrimp - 1 pound
- Green bell pepper, chopped - ½ medium
- Chopped onion - 1 medium
- Tinned tomatoes, undrained and coarsely chopped - 14½ ounces
- Garlic, minced - 2 cloves
- Tomato sauce - 8 ounces
- Chicken broth with low sodium - 14½ ounces
- Orange juice - 1/2 cup
- Sliced mushrooms - 2½ ounces
- Sliced ripe olives - ¼ cup
- Dry white wine - ½ cup
- Dried basil leaves - 1 teaspoon
- Bay leaves - 2
- Black pepper, ground - ¼ teaspoon
- Crushed fennel seed - ¼ teaspoon

Directions: Excluding shrimp, combine all ingredients in a slow cooker. Close the slow cooker and slow cook for 4½ hours. After cooking add the shrimp and stir. Close the slow cooker and cook for 30 minutes. Discard the bay leaves before serving.

Nutritional Value: Calories: 117, Carbohydrate: 7g, Fat: 1g

HEARTY CROCK POT SHRIMP STEW

(Perfect Mediterranean Diet recipe)

Preparation Time: 30 minuts | Cooking Time: 8 hours | Serves: 6

Ingredients:

- Catfish cut into 2" sized pieces - 1½ pounds
- Olive oil - 2 tablespoons
- Onion sliced - 1 large
- Garlic minced - 1 large clove
- Zucchini squash, sliced - 2
- Green bell pepper - 1
- Basil leaf dried - ½ teaspoon
- Tinned tomatoes whole - 14½ ounces
- Salt - 1 teaspoon
- Dried leaf oregano - ½ teaspoon
- Dry white wine - ¼ cup
- Pepper - ⅛ teaspoon
- Sliced mushrooms - 4 ounces

For Garnish:
- Parsley, chopped - ¼ cup

Directions: Put all the ingredients in a 6-quart crockpot and combine it gently. Close the cooker and cook on low heat for 8 hours. While serving, garnish with chopped parsley.

Nutritional Value: Calories: 225, Carbohydrate: 17g, Fat: 8g

MEDITERRANEAN COD WITH PEPPER & TOMATO

(Perfect Mediterranean Diet recipe)

Preparation Time: 15 minuts | Cooking Time: 3 hours 45 minutes | Serves: 2

Ingredients:

- Cod fillet, boneless, skinless in 5cm cut size - ½ pound
- Sliced red peppers - 2
- Olive oil - 2 teaspoons
- Tinned cherry tomatoes – 14 ounces
- Sliced garlic - 2 cloves
- Basil - ½ ounce
- Sprigs - 2 tablespoons
- Sherry vinegar - 1 teaspoon
- Roughly chopped green olives - ¼ cup
- Rinsed and drained capers - 2 teaspoons
- Ciabatta shredded into pieces - 1¾ ounces

Directions: In a slow cooker pour one teaspoon of olive oil and bring to medium-high heat. Once the oil starts to sizzle, fry the peppers for 10 minutes or until the peppers turn soft. Add garlic to the slow cooker and fry it for a minute. Later on, add sherry vinegar, tomatoes, and basil sprigs. Bring these ingredients to a boil. Close slow cooker and cook on low heat for 3 hours. Check the sauce consistency and maintain as you required. After cooking, remove the basil sprigs. Stir in the olives, capers and the fillet. Let it simmer for 30 minutes on low heat. Now, using a food processor quick stir the chopped basil and ciabatta. Fry the whizzed mixture in a non-stick pan in one teaspoon olive oil. Scatter the toasted bread mixture over the fish before serving. Garnish with chopped basil.

Nutritional Value: Calories: 164, Carbohydrate: 25.2g, Fat: 6g

MEDITERRANEAN SEAFOOD STEW

(Perfect Mediterranean Diet recipe)

Preparation Time: 20 minuts | Cooking Time: 5 hours 30 minutes | Serves: 8

Ingredients:

- Shrimp, veined, peeled – 1 pound
- Haddock fillets, 1"cut size – 1 pound
- Tinned crabmeat, drained – 6 ounces
- Tinned clams, chopped, undrained – 6 ounces
- Tinned tomatoes, diced – 28 ounces
- Celery ribs, shredded – 3
- Onions, sliced – 2 medium
- Tomato paste – 6 ounces
- Vegetable broth - ½ cup
- Garlic, minced – 5 cloves
- Olive oil – 1 tablespoon
- Red wine vinegar – 1 tablespoon
- Italian seasoning – 2 tablespoons
- Sugar - ½ teaspoon
- Bay leaf -1
- Parsley, finely chopped – 2 tablespoons
- Bottled clam juice – 8 ounces

Directions: Combine all the ingredients except shrimp, haddock, crabmeat, clams and parsley in a 6-quart slow cooker. Cover the lid and slow cook for 5 hours. Add all the seafood, cover and cook for 30 minutes. Discard bay leaf at the time of serving. Garnish with parsley.

Nutritional Value: Calories: 205, Carbohydrate: 15g, Fat: 3g

MEDITERRANEAN DESSERT RECIPES

MEDITERRANEAN SLOW COOKER APPLE OLIVE CAKE

(Perfect Mediterranean Diet recipe)

Preparation Time: 20 minuts | Cooking Time: 2 hours | Serves: 4

Ingredients:

- Peeled and chopped Gala apples - 2 large
- Ground cinnamon - ½ teaspoon
- Whole wheat flour - 3 cups
- Orange juice – 2 cups
- Baking powder - 1 teaspoon
- Ground nutmeg - ½ teaspoon
- Sugar - 1 cup
- Baking soda - 1 teaspoon
- Large eggs - 2
- Extra virgin olive oil - 1 cup
- Gold raisins, soaked and drained - $^2/_3$ cup
- Confectioner's sugar - for dusting purpose

Directions: In a small bowl, soak the gold raisins in lukewarm water for 15 minutes and drain. Keep aside. Put the chopped apple in a medium bowl and pour orange juice over it. Toss and make sure the apple gets well coated with the orange juice. Combine cinnamon, flour, baking powder, nutmeg in a large bowl and keep aside. Add extra virgin olive oil and sugar into the mixture and combine thoroughly. This particular mixture must be thicker in texture and not a runny one. In the large bowl that contains the dry ingredients, make a circular path in the middle part of the flour mixture. Add the olive oil and sugar mixture into this path. Make use of a wooden spoon and stir them well until they blend well with one another. It must be a thick batter. Drain the excess juice from the apples. Add the apples and raisins to the batter and mix it with a spoon to combine. Once again, the batter must be reasonably thick in terms of texture. In a six quart slow cooker, place a parchment paper and add the batter over it. Turn the heat setting to low and the timer to two hours or cook until the cake does not have any wet spots over it. Once the cake has cooked well, wait until the cake cools down before cutting them into pieces. Transfer the cake to a serving dish and sprinkle confectioner's sugar on top.

Nutritional Value: Calories: 294, Carbohydrate: 47.7g, Fat: 11g

MEDITERRANEAN CROCKPOT STRAWBERRY BASIL COBBLER

(Perfect Mediterranean Diet recipe)

Preparation Time: 20 minuts | Cooking Time: 2 hours 30 minutes | Serves: 5

Ingredients:

- Divided granulated sugar - 1¼ cups
- Divided whole wheat flour - 2½ cups
- Ground cinnamon - ½ teaspoon
- Canola oil - 4 tablespoons
- Rolled oats - ¼ cup
- Frozen strawberries - 6 cups

- Baking powder - 2 teaspoons
- Skim milk - ½ cup
- Eggs - 2
- Divided salt - ¼ teaspoon
- Vanilla frozen yogurt – 3 cups
- Chopped fresh basil - ¼ cup
- Cooking spray – as required

Directions: Combine sugar, flour, baking powder, salt and cinnamon in a large bowl. Add milk, oil, and eggs into the bowl and combine thoroughly. Coat some olive oil in the bottom of the slow cooker. Transfer and spread the mixed batter evenly into the slow cooker. Take another large bowl and combine flour, salt, and sugar. Add basil and strawberries to the bowl and toss it to coat. Pour this mixture on the top of the batter in the slow cooker. Top up with the rolled oat mixture. Close the slow cooker and cook on high heat setting for 2½ hours. You can check the cooking status by inserting a toothpick. If it comes out clean, your cake is ready. Serve topped with frozen vanilla yogurt and basil.

Nutritional Value: Calories: 727, Carbohydrate: 126.8g, Fat: 16.2g

SLOW COOKER MEDITERRANEAN PUMPKIN PECAN BREAD PUDDING

Preparation Time: 15 minuts | Cooking Time: 4 hours | Serves: 3

Ingredients:

- Chopped toasted pecans - ½ cup
- Day old whole wheat bread cubes - 8 cups
- Eggs - 4
- Cinnamon chips - ½ cup
- Half n half - 1 cup
- Canned pumpkin - 1 cup
- Melted butter - ½ cup
- Brown sugar - ½ cup
- Vanilla - 1 teaspoon
- Ground ginger - ¼ teaspoon
- Nutmeg - ½ teaspoon
- Vanilla ice cream - ¼ cup
- Ground cloves - ⅛ teaspoon
- Caramel ice cream topping - ¼ cup
- Cinnamon - ½ teaspoon

Directions: Grease a 6-quart crock pot and put the bread cubes, cinnamon, and chopped pecans into it. In a medium bowl, whisk together pumpkin, eggs, brown sugar, half-n-half, vanilla, melted butter, nutmeg, cinnamon, cloves, ginger and pour the mixture over the bread cubes. Stir the mix gently. Cover up the slow cooker and cook for 4 hours. It will be well prepared within 4 hours, which you can check by inserting a toothpick and if it comes clean, it is ready to serve. Before serving, top up with caramel ice cream and vanilla ice cream.

Nutritional Value: Calories: 289, Carbohydrate: 28g, Fat: 17g

SLOW COOKER CHOCOLATE FONDUE

Preparation Time: 15 minuts | Cooking Time: 2 hours | Serves: 3

Ingredients:

- Chocolate Almonds candy bars - 4½ ounces
- Miniature marshmallows - 1½ cup
- Heavy whipping cream - ½ cup

- Butter - 1½ tablespoons
- Milk - 3 tablespoons

Directions: Grease a 2-quart slow cooker and put chocolate, butter, milk, marshmallows into it. Close the cooker and cook on low heat setting for 1½ hours. Stir the mix every 30 minutes to melt and mix whipping cream gradually. After adding whipping cream allow it to settle for 2 hours. Use it as a chocolate dip.

Nutritional Value: Calories: 463, Carbohydrate: 3901g, Fat: 31.8g

CHOCOLATE ORANGE VOLCANO PUDDING

Preparation Time: 20 minuts | Cooking Time: 2 hours | Serves: 6

Ingredients:

- Self-raising flour – ½ pound
- Melted butter - 3½ ounces
- Sifted cocoa - 2¾ ounces
- Caster sugar - 5¼ ounces
- Zest and juice of orange - 1
- Baking powder - 1 teaspoon
- Orange flavored milk chocolate, chopped into chunks - 5¼ ounces
- Milk - 1½ cup
- Salt – a pinch
- Water – 2 cups

For the Sauce:

- Cocoa – 1 ounce
- Light brown soft sugar - 7½ ounces

Topping:

- Vanilla ice cream - ¼ cup
- Orange wedges – 1 orange
- Cream - ¼ cup

Directions: Grease the slow cooker with butter. Combine the caster sugar, flour, baking powder, and cocoa, pinch of salt and orange zest in a large mixing bowl thoroughly. Whisk the eggs, orange juice, milk and buttermilk in a medium bowl. Add it to the dry ingredients and combine to form a smooth mixture. Stir in chocolate pieces and then transfer the mixture into the slow cooker. Prepare the sauce by mixing cocoa and sugar in two cups of boiling water. Pour the sauce over the pudding mixture. Cover the slow cooker and cook on high heat for two hours. Before serving, top the pudding with vanilla ice cream or cream and orange wedges.

Nutritional Value: Calories: 733, Carbohydrate: 120.8g, Fat: 25.4g

SLOW COOKER NUTELLA FUDGE

Preparation Time: 10 minuts | Cooking Time: 1 hours 30 minutes | Serves: 5

Ingredients:

- Vanilla essence - 1 teaspoon
- Condensed milk – 14 ounces
- 70 percent dark chocolate - 7 0unces
- Nutella - 1 cup
- Chopped toasted hazelnuts - 4 ounces
- Icing sugar - 3 ounces

Directions: In a slow cooker add vanilla essence, condensed milk, dark chocolate, and Nutella. Cook it for 1½ hours without covering the lid. Make sure to stir the ingredients every ten minutes until they melt completely. After cooking turn off the slow cooker and transfer its content into a large sized mixing bowl. Stir in the sieved icing sugar. Take the warm fudge and carefully scrape it flat and allow it cool. Sprinkle the hazelnuts over the fudge and slightly press them downwards, so that they get attached well. Refrigerate this well for 4 hours and then cut them into squares.

Nutritional Value: Calories: 191, Carbohydrate: 24.7g, Fat: 9.3g

GREEK YOGURT CHOCOLATE MOUSSE

(Perfect Mediterranean Diet recipe)

Preparation Time: 5 minuts | Cooking Time: 2 hours | Serves: 4

Ingredients:

- Dark chocolate - 3½ ounces
- Milk - ¾ cup
- Maple syrup - 1 tablespoon
- Greek yogurt - 2 cups
- Vanilla extract - ½ teaspoon

Directions: Pour milk into a glass bowl that can be placed inside the slow cooker. Add the chocolate, either as finely chopped or as a grated one into the glass bowl. Place the bowl inside the slow cooker. Pour water surrounding the bowl. Cook it for 2 hours on low heat by stirring intermittently. Once the chocolate is combined thoroughly with the milk, turn off the cooker and remove the glass bowl from the slow cooker. Add vanilla extract and maple syrup to the bowl and stir well. Spoon in the Greek yogurt in a large bowl and add the chocolate mixture on top of it. Mix it well together before serving. Refrigerate for two hours before serving.

Nutritional Value: Calories: 170, Carbohydrate: 20.4g, Fat: 8.3g

PEANUT BUTTER BANANA GREEK YOGURT BOWL

(Perfect Mediterranean Diet recipe)

Preparation Time: 5 minuts | Cooking Time: 2 hours | Serves: 4

Ingredients:

- Sliced bananas - 2
- Vanilla Greek yogurt - 4 cups
- Flaxseed meal - ¼ cup
- Creamy natural peanut butter - ¼ cup
- Nutmeg - 1 teaspoon

Directions: Divide the yogurt between four different bowls and top it with banana slices. Add peanut butter into a small sized glass bowl and place in the slow cooker. Pour water surrounding the glass bowl. Under low heat setting, cook without covering the slow cooker until the peanut butter starts to melt. The peanut butter should be in a thick consistency. Once the butter turns to the required consistency, remove the bowl from the slow cooker. Now, scoop one tablespoon of melted peanut butter and serve into the bowl with yogurt and bananas. For each bowl, add about one tablespoon of melted peanut butter. Sprinkle ground nutmeg and flax seed.

Nutritional Value: Calories: 187, Carbohydrate: 19g, Fat: 10.7g

ITALIAN SLOW COOKER BANANA FOSTER

Preparation Time: 10 minuts | Cooking Time: 2 hours | Serves: 4

Ingredients:

- Bananas – 4
- Butter, melted – 4 tablespoons
- Rum - ¼ cup
- Brown sugar – 1 cup
- Cinnamon, ground - ½ teaspoon
- Vanilla extract – 1 teaspoon
- Coconut, shredded - ¼ cup
- Walnuts, chopped - ¼ cup

Directions: Peel the bananas, slice and keep ready to use. Place the sliced bananas in the slow cooker in layers. Mix the brown sugar, vanilla, butter, rum and cinnamon in a medium bowl thoroughly. Pour the mix over the bananas. Close the slow cooker and cook on low heat for 2 hours. Sprinkle shredded coconut and walnuts on top before 30 of the end process.

Nutritional Value: Calories: 539, Carbohydrates: 83.7g, Protein: 3g

MEDITERRANEAN RICE PUDDING

Preparation Time: 10 minutes | Cooking Time: 2 hours | Serves: 8

Ingredients:

- Glutinous white rice, uncooked – 1 cup
- Evaporated milk – 12 ounces
- Cinnamon stick – 1 ounce
- White sugar – 1 cup
- Nutmeg, ground – 1 teaspoon
- Vanilla extract – 1 teaspoon

Directions: In a 6-quart slow cooker, put all the ingredients. Cover the lid and cook on low heat for 1½ hours. Stir intermittently, while cooking in progress. Once ready, discard cinnamon stick and serve.

Nutritional Value: Calories: 321, Carbohydrates: 56.4g, Protein: 8.2g

CONCLUSION

A slow cooker is your easy food partner. It alleviates your tension and does not demand that you stand near it while it's cooking. It has the ability to stop cooking by itself when the food is cooked, and it will never burn your food. It is made to make your life easier, so it's a good idea to purchase one.

Made in the USA
Middletown, DE
06 September 2023